PRACTICE
MAKES
PERFECT™

# French
*Sentence*
*Builder*

PRACTICE
MAKES
PERFECT™

# French
## *Sentence Builder*

**Premium Third Edition**

**Eliane Kurbegov**

New York   Chicago   San Francisco   Athens   London   Madrid   Mexico City
Milan   New Delhi   Singapore   Sydney   Toronto

1 2 3 4 5 6 7 8 9   LON   27 26 25 24 23 22

ISBN        978-1-264-28602-7
MHID        1-264-28602-3

e-ISBN      978-1-26428603-1
e-MHID      1-264-28603-4

Trademarks: McGraw Hill, the McGraw Hill logo, Practice Makes Perfect, and related trade dress are trademarks or registered trademarks of McGraw Hill and/or its affiliates in the United States and other countries and may not be used without written permission. All other trademarks are the property of their respective owners. McGraw Hill is not associated with any product or vendor mentioned in this book.

Interior design by Village Typographers, Inc.

McGraw Hill books are available at special quantity discounts to use as premiums and sales promotions, or for use in corporate training programs. To contact a representative please visit the Contact Us pages at www.mhprofessional.com.

McGraw Hill is committed to making our products accessible to all learners. To learn more about the available support and accommodations we offer, please contact us at accessibility@mheducation.com. We also participate in the Access Text (www.accesstext.org), and ATN members may submit requests through ATN.

---

McGraw Hill Language Lab App

Additional exercises and audio recordings of answers to select exercises in the book are available to support your study of this book. Go to mhlanguagelab.com to access the online version of this application, or to locate links to the mobile app for iOS and Android devices. Search "McGraw Hill Language Lab" in the iTunes app store or Google Play store for Android.

# Contents

# Introduction

English and French have many similarities such as common vocabulary words derived from Latin. Knowing these words makes it easier for a speaker of English to learn and remember French words. However, when it comes to word order, French and English sentences may sometimes differ. For example, adverbs are usually placed before a verb in English but after the verb in French.

This book will help you compare the syntax of French and English sentences, allow you to revisit grammatical concepts such as object pronouns (focusing on their position in the French sentence), and provide you with many opportunities to write the least as well as the most complex sentences. This book and a little determination will undoubtedly make you a better writer.

A step-by-step approach to analyzing the components of a sentence paired with a guided structuring of phrases, sentences, and ultimately paragraphs will allow you to hone your writing skills.

The structures that are explained and practiced in this book progress from basic phrases, such as **À demain** (*See you tomorrow*), to increasingly complex sentences including relative and subjunctive clauses. Many diagrams accompany information to illustrate the functions and positions of the various parts of a sentence.

This book provides an abundance of exercises to help you practice building and structuring a great variety of sentences. Some exercises aim at helping you understand structures by identifying or matching components, while others require restructuring, modifying, and writing new sentences. The ultimate goal is to write full sentences independently. The last few chapters of this book allow you to progress from writing sentences to writing paragraphs, e-mails, and letters.

New to this third edition are audio recordings, accessible through the McGraw Hill Language Lab app. Spoken by native French speakers, these recordings provide the answers to selected exercises throughout the book, to help improve your listening and speaking skills.

An answer key is provided with actual or suggested answers for all exercises or with models for such activities as letter writing.

Writing can be challenging in any language, but rest assured that close attention to the rules of sentence building combined with regular practice will make you a better writer. This book will provide you with ample opportunities to build sentences while at the same time building your confidence as a writer.

# PRACTICE MAKES PERFECT™

# French

*Sentence
Builder*

# Declarative sentences and word order

It is important to understand the difference between a phrase and a sentence. They are different in nature and serve different purposes.

## What is a phrase?

A phrase consists of more than one word but does not have the subject + verb organization of a sentence.

> one or more words excluding a verb → phrase

Some examples of phrases are as follows:

| | | |
|---|---|---|
| Noun phrase including two nouns: | une salle de séjour | a living room |
| Noun phrase with adjective + noun: | une belle maison | a beautiful house |
| Noun phrase with noun + adjective: | un film amusant | an amusing movie |
| Adverbial phrase: | sans doute | without a doubt |
| Prepositional phrase: | à la maison | at home |

Some phrases are formulas used frequently in social situations. Other phrases are common sayings or proverbs. Notice that they do not have a subject + verb structure:

| | |
|---|---|
| À ce soir. | *See you tonight.* |
| Pas maintenant. | *Not now.* |
| la prunelle de mes yeux | *the apple of my eyes* |

## What is a sentence?

Unlike a phrase, a sentence is defined as a grammatical unit. To build this unit in French, you need nouns, verbal structures, object pronouns, adverbs, etc.—elements you may have previously learned. Think of these elements as the blocks that help you build a structure, the sum of the pieces of a whole that has a meaning of its own. A sentence includes a *subject*—a word or a group of words that tell you what or whom the sentence is about—and a *predicate*—a word or words that tell us something about the subject. Spelling and punctuation require a capital letter to start a sentence and a period to indicate the end of the message.

| | |
|---|---|
| On se verra ce soir. | *We will see each other tonight.* |

This is a sentence because there is a subject (**on**) and a predicate (**se verra ce soir**), as well as the verb **verra**.

| | |
|---|---|
| La mère veille à ses enfants. | *The mother watches her children.* |

This is a sentence because there is a subject (**la mère**) and a predicate (**veille à ses enfants**), as well as the verb **veille**.

In addition, in this sentence, the verb has an indirect object (**à ses enfants**).

# Declarative sentences

According to the function they perform, sentences are classified in categories. First, we will study the category of *declarative sentences*. A declarative sentence (from the Latin **declarare**) makes an affirmative or negative statement about a subject. A declarative sentence communicates information; it does not ask a question, it does not express exclamations, nor does it give a command. A declarative sentence consists of the following elements:

**subject + predicate**
Le pilote + atterrit sur la piste.
Le pilote atterrit sur la piste.              *The pilot lands (is landing) on the runway.*
Le pilote a atterri sur la piste.             *The pilot landed on the runway.*
Le pilote atterrira sur la piste.             *The pilot will land on the runway.*

All three of these examples are simple declarative sentences with one subject and one verb. Note that the tense of the verb in each example varies from one sentence to the next, using present, past, and future tenses. Now consider the following sentence and note how it meets the requirements of a declarative sentence:

Elle n'aime pas le bruit.                     *She does not like noise.*

It is a sentence. It includes a subject: **elle**, and a predicate including the verb: **aime**. It makes a negative statement about the subject **elle**. It is not a question, nor is it a command.

Now consider the following sentences and note that they all meet the subject + verb requirements of a declarative sentence, that the verb in each sentence is either in the affirmative or negative form, and that the verb is in various tenses of the *indicative mood*:

Nous partons à quatre heures.                *We leave at four o'clock.*
Nous ne sommes pas partis hier.              *We did not leave yesterday.*
Nous partirons demain.                        *We will leave tomorrow.*

**partons**                                   present tense *indicative mood*
**ne sommes pas partis**                      passé composé of the *indicative mood*
**partirons**                                 future tense of the *indicative mood*

In a declarative sentence, the subject of the verb may be a *simple subject* as in the previous examples, or it may be a *compound subject*. A compound subject consists of two or more subjects. These subjects are joined by a coordinating conjunction such as **et** (*and*), and **ou** (*or*). They govern the same verb.

Jean, Paul **et** Raymond vont à Nice.        *Jean, Paul, **and** Raymond go to Nice.*
Gérard **ou** Arthur va venir me chercher.    *Gerard **or** Arthur is going to pick me up.*

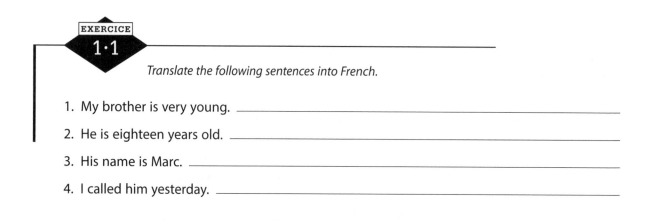

EXERCICE
## 1·1

*Translate the following sentences into French.*

1. My brother is very young. _____

2. He is eighteen years old. _____

3. His name is Marc. _____

4. I called him yesterday. _____

5. He was not home. _____

6. He will answer me soon. _____

EXERCICE

1·2

*Underline the subject of each sentence and circle the verb.*

1. Lili et Mélanie jouent ensemble.

2. Leur maman fait à manger.

3. Le papa travaille jusqu'à dix-huit heures.

4. Les dessins animés à la télé sont finis.

5. Le poulet rôtit dans le four.

6. Les petites filles se lavent les mains.

# Word order in affirmative declarative sentences

The order of words within a simple French declarative sentence is often the same as the word order in an English sentence. However, it will differ when the sentence includes object pronouns, adjectives, adverbs, and adverbial phrases (see subsequent units).

## Simple declarative sentences with direct object nouns

In English and in French alike, the natural word order of simple sentences (sentences limited to subject, verb, and object noun) is as follows:

**subject + verb + object noun**
*Marie + loves + Paul.*
Marie aime Paul.

Frequently, pronouns take the place of nouns. Just like nouns, they can play the role of subject or object in the sentence. (See Unit 12 for more on personal pronouns.) In the following examples, the subjects are pronouns:

**Tu** appelles Jean.                    *You* call John.
**Elle** lave la vaisselle.              *She washes the dishes.*

In the previous sentences, the following syntactical elements can be identified:

◆ **Tu** and **Elle** are the subjects of the verbs. They are personal pronouns and represent who completes the action of the verb.
◆ **Appelles** and **lave** are the verbs. They are in the present tense and represent the action that takes place.

◆ **Jean** and **la vaisselle** are the direct objects. They are the person or thing receiving the action of the verb.

Now consider the following sentence and note its syntactical elements:

Elise appellera Marie.                    *Elise will call Marie.*

◆ **Elise** is the subject of the verb. The subject here is a noun and represents who completes the action of the verb.
◆ **Appellera** is the verb. It is in the future tense and represents the action that will take place.
◆ **Marie** is the direct object. She is the person who receives the action of the verb.

**EXERCICE**
**1·3**

*Identify the subject in each sentence by writing S, the verb by writing V, and the object by writing O under each element, respectively.*

EXAMPLE:        Le chat attrape la souris.

                S        V        O

1. Le contrôleur demande les billets.

2. Les passagers ont composté leurs billets.

3. Je lis mon livre.

4. J'admire les illustrations.

5. Mon voisin regarde le journal.

6. Il parle à sa femme.

**EXERCICE**
**1·4**

*In the previous exercise, were the subjects nouns or pronouns? Write N for noun and P for pronoun on the lines provided.*

1. _____          4. _____

2. _____          5. _____

3. _____          6. _____

# Declarative sentences with direct and indirect object nouns

In every language, words must be arranged in the proper and logical order to avoid misunderstandings and to express ideas clearly. Consider the following declarative sentence that includes a *direct object* and an *indirect object*:

**subject + verb + direct object + indirect object**
Rémy + a acheté + un livre + à son père.
*Rémy bought a book for his father.*

Note in the previous sentences that the word order is the same in both the French and English. (*Father* is the object of a preposition.) Now consider this English variation: *Rémy bought his father a book.* The order of object nouns in this sentence has been reversed, which cannot be done in French. This demonstrates that word order is *more* flexible in the English sentence than in the French sentence when it comes to direct and indirect objects.

**EXERCICE**
**1·5**

*Is there a direct object in the following sentences? If there is, underline it; if not, write* None.

1. Nous fêtons l'anniversaire de Viviane.

2. Ses amis ont organisé une fête chez Dorine.

3. Les invités vont arriver à dix-neuf heures.

4. Ils vont tous féliciter Viviane.

5. On servira le repas sur la terrace de Dorine.

6. Dorine allumera la chaîne hi-fi.

**EXERCICE**
**1·6**

*Complete each sentence with an appropriate direct object from the following list to find out what car this couple will buy.*

son mari / des sièges de velours / les voitures confortables / un rêve / une voiture/
la performance de la voiture

1. Mimi et Jojo veulent _____

2. Mimi préfère _____

3. Mais Jojo a _____

4. Il imagine _____ sur l'autoroute.

5. Mimi, elle, imagine _____

6. Elle persuade _____ d'acheter un monoespace.

*Complete each French sentence with the direct and/or indirect object(s).*

1. *The teacher shows a movie to the students.*

   Le professeur montre _____.

2. *Mr. Dumont gives a grade to his students.*

   M. Dumont donne _____.

3. *The students do their assignment.*

   Les élèves font _____.

4. *The children bring their work to their parents.*

   Les enfants apportent _____.

5. *Some parents give a little gift to their children.*

   Certains parents donnent _____.

*Place the following sentence fragments in the appropriate order to find out a few facts about Jean and Lucie. Be sure to use the appropriate spelling and punctuation.*

1. habite / Jean / la ville de Paris

   _____

2. est / Lucie / la femme / de Jean

   _____

3. à Jean et à Lucie / les parents de Jean / une maison / achètent

   _____

4. partent / Lucie et Jean / en lune de miel / aujourd'hui

   _____

5. l'annonce / nous avons lu / de leur mariage / dans le journal

   _____

6. vont passer / à Tahiti / une semaine / ils

   _____

*Translate the following sentences into French.*

1. Today my friend Jean and I study French.

   _____

2. We already speak French.

   _____

3. We always finish our work.

   _____

4. We give our work to the teacher.

   _____

5. Sometimes I help my friend.

   _____

6. He helps me, too.

   _____

# Word order in negative declarative sentences

Negative sentences must include negative words. To make an affirmative sentence negative, place the word **ne** (or **n'** before a vowel sound) directly before the verb and place the word **pas** directly after the verb.

| | |
|---|---|
| Michelle joue au basket. | *Michelle plays basketball.* |
| Michelle **ne** joue **pas** au basket. | *Michelle does **not** play basketball.* |
| Marius habite à Marseille. | *Marius lives in Marseille.* |
| Marius **n'**habite **pas** à Marseille. | *Marius does **not** live in Marseille.* |

Other negative words and phrases that are used to create negative declarative sentences are: **rien** (*nothing*), **plus** (*no longer*), **jamais** (*never*), **personne** (*nobody*), **ni** (*neither, nor*), and **nulle part** (*nowhere*). They are placed after the verb just like **pas** and also require **ne** or **n'** before the verb.

| | |
|---|---|
| Je **ne** sais **rien**. | *I do **not** know **anything** (I know **nothing**).* |
| Nous **ne** partons **jamais** en hiver. | *We **never** leave in the winter.* |
| Il **ne** veut **plus** fumer. | *He does **not** want to smoke **anymore**.* |

Unlike English, two or three negative words can be used in a single French sentence.

| | |
|---|---|
| Je ne veux **plus jamais rien** faire de mal. | *I do **not** ever want to do **anything** bad **again**.* |
| Cela ne se fait **jamais nulle part**. | *This should **never** be done **anywhere**.* |
| Il n'y a **plus personne**. | *There is **nobody** left.* |

*Write the following sentences in French making sure the negative word used is correct. Use only one negative construction in each sentence.*

1. I never buy wine here. _____

2. The clerk is not very kind. _____

3. I do not like to pay high prices. _____

4. The owner never says hello. _____

5. We do not waste our time here. _____

*Add another negative word that makes sense in the following sentences:*

1. Nous n'irons jamais _____ nager dans le lac quand il fera froid.

2. Nous ne ferons plus _____ d'aussi grosses bêtises.

3. Nous n'inviterons jamais _____ ici. C'est notre cachette.

4. Il n'y a plus _____ à voir. Il est tard.

5. Nous ne verrons plus _____ après que le soleil se couchera.

*Translate the following sentences into French.*

1. I threw out my old phone because I did not want it anymore.

_____

2. But I cannot find my new cell phone anywhere.

_____

3. These days I do not remember anything anymore.

_____

4. Well, I cannot call anyone else tonight.

_____

5. I will never again forget to put it back into my purse.

_____

# Interrogative sentences and word order

An *interrogative* sentence serves to ask a question. We use interrogative sentences for different purposes: to obtain information, and to elicit confirmation or denial about something or someone.

| | |
|---|---|
| Tu peux répondre, n'est-ce pas? | *You can answer, can't you?* (confirmation or denial) |
| Ginette n'est pas là? | *Is Ginette not there?* (confirmation or denial) |
| Quelle heure est-il? | *What time is it?* (information) |
| Où allons-nous? | *Where are we going?* (information) |

To communicate effectively, you often must be able to ask precise questions in order to get the information you seek; furthermore you must understand a variety of questions in order to give others the information they seek from you. Consider the following sentence and the many questions that can be asked about it. Note the word order and the different question words used.

| | |
|---|---|
| Chaque jour les fleurs devenaient de plus en plus belles grâce à l'attention diligente que papa leur accordait. | *Each day, the flowers grew more and more beautiful thanks to the diligent care Dad gave them.* |
| Est-ce que les fleurs devenaient de plus en plus belles? | *Did the flowers grow more and more beautiful?* |
| Les fleurs devenaient de plus en plus belles, n'est-ce pas? | *The flowers became more and more beautiful, did they not?* |
| Quand est-ce que les fleurs devenaient de plus en plus belles? | *When did the flowers grow more and more beautiful?* |
| Qu'est-ce qui devenait de plus en plus beau? | *What grew more and more beautiful?* |
| Pourquoi est-ce que les fleurs devenaient de plus en plus belles? | *Why did the flowers grow more and more beautiful?* |
| Grâce à qui est-ce que les fleurs devenaient de plus en plus belles? | *Thanks to whom did the flowers grow more and more beautiful?* |

## Interrogative sentences and intonation

In French the intonation or rising pitch at the end of a sentence signals for the listener that a question is being asked. This manner of asking a question is familiar and preferred in oral interactions. To transcribe this oral question into writing, a question mark helps identify an interrogative sentence. Sometimes a *yes* or *no* answer may suffice as is shown in the following examples:

| | |
|---|---|
| Le train est arrivé? —Oui. / Non. | *Did the train arrive? —Yes. / No.* |
| Tu passes un examen? —Oui. / Non. | *Are you taking an exam? —Yes. / No.* |
| Elle ne viendra pas aujourd'hui? | *Will she not come today? —Yes. / No.* |
|    —Oui. / Non. | |

Other times a question solicits specific information as in the following examples:

| | |
|---|---|
| Qui a peint ce portrait? —Monet. | *Who painted this portrait? —Monet.* |
| À quelle heure on dîne? —À huit heures. | *At what time do we have dinner?* |
| |    *—At eight o'clock.* |
| Où tu vas? —À la pharmacie. | *Where are you going? —To the pharmacy.* |

## Affirmative interrogative sentences

There are several ways to communicate a question. One way to create an interrogative sentence is to use an affirmative sentence and end it with a rising inflection. The intonation alone communicates a question in spoken language; a question mark follows the interrogative sentence in written texts.

**declarative sentence + ? → interrogative sentence**

Note how the message of a straightforward declarative sentence changes when it becomes a question:

| | |
|---|---|
| Le magasin est fermé. | *The store is closed.* |
| Le magasin est fermé? | *The store is closed?* |

**EXERCICE**

**2·1**

*Rewrite each statement, changing it to a question by using the appropriate punctuation.*

1. Mon copain est en retard. _____

2. Tu as ma liste. _____

3. Le passager est patient. _____

4. Nous attendons. _____

5. Il y a un taxi au coin. _____

6. Il fait chaud ici. _____

**EXERCICE**

**2·2**

*Using appropriate punctuation and capitalization, compose questions with the following sentence fragments, making sure to follow the word order of a declarative sentence.*

1. les instructions / tu as compris

_____

2. à ton avis / étaient claires / elles

_____

3. à faire ce travail / on va / arriver

_____

4. que ce ne sera pas trop difficile / certain / tu es

_____

5. ce soir / commencer / tu veux

_____

6. d'échouer / tu ne crains pas

_____

## Negative interrogative sentences

Another way of forming a question is to start with a negative declarative sentence. Add a question mark to a negative declarative sentence and as a result you have an interrogative sentence.

**negative declarative sentence + ? → interrogative sentence**
| | |
|---|---|
| Vous ne travailliez pas pour nous. | *You were not working for us.* |
| Vous ne travailliez pas pour nous? | *Were you not working for us?* |

This type of construction (**ne...pas**) is used when the questioner expects an affirmative answer or an affirmation. Consider the following sentences and note that a *yes* answer starts with **oui** when the interrogative sentence is affirmative; it starts with *si* when the interrogative sentence is negative.

**affirmative interrogative sentence: oui** (*yes*)
| | |
|---|---|
| Ils **vont** au cours? —**Oui**, mais plus tard! | *Do they **go** to class? —**Yes**, but later!* |
| Vous **avez** de l'argent? —**Oui**, un peu. | *Do you **have** some money? —**Yes**, a little.* |

**negative interrogative sentence: si** (*yes*)
| | |
|---|---|
| Ils **ne vont pas** au cours? —**Si**, mais plus tard! | *Don't they **go** to class? —**Yes**, but later!* |
| Vous **n'avez pas** d'argent? —**Si**, un peu. | *You **do not have** any money? —**Yes**, a little.* |

Adverbs such as **encore** or **toujours** can be added to **pas** to build interrogative sentences.

| | |
|---|---|
| pas encore | *not yet* |
| pas toujours | *not always* |
| pas ici | *not here* |
| pas bien | *not well* |

And as always, by adding a question mark, the declarative sentence then becomes an interrogative sentence.

| | |
|---|---|
| Ils **ne** sont **pas encore** ici. | *They are **not** here yet.* (declarative) |
| Ils **ne** sont **pas encore** ici? | *They are **not** here yet?* (interrogative) |
| Tu **n'es pas toujours** en forme. | *You are **not always** in shape.* (declarative) |
| Tu **n'es pas toujours** en forme? | *You are **not always** in shape?* (interrogative) |
| Cette montre **ne** marche **pas** bien. | *This watch does **not** work **well**.* (declarative) |
| Cette montre **ne** marche **pas** bien? | *This watch does **not** work **well**?* (interrogative) |

As discussed in Unit 1, other negative expressions can be used instead of **ne...pas** to build interrogative sentences. They are: **ne...plus** (*no longer*), **ne...rien** (*nothing/not anything*), **ne... jamais** (*never*), **ne...personne** (*nobody/not anybody*).

| | |
|---|---|
| Elle **ne** joue **plus** au piano? | *She does **not** play the piano **anymore**?* |
| Elle **ne** joue **jamais** au piano? | *She **never** plays the piano?* |
| Elle **ne** voit **rien**? | *She does **not** see **anything**?* |
| Elle **ne** voit **personne**? | *She does **not** see **anyone**?* |

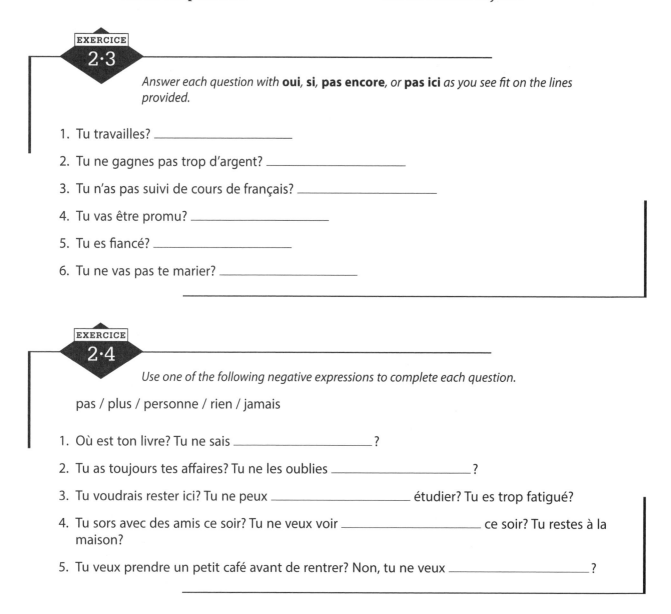

**EXERCICE 2·3**

*Answer each question with **oui, si, pas encore**, or **pas ici** as you see fit on the lines provided.*

1. Tu travailles? _____

2. Tu ne gagnes pas trop d'argent? _____

3. Tu n'as pas suivi de cours de français? _____

4. Tu vas être promu? _____

5. Tu es fiancé? _____

6. Tu ne vas pas te marier? _____

**EXERCICE 2·4**

*Use one of the following negative expressions to complete each question.*

pas / plus / personne / rien / jamais

1. Où est ton livre? Tu ne sais _____?

2. Tu as toujours tes affaires? Tu ne les oublies _____?

3. Tu voudrais rester ici? Tu ne peux _____ étudier? Tu es trop fatigué?

4. Tu sors avec des amis ce soir? Tu ne veux voir _____ ce soir? Tu restes à la maison?

5. Tu veux prendre un petit café avant de rentrer? Non, tu ne veux _____?

## Interrogative sentences with **est-ce que**

There are several ways to communicate a simple question in French. We have previously seen that one way to create an interrogative sentence is to use an affirmative sentence and end it with a rising inflection. Another way to create an interrogative sentence in French is to place the phrase **est-ce que** before the declarative sentence.

> **est-ce que + declarative sentence → interrogative sentence**
> Le magasin est fermé. *The store is closed.*
> **Est-ce que** le magasin est fermé? *Is the store closed?*

Compare the following French and English interrogative sentences and note that the structure in the French sentence is always the same. The structure in the English sentence varies depending on the tense used and depending on whether the verb *to be* or *to have* is a part of the structure.

| **est-ce que/qu'** + subject + predicate | verb (*to be/to have*) + subject + predicate |
|---|---|
| Est-ce qu'il ne fait pas beau? | *Is the weather not nice?* |
| Est-ce que vous êtes triste? | *Are you sad?* |
| Est-ce qu'elle ne va pas se marier? | *Is she not going to get married?* |
| Est-ce que tu as mangé? | *Have you eaten?* |

| **est-ce que/qu'** + subject + predicate | helping verb (*do/does/did/will*) + subject + predicate |
|---|---|
| Est-ce que vous faites du ski? | *Do you ski?* |
| Est-ce que tu ne me dois pas d'argent? | *Don't you owe me money?* |
| Est-ce qu'ils ne sont pas arrivés? | *Did they not arrive?* |
| Est-ce que tu les chercheras ? | *Will you pick them up?* |

**EXERCICE**
**2·5**

*Translate each question into French using* **est-ce que***.*

1. Does the sun shine today?

   _____

2. Are we going to the beach?

   _____

3. Do you (tu) want to have breakfast on the terrace?

   _____

4. Will we go swim in the sea after breakfast?

   _____

5. Are you (tu) still a little sleepy?

   _____

6. Do you (tu) need a good shower?

   _____

## Interrogative sentences with inversion

Another way to create interrogative sentences is to use the inversion method. The inverted interrogative structure is somewhat formal but is sometimes used in informal situations, for example, when asking for the time: **Quelle heure est-il?** To create such an interrogative structure, we will once again start with the declarative sentence. It will be important, however, to distinguish between a subject pronoun and a subject noun in the sentence when using this method.

# When the subject is a pronoun

If the subject of the verb in the declarative sentence is a personal pronoun, it suffices to invert the subject and the verb while separating the two with a hyphen. The result is an interrogative sentence.

**subject pronoun + verb** → declarative sentence
**verb + subject pronoun** → interrogative sentence

| | |
|---|---|
| Il est fermé. | *It is closed.* |
| **Est-il** fermé? | ***Is it*** *closed?* |
| Elle chantera fort. | *She will sing loud.* |
| **Chantera-t-elle** fort? | ***Will she sing*** *loud?* |
| Nous boirons à ta santé. | *We will drink to your health.* |
| **Boirons-nous** à ta santé? | ***Will we drink*** *to your health?* |
| Vous êtes allés au cinéma. | *You went to the movies.* |
| **Etes-vous allés** au cinéma? | ***Did you go*** *to the movies?* |
| On ne fait pas de bêtises. | *We are not doing anything silly.* |
| **Ne fait-on pas** de bêtises? | ***Are we not being*** *silly?* |
| Il y a beaucoup de gens ici. | *There are a lot of people here.* |
| **Y a-t-il** beaucoup de gens ici? | ***Are there*** *a lot of people here?* |

You can always invert the subject pronoun and the verb except when the subject pronoun is **je**. The subject pronoun **je** and the verb are only inverted in very rare cases such as in **Puis-je?** (*May I?*) This phrase is commonly used, especially in the service business. **Puis** is a modified form of the verb **pouvoir** (*to be able*). In other cases, the inversion with the pronoun **je** can also be used but only to make an emphatic statement. Look at the following examples:

| | |
|---|---|
| **Puis-je** vous aider, monsieur? | ***May I*** *help you, sir?* |
| **Ai-je** autant de cheveux gris? | ***Do I have*** *so much gray hair?* (sense of humor) |
| **Vais-je** y aller? | ***Am I going*** *to go?* (*Should I?*) |
| **Dois-je** le faire? | ***Must I*** *do it?* (emphasis) |
| **Saurais-je** le dire? | ***Dare I*** *say it?* (emphasis) |

# When the subject is a noun

If the subject of the verb in the declarative sentence is a noun, the subject + verb structure of the declarative sentence will remain the same, but the appropriate subject pronoun that can replace the subject noun is added after the verb and is linked to the verb with a hyphen.

**subject noun + verb** → declarative sentence
**subject noun + verb + - + pronoun** → interrogative sentence

| | |
|---|---|
| Le magasin est fermé. | *The store is closed.* |
| Le magasin **est-il** fermé? | ***Is the store closed?*** |

Compare the following declarative and interrogative sentences. Note that the pronoun to be added must have the same gender and number as the noun it completes; therefore it is either **il**, **ils**, **elle**, or **elles**. Also note that whenever a verb ends in a vowel, the letter **-t-** is inserted between the verb and the pronoun; the inserted **-t-** is wrapped between two hyphens.

| | |
|---|---|
| La maison sera vendue. | *The house will be sold.* |
| La maison **sera-t-elle** vendue? | ***Will the house be sold?*** |
| (la maison = elle) | |
| La petite fille va à l'école. | *The little girl goes to school.* |
| La petite fille **va-t-elle** à l'école? | ***Will*** *the little girl* ***go*** *to school?* |
| (la fille = elle) | |
| Le marché aux fleurs n'existe plus. | *The flower market no longer exists.* |
| Le marché aux fleurs **n'existe-t-il** plus? | ***Does*** *the flower market no longer* ***exist?*** |
| (le marché = il) | |

Les personnes présentes voteront.  
Les personnes présentes **voteront-elles**?  
(les personnes = elles)

*The people in attendance will vote.*  
*Will the people in attendance **vote**?*

EXERCICE 2·6

*Change the following declarative sentences into questions by using inversion.*

1. Marie écoute bien les conseils de sa maman. _____

2. Elle est attentive. _____

3. Les frères jumeaux travaillent ensemble. _____

4. Ils sont inséparables. _____

5. Tu ne vois pas le bus. _____

6. Il faut se dépêcher. _____

## Polite phrases in interrogative sentences

To demonstrate courtesy in asking a question, use a phrase such as **Pardon** or **Pardonnez-moi** (*Pardon, Pardon me*), **Excusez-moi** (*Excuse me*), **Excusez-moi de vous déranger** (*Forgive me for interrupting*), or **S'il vous plaît** (*Please*) before the question. Also be sure to use the appropriate title: **monsieur** (*sir*), **madame** (*madam*), or **mademoiselle** (*miss*). Consider the following examples and note the punctuation:

**polite phrase + title + verb + subject pronoun + . . . ?**

**Pardonnez-moi, madame, avez-vous** de la monnaie**?**

*Pardon me, madam. Do you have change?*

**S'il vous plaît, monsieur, pouvez-vous** ouvrir la porte**?**

*Please, sir, could you open the door?*

**Excusez-moi, mademoiselle, êtes-vous** la caissière**?**

*Excuse me, miss. Are you the cashier?*

EXERCICE 2·7

*Play the role of a saleslady and write the following questions in French, in a very polite and formal manner.*

1. Do you like this dress, miss?

_____

2. Can I recommend a pair of shoes, miss?

_____

3. Do you need a scarf, miss?

_____

4. Are you ready to pay, miss?

_____

5. Do you have a credit card, miss?

_____

6. Would you like a bag, miss?

_____

EXERCICE
2·8

*Go back to the previous exercise and for each of those questions add one of the following polite phrases:* **s'il vous plaît**, **excusez-moi**, **pardonnez-moi**, **pardon**, *or* **excusez-moi de vous déranger**.

1. _____

2. _____

3. _____

4. _____

5. _____

6. _____

EXERCICE
2·9

*With the sentence fragments provided write a question using the inversion method and the present tense of the indicative mood.*

1. préférer (tu) **/** un citron pressé / un coca / une bière

_____

2. arriver (vous) cet après-midi / demain

_____

3. désirer (ils) / aller à la plage / nager dans la piscine

_____

4. acheter (nous) le parasol / la chaise-longue / une serviette

_____

5. vouloir (elles) voir un film / dîner au restaurant

_____

6. dormir (vous) dans le lit / sur le canapé

_____

# Tag questions

Another way of forming a question both in English and French is to add a "tag" at the end of a declarative sentence.

**declarative sentence, + tag + ? → tag question**

The tag phrase **n'est-ce pas** is used in all registers of the French language (familiar and formal), but it is more frequently used in formal situations.

**Tu as mon sac, + n'est-ce pas + ? → tag question**

| | |
|---|---|
| Cette écharpe est chère, **n'est-ce pas?** | *This scarf is expensive, **isn't it?*** |
| Elle a très bien parlé, **n'est-ce pas?** | *She spoke very well, **did she not?*** |
| Tu nous rejoindras, **n'est-ce pas?** | *You will join us, **won't you?*** |

However, some other tags are only used in informal spoken communication. In any case, a questioner who poses a tag question expects agreement, not a *no* answer. In French, some common and familiar tags added to declarative sentences to create questions are: **non?** (*no?*), **pas vrai?** (*not true? / right?*), and **tu ne crois pas? / tu ne penses pas?** (*don't you think?*)

| | |
|---|---|
| La gérante est intelligente, **non?** | *The manager is smart, **isn't she?*** |
| Marc nage bien, **tu ne penses pas?** | *Marc swims very well, **don't you think?*** |
| Cette fille a du talent, **pas vrai?** | *This girl has talent, **right?*** |

---

**EXERCICE 2·10**

*Write the letter of the correct answer to each question on the lines provided.*

1. Il est intelligent, non? _____

2. Il est grand, tu ne penses pas? _____

3. Tu veux une limonade, non? _____

4. Elles sont américaines, n'est-ce pas? _____

5. Tu viendras demain, pas vrai? _____

a. Non, un thé chaud.

b. Non, canadiennes.

c. Oui, mais le soir.

d. Oui, brillant même.

e. Non, au contraire, il est petit.

---

**EXERCICE 2·11**

*Translate the following questions into French using tag phrases. Use **tu** for you.*

1. You like this book, right?

_____

2. You know who wrote it, don't you?

_____

3. This author is good, don't you think?

_____

4. He is a master of suspense, no?

_____

5. You have read his previous book, right?

_____

# Precise questions

·3·

In Unit 2, you learned the various ways to form a question such as using intonation, using the phrase **est-ce que**, and making subject-verb inversions. In this unit, you will continue practicing these interrogative structures while focusing on asking for very precise information.

## Complex questions

Questions in which you expect more specific information than a simple choice-answer or a straightforward *yes* or *no* response are referred to as complex questions. They start with an interrogative pronoun, an interrogative adverb, or any other interrogative word or phrase.

## Questions with qui

There are several ways to create an interrogative sentence with the interrogative pronoun **qui**. The elements and word order in the sentence will vary according to the function performed by **qui**, which can be either *subject* or *direct object*. The various possible structures for an interrogative sentence introduced by **qui** are as follows:

### Qui + verb

In this interrogative sentence, **qui** is the subject and is followed directly by the verb.

| | |
|---|---|
| **Qui** était ce monsieur?<br>(**qui** = subject of **était**) | ***Who*** *was that gentleman?* |
| **Qui** dit cela?<br>(**qui** = subject of **dit**) | ***Who*** *says that?* |
| **Qui** a compris la leçon?<br>(**qui** = subject of **a compris**) | ***Who*** *understood the lesson?* |

### Qui est-ce qui + verb

In this interrogative sentence, **qui** is the subject, but the word order is the one used in the **est-ce que** method with one difference: The phrase used is **est-ce qui**.

| | |
|---|---|
| **Qui est-ce qui** dit cela? | ***Who*** *says that?* |
| **Qui est-ce qui** a compris? | ***Who*** *understood?* |
| **Qui est-ce qui** est le plus grand? | ***Who*** *is the tallest?* |

18

## Qui est-ce que + subject + verb

In this interrogative sentence structure, **qui** is the *direct object*, but the word order is the one used in the **est-ce que** method.

| | |
|---|---|
| **Qui est-ce que** tu as vu? | **Whom** *did you see?* |
| **Qui est-ce que** nous inviterons? | **Whom** *will we invite?* |
| **Qui est-ce que** tu préfères? | **Whom** *do you prefer?* |

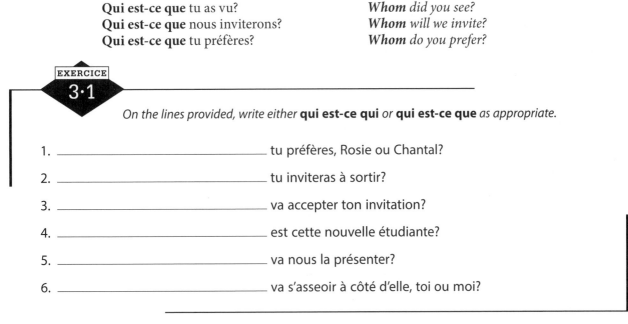

**EXERCICE**
**3·1**

*On the lines provided, write either* **qui est-ce qui** *or* **qui est-ce que** *as appropriate.*

1. _____ tu préfères, Rosie ou Chantal?

2. _____ tu inviteras à sortir?

3. _____ va accepter ton invitation?

4. _____ est cette nouvelle étudiante?

5. _____ va nous la présenter?

6. _____ va s'asseoir à côté d'elle, toi ou moi?

## Qui + interrogative sentence including inversion

In this interrogative sentence, **qui** is also the *direct object*, but the word order is the one used in the inversion method.

| | |
|---|---|
| **Qui** Marielle a-t-elle épousé? <br> (**qui** = direct object of **a épousé**) | **Whom** *did Marielle marry?* |
| **Qui** as-tu vu? <br> (**qui** = direct object of **as vu**) | **Whom** *did you see?* |
| **Qui** inviterons-nous? <br> (**qui** = direct object of **inviterons**) | **Whom** *will we invite?* |
| **Qui** avez-vous embauché? <br> (**qui** = direct object of **avez embauché**) | **Whom** *did you hire?* |
| **Qui** aimez-vous le mieux ? <br> (**qui** = direct object of **aimez**) | **Whom** *do you love the most?* |

**EXERCICE**
**3·2**

*Translate each question and answer into English.*

1. Qui as-tu rencontré hier soir? —Un vieil ami.

_____

2. Qui as-tu invité? —La famille.

_____

3. Qui est-ce que Raymond va féliciter? —Son nouvel employé.

_____

4. Qui cherchez-vous? —La vendeuse.

_____

5. Qui est-ce que tes parents préfèrent? —Moi bien sûr.

_____

6. Qui Suzanne embrasse-t-elle? —Son copain.

_____

EXERCICE
3·3

*Complete the following questions using **qui** with an inversion. Use the formal pronoun* **vous** *for* you.

1. Whom are you calling? (appeler)

Qui _____?

2. Whom are you inviting? (inviter)

Qui _____?

3. Whom did you see? (voir)

Qui _____?

4. Whom do you prefer? (préférer)

Qui _____?

5. Whom are you going to pick up? (chercher)

Qui _____?

6. Whom are you going to send back? (renvoyer)

Qui _____?

## Questions with **qu'est-ce que** and **que**

The phrase **qu'est-ce que/qu'** as well as the pronoun **que** express *what* and play the role of direct object in a sentence.

### Qu'est-ce que/qu' + subject + verb

In this interrogative sentence, the phrase **qu'est-ce que** (*what*) is followed by a subject and a verb.

| | |
|---|---|
| **Qu'est-ce qu'**Anne fait? | *What is Anne doing?* |
| **Qu'est-ce que** tu désires? | *What would you like?* |
| **Qu'est-ce que** nous allons manger? | *What are we going to eat?* |

## Que/Qu' + verb + subject

In this interrogative sentence, **que** (*what*) is followed by a verb and a subject.

Que **fait Anne**?                    *What **is Anne doing**?*

(The noun, **Anne**, and the verb, **fait**, have been inverted.)

Que **désires-tu**?                    *What **would you like**?*
Qu'**allons-nous** manger?          *What **are we going** to eat?*

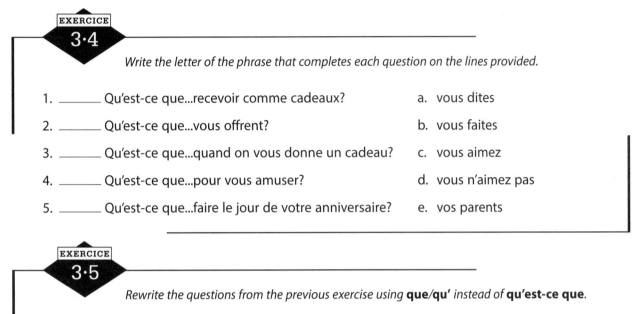

EXERCICE
3·4

*Write the letter of the phrase that completes each question on the lines provided.*

1. _____ Qu'est-ce que...recevoir comme cadeaux?          a.  vous dites

2. _____ Qu'est-ce que...vous offrent?          b.  vous faites

3. _____ Qu'est-ce que...quand on vous donne un cadeau?          c.  vous aimez

4. _____ Qu'est-ce que...pour vous amuser?          d.  vous n'aimez pas

5. _____ Qu'est-ce que...faire le jour de votre anniversaire?          e.  vos parents

EXERCICE
3·5

*Rewrite the questions from the previous exercise using **que/qu'** instead of **qu'est-ce que**.*

1. Qu' _____ ?

2. Que _____ ?

3. Que _____ ?

4. Que _____ ?

5. Que _____ ?

## Questions with qu'est-ce qui

The phrase **qu'est-ce qui** is used to express *what*. It plays the role of *subject* in the sentence.

Qu'**est-ce qui** arrive?                    *What **is happening**?*
Qu'**est-ce qui** s'est passé?          *What **happened**?*
Qu'**est-ce qui** prouve ce fait?          *What **proves this fact**?*

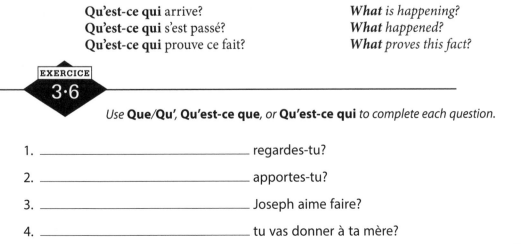

EXERCICE
3·6

*Use **Que/Qu'**, **Qu'est-ce que**, or **Qu'est-ce qui** to complete each question.*

1. _____ regardes-tu?

2. _____ apportes-tu?

3. _____ Joseph aime faire?

4. _____ tu vas donner à ta mère?

5. _____ ne va pas?

6. _____ fait-il?

## Questions with interrogative adverbs

With the interrogative adverbs **pourquoi** (*why*), **comment** (*how*), **quand** (*when*), **combien de** (*how many/how much*), and **où** (*where*), French uses the following methods to create interrogative sentences:

### Interrogative adverb + **est-ce que** + word order of simple declarative sentence

In the following questions, the interrogative adverb is followed by the phrase **est-ce que**, the subject, and the verb.

| | |
|---|---|
| Pourquoi **est-ce que Patrick n'aime pas** son travail? | *Why **doesn't Patrick like** his work?* |
| Comment **est-ce que tu vas?** | *How **are you?*** |
| Quand **est-ce que tu vas** au travail? | *When **are you going** to work?* |
| Combien de jours **est-ce que tu resteras?** | *How many days **will you stay?*** |
| Où **est-ce qu'Anne va** avec tous ces livres? | *Where **is Anne going** with all those books?* |
| Où **est-ce qu'elle habite?** | *Where **does she live?*** |

### Interrogative adverb + word order appropriate to inversion method

In using this method, apply what you have previously learned about the inversion method (remember not to invert a noun-subject with the verb; instead add a hyphen and a subject pronoun after the verb).

| | |
|---|---|
| Pourquoi **Patrick n'aime-t-il pas** son travail? | *Why **doesn't Patrick like** his work?* |
| Comment **vas-tu?** | *How **are you?*** |
| Quand **vas-tu** au travail? | *When **do you go** to work?* |
| Combien de jours **resteras-tu?** | *How many days **will you stay?*** |
| Où **Anne va-t-elle** avec tous ces livres? | *Where **does Anne go** with all these books?* |
| Où **habite-t-elle?** | *Where **does she live?*** |

### Interrogative adverb + word order of simple declarative sentence

Using this method means simply adding the interrogative adverb to the declarative sentence and using a higher pitch intonation at the end of the sentence. This is used in very familiar settings only.

| | |
|---|---|
| Pourquoi **Patrick n'aime pas** son travail? | *Why **doesn't Patrick like** his work?* |

Note in the following sentences that the words **comment**, **quand**, **combien de jours**, and **où** can be placed at the head of the question or after the verb:

| | |
|---|---|
| **Comment** tu vas? | *How are you?* |
| Tu vas **comment?** | *How are you?* |
| **Quand** tu vas au travail? | *When do you go to work?* |
| Tu vas au travail **quand?** | *When do you go to work?* |
| **Combien de jours** tu resteras? | *How many days will you stay?* |

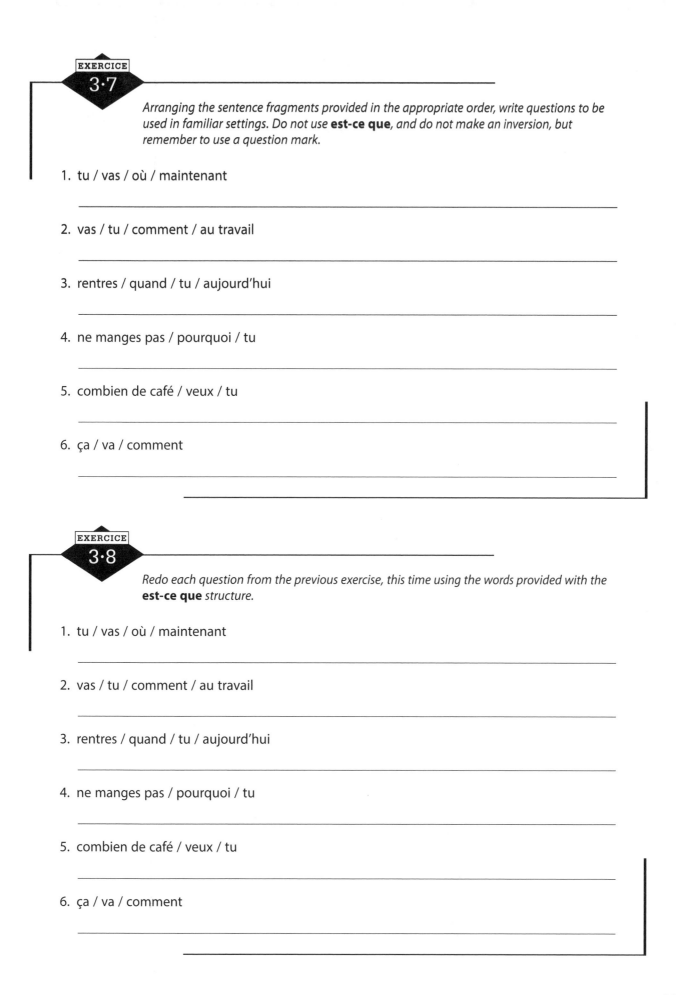

## EXERCICE 3·7

*Arranging the sentence fragments provided in the appropriate order, write questions to be used in familiar settings. Do not use **est-ce que**, and do not make an inversion, but remember to use a question mark.*

1. tu / vas / où / maintenant

   _____

2. vas / tu / comment / au travail

   _____

3. rentres / quand / tu / aujourd'hui

   _____

4. ne manges pas / pourquoi / tu

   _____

5. combien de café / veux / tu

   _____

6. ça / va / comment

   _____

## EXERCICE 3·8

*Redo each question from the previous exercise, this time using the words provided with the **est-ce que** structure.*

1. tu / vas / où / maintenant

   _____

2. vas / tu / comment / au travail

   _____

3. rentres / quand / tu / aujourd'hui

   _____

4. ne manges pas / pourquoi / tu

   _____

5. combien de café / veux / tu

   _____

6. ça / va / comment

   _____

# Questions with the adjective quel

Many very common interrogative questions include a form of the adjective **quel**. Here are a few. Note how the form of **quel** changes according to the gender (masculine or feminine) and the number (singular or plural) of the noun it accompanies. As previously seen, there are again three ways to create this type of question: the **est-ce que** method, the inversion method, and the voice pitch method.

| | |
|---|---|
| **Quel** train **est-ce que tu prends?** | *Which train **are you taking**?* |
| **Quel** train **prends-tu?** | |
| **Quel** train **tu prends?** | |
| | |
| **Quelle** heure **est-ce qu'il est?** | *What time **is it**?* |
| **Quelle** heure **est-il?** | |
| **Quelle** heure **il est?** | |
| | |
| **Quels** livres **est-ce que tu as lus?** | *What books **have you read**?* |
| **Quels** livres **as-tu lus?** | |
| **Quel** livres **tu as lus?** | |
| | |
| **Quelles** dates **est-ce que tu préfères?** | *What dates **do you prefer**?* |
| **Quelles** dates **préfères-tu?** | |
| **Quelles** dates **tu préfères?** | |

Now consider these examples in which **quel** does not directly precede the noun, and note the word order in this type of interrogative sentence:

**Quel + être + subject**

| | |
|---|---|
| Quel + est + ton nom? | *What is your name?* |
| Quels sont tes numéros de téléphone? | *What are your phone numbers?* |
| Quelles sont les prévisions météorologiques? | *What is the weather forecast?* |
| Quelle est ton opinion? | *What is your opinion?* |

EXERCICE

3·9

*Translate the following questions into French using the correct form of* **quel**.

1. What time is it? _____

2. What is his date of birth? _____

3. What is her telephone number? _____

_____

4. What is the weather today? _____

_____

5. What are his favorite colors? _____

_____

6. What choice do I have? _____

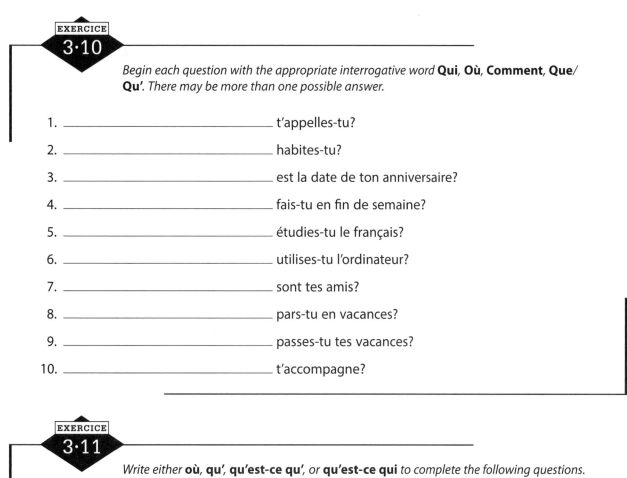

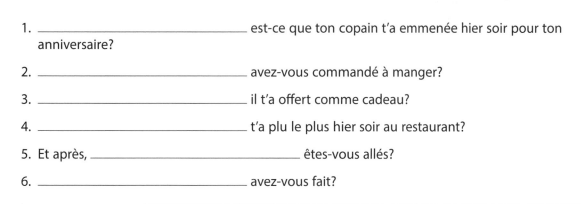

**EXERCICE 3·10**

*Begin each question with the appropriate interrogative word* **Qui, Où, Comment, Que/ Qu'**. *There may be more than one possible answer.*

1. _____ t'appelles-tu?

2. _____ habites-tu?

3. _____ est la date de ton anniversaire?

4. _____ fais-tu en fin de semaine?

5. _____ étudies-tu le français?

6. _____ utilises-tu l'ordinateur?

7. _____ sont tes amis?

8. _____ pars-tu en vacances?

9. _____ passes-tu tes vacances?

10. _____ t'accompagne?

**EXERCICE 3·11**

*Write either* **où, qu', qu'est-ce qu'**, *or* **qu'est-ce qui** *to complete the following questions.*

1. _____ est-ce que ton copain t'a emmenée hier soir pour ton anniversaire?

2. _____ avez-vous commandé à manger?

3. _____ il t'a offert comme cadeau?

4. _____ t'a plu le plus hier soir au restaurant?

5. Et après, _____ êtes-vous allés?

6. _____ avez-vous fait?

# Questions with prepositions

Complex questions sometimes start with prepositions followed by question words; these are used to elicit concrete or fuller responses to a question. As previously seen, there are usually several ways to form a question: the **est-ce que** method, the inversion method, and using intonation in a declarative sentence. The word order in the complex interrogative sentence introduced by a preposition may be as follows:

> **preposition + interrogative word + est-ce que + declarative sentence**

or

> **preposition + interrogative word + inversion method word order**

or

**preposition + interrogative word + declarative sentence (use of intonation in speaking, use of question mark in writing)**

The following is a list of prepositions followed by an interrogative adverb often used to create complex questions:

| | |
|---|---|
| À qui? | *To whom?* |
| Avec qui? | *With whom?* |
| De qui? | *From whom?* |
| Pour qui? | *For whom?* |
| D'où? | *From where? / Where from?* |
| Par où? | *Through where?* |
| Depuis quand? | *Since when?* |
| Jusqu'à quand? | *Until when?* |
| Pendant combien de temps? | *For how long?* |
| Dans combien de temps? | *When? / In how much time?* |

**Pour qui** est-ce qu'elle achète le bijou?     *For whom does she buy the jewel?*
**Pour qui** achète-t-elle le bijou?
**Pour qui** elle achète le bijou?

**Depuis quand** est-ce qu'Anne habite Paris?     *Since when does Anne live in Paris?*
**Depuis quand** Anne habite-t-elle Paris?
**Depuis quand** Anne habite Paris?

**Pendant combien de temps** est-ce qu'ils ont attendu?     *For how long did they wait?*
**Pendant combien de temps** ont-ils attendu?
**Pendant combien de temps** ils ont attendu?

---

**EXERCISE**

**3·12**

*Using **tu** for* you *and the inversion method, translate the sentences into French.*

1. Where are you from? _____

2. Where are you going? _____

3. Since when do you study French? _____

_____

4. When are you going to finish this exercise? _____

_____

5. Until when are you going to wait? _____

_____

6. To whom do you write most of your e-mails? _____

_____

*Complete the following questions for your favorite singer using* **vous** *to address him/her and the present indicative of the verbs in parentheses.*

1. Quel âge _____? (avoir)

2. _____ la couleur naturelle de vos cheveux? (être)

3. Où _____? (habiter)

4. _____ votre vrai nom? (être)

5. Pourquoi _____ à Paris? (ne pas venir)

6. Combien d'enfants _____? (avoir)

*Translate the following questions into French, using* **vous** *for you and the inverted word order structure.*

1. Where would you like to go? _____

2. How much can you spend? _____

3. Who is traveling with you? _____

4. What airline do you prefer? _____

5. Why do you want to travel first class? _____

*Complete each of the following sentences with the appropriate interrogative term.*

1. Pour _____ est-ce que tu vas voter?

2. D' _____ est-il? De Bretagne?

3. _____ est-ce que tu vas voter?

4. _____ est le slogan de sa campagne électorale?

5. _____ seront les élections?

6. _____ prendras-tu ta décision?

*Read the paragraph below and complete the following questions for each of the underlined sentences.*

Aman Ary, à l'âge de dix-neuf ans, est un grand athlète. Comme enfant, il jouait déjà au foot et cette expérience l'a inspiré pour le reste de sa vie. Son père l'emmenait aussi régulièrement à des matchs de football. Aman voulait devenir célèbre, comme ses idoles, et il voulait jouer comme eux pour une équipe professionnelle aux États-Unis. Actuellement, Aman joue pour l'équipe nationale de France. Aman est très discipliné: il ne rate jamais l'entraînement et il maintient la forme. Son rêve s'est réalisé!

1. _____ a Aman Ary?

2. _____ faisait-il déjà comme enfant?

3. _____ est-ce que son père l'emmenait régulièrement?

4. _____ voulait devenir célèbre?

5. _____ voulait-il jouer un jour?

6. _____ est-ce qu'Aman joue actuellement?

7. _____ est Aman?

8. _____ il ne rate jamais?

9. _____ il maintient?

10. _____ s'est réalisé?

# Limiting questions

Some interrogative terms are used to ask limiting or partial questions. Some elicit a specific answer about a noun such as the adverbial phrase **combien de** (*how much*) or the adjectives **lequel, laquelle, lesquels,** and **lesquelles** (*which one/which ones*).

| | |
|---|---|
| **Lequel** de ces tableaux préfères-tu? | ***Which one*** *of these paintings do you prefer?* |

(**Lequel** is in the masculine singular form; it refers to one **tableau**.)

| | |
|---|---|
| **Laquelle** de ces serveuses est la plus serviable? | ***Which one*** *of these waitresses is the most helpful?* |

(**Laquelle** is in the feminine singular form; it refers to one **serveuse**.)

| | |
|---|---|
| **Combien d'**euros as-tu? | ***How many*** *euros do you have?* |
| **Combien de** temps avons-nous? | ***How much*** *time do we have?* |

**EXERCICE**
**3·17**

*Complete the following questions with a form of* **lequel** *or with the phrase* **combien de**.

1. Regardez ces deux filles! _____ des deux est la plus grande?

2. Il y a deux bons films à la télé. _____ des deux veux-tu voir?

3. Nous pouvons acheter deux CD récents. _____?

4. Jacques a téléphoné? _____ fois?

5. _____ baguettes est-ce qu'il nous faut?

6. Les bananes sont mûres? _____ veux-tu?

# Exclamatory sentences

Exclamatory sentences communicate strong feelings. The speaker often adds voice modulation and facial expressions to stress emotions. Exclamatory sentences are more common in speech than in writing.

## Basic exclamatory sentences

There are three basic ways of expressing yourself in an exclamatory manner in French. You may use a declarative sentence and add intonation (an exclamation mark in writing), or start a sentence with one of the conjunctions **que** or **comme** followed by the declarative sentence.

| | |
|---|---|
| Ce souper est délicieux! | *Supper is delicious!* (intonation) |
| **Que** tu es gentil! | *How nice you are!* |
| **Comme** il fait froid! | *How cold it is!* |

## Declarative sentence with intonation or punctuation

With the appropriate punctuation you can use declarative sentences (Unit 1) to express strong feelings. For some, a definition of an exclamatory sentence in English and in French alike is a forceful declarative sentence that shows strong emotion. In writing, an exclamation mark ends the sentence.

**declarative sentence + ! → exclamatory sentence**

The exclamation mark adds emphasis, an element of surprise, astonishment, admiration, or happiness to what was initially a simple declarative sentence (affirmative or negative).

| | |
|---|---|
| Ce monsieur a gagné la loterie! | *This man won the lottery!* |
| Je suis la meilleure! | *I am the best!* |
| Il a du courage! | *He has courage!* |
| Tu n'as pas fait ton devoir! | *You did not do your homework!* |
| Regarde ma nouvelle voiture! | *Look at my new car!* |
| Bon, je ne dirai pas un mot! | *Fine, I will not say one word!* |

**EXERCICE**
**4·1**

*Fill in the blanks to complete the French translations of the following sentences.*

1. *The moon is so beautiful!* Comme _____!

2. *We love the beach so much!* _____ tant la plage!

3. *It is hot outside!* Qu' _____!

4. *The lemonade is cold!* Que _____!

5. *Lucie is so tired!* _____

6. *Good! Now we* (fem.) *are ready!* _____

EXERCICE
4·2

*Express the following English statements in French as affirmative exclamations.*

1. I am so cute! _____

2. I dance so well! _____

3. I have so many friends! _____

4. My boss loves me a lot! _____

5. I am very rich! _____

6. Everybody admires me! _____

# Exclamatory sentences introduced by exclamatory conjunctions, adverbs, or adjectives

Exclamation words express the attitudes and emotions of the speaker. A definition of a formal exclamatory sentence (used in writing) is one that begins with an exclamation word.

## Exclamations with **que** and **comme**

Some exclamatory sentences start with **que** (*how*) or **comme** (*how*). These words underscore the quality, nature, or intensity of the adjective or verb that follows them.

**que + declarative sentence + ! → exclamatory sentence**

| | |
|---|---|
| **Que** c'est beau! | *How beautiful this is!* |
| **Qu'**il est grand! | *How tall he is!* |
| **Que** vous êtes polis! | *How polite you are!* |
| **Que** vous avez l'air content! | *How happy you look!* |

**comme + declarative sentence + ! → exclamatory sentence**

| | |
|---|---|
| **Comme** vous travaillez bien! | *How well you work!* |
| **Comme** ils sont mignons! | *How cute they are!* |
| **Comme** ils nagent vite! | *How fast they swim!* |
| **Comme** tu es amusante! | *How funny you are!* |
| **Comme** ils sont adorables! | *How adorable they are!* |

## Exclamations with **combien, combien de/d'**, and **que de/d'**

Exclamatory sentences are also introduced by the exclamatory adverbs **combien** (*how much*), **combien de/d'**, and **que de/d'** (*how much/how many*). These words stress the quantity or intensity of the verb or noun that follows.

**combien + declarative sentence + ! → exclamatory sentence**

Combien j'aime ce pays! | *How I love this country!*
Combien j'ai attendu ce moment! | *How I waited for this moment!*

**combien de + noun + ! → exclamatory phrase**

Combien de roses! | *How many roses!*
Combien de compliments! | *How many compliments!*
Combien d'argent il a hérité! | *How much money he inherited!*

**que de + noun + ! → exclamatory phrase**

Que de cadeaux sous l'arbre de Noël! | *How many gifts under the Christmas tree!*
Que d'amour! | *How much love!*

**que de + noun + declarative sentence + ! → exclamatory sentence**

Que de confettis on jette dans les rues! | *How much confetti they throw into the streets!*
Que de papier vous gaspillez! | *How much paper you waste!*
Que de sucreries elle mange! | *How many sweets she eats!*

## Exclamations with quel

Exclamations can also be introduced by a form of the adjective **quel** (*what*). This exclamation word underscores the quality, nature, or intensity of the noun or noun phrase it describes.

**quel/quelle/quels/quelles + noun + ! → exclamatory phrase**

Quel conducteur! | *What a driver!*
Quels sportifs! | *What athletes!*
Quelles magnifiques couleurs! | *What magnificent colors!*

**quel/quelle/quels/quelles + noun + ! → exclamatory sentence**

Quelle imagination elle a! | *What imagination she has!*
Quelle peur bleue j'ai eue hier soir! | *What horrible fright I had last night!*
Quelle force ils ont! | *What strength they have!*

These exclamations may have several meanings. For example, the exclamation **Quelle voiture!** (*What a car!*) could praise the size, value, performance, beauty, or other qualities of the car; or the context may suggests the car is ugly, old, or otherwise despicable.

Quel costume! | *What a cool (or awful) suit!*
Quelle maison il a achetée! | *What a great (or horrible) house he bought!*

**EXERCICE**
**4·3**

*Translate the following sentences into English.*

1. Que de plaisirs on trouve dans la vie!

   _____

2. Combien de surprises elle nous réserve!

   _____

3. Quelle innocence on voit dans les enfants!

   _____

4. Combien nous sommes attachés à la vie!

   _____

5. Comme nous sommes heureux!

_____

6. Quelle chance nous avons!

_____

EXERCICE
4·4

*Place the sentence fragments provided in the right order to create exclamatory sentences about crazy drivers. Beware of capitalization and punctuation.*

1. conduit vite / que / ce monsieur

_____

2. il y a / accidents / combien d' / sur les routes

_____

3. dangereux / comme / les chauffards / sont

_____

4. que d' / sur la route / obstacles / il y a

_____

5. les feux rouges / fous / combien de / brûlent

_____

# Interjections and exclamatory sentences

Interjections are words or phrases used in an exclamation to add emotion. These utterances frequently appear in or with exclamatory sentences to express a reaction to what we perceive around us. Interjections end in an exclamation mark.

| | |
|---|---|
| **Tiens!** Le temps s'éclaircit. | ***Look at that!*** *The weather is clearing up.* |
| **Ah tiens!** Voilà finalement l'autobus. | ***Look at that!*** *There is the bus finally!* |

The following interjections are used to express pain or relief:

| | | | |
|---|---|---|---|
| Aïe! | *Ouch!* | Ouïlle! | *Ouch!* |
| Dieu merci! | *Thank goodness!* | Ouf! | *Phew! (as in escaping a bad situation; sign of relief)* |

The following interjections are used to express annoyance:

| | | | |
|---|---|---|---|
| Zut! | *Darn!* | Zut alors! | *Darn!* |
| Oups! | *Oops!* | Bon sang! | *Good grief!* |
| Que diable! | *What in the dickens!* | | |

The following interjections are used to express spite, disgust, or indifference:

| | | | |
|---|---|---|---|
| Bah! | *Nonsense!* | Hélas! | *Alas!* |
| Pouah! | *Berk!* | Bof! | *So what!* |

The following interjections are used to get somebody's attention:

| | | | |
|---|---|---|---|
| Hé! Eh! Hep! | *Hey!* | Coucou! | *Hi!* |
| Allons! | *Come on!* | Attention! | *Watch out!* |
| Vite! | *Quick!* | | |

The following interjections are used to express helplessness or to call for help:

| | | | |
|---|---|---|---|
| Ciel! | *Heavens!* | Mon dieu! | *My goodness!* |
| Au secours! | *Help!* | A l'aide! | *Help!* |

The following interjections are used to express surprise, disbelief, or cynicism:

| | | | |
|---|---|---|---|
| Espérons! | *Let's hope!* | Tu parles! | *You bet!* |
| Quoi! | *What!* | Comment! | *What!* |
| Eh ben dis donc! | *You don't say!* | Sans blague! | *No kidding!* |
| Tiens! | *Look at that!* | Ah tiens! | *Look at that!* |
| Oh la la! | *Oh my!* | | |

The following interjections are used to express admiration, gratitude, and enthusiasm:

| | | | |
|---|---|---|---|
| Chouette! | *Cool!* | Super! | *Great!* |
| Bravo! | *Great!* | Hourra! | *Hurrah!* |
| Pardi! | *For sure!* | Tant mieux! | *So much the better!* |

The following interjections are used to ask for quiet:

| | | | |
|---|---|---|---|
| Chut! | *Hush!* | Silence! | *Quiet!* |

Some interjections are euphemisms, inoffensive expressions that replace those that may offend the listeners, or expressions that suggest something not pleasant. They are more common in speech.

| | |
|---|---|
| **Zut!** Cet examen est difficile! | ***Darn,*** *this exam is hard!* |
| **Eh ben dis donc!** Je ne l'aurais jamais cru! | ***You don't say!*** *I would have never believed it!* |
| Tu vas au concert? —**Tu parles!** | *Are you going to the concert?* —***You bet!*** |
| Ce poulet est atroce! **Pouah!** | *This chicken is awful.* ***Berk!*** |
| **Quoi!** Ils n'ont pas encore fini? | ***What!*** *They have not yet finished?* |
| **Sans blague!** Tu vas faire le tour du monde? | ***No kidding!*** *You are going to take a trip around the world?* |

EXERCICE
4·5

*Write the letter of the word on the right that describes the emotion expressed in the following sentences. There may be more than one answer, depending on how you interpret the message.*

1. \_\_\_\_\_ Zut! J'ai la migraine!

2. \_\_\_\_\_ Oh la la! Que j'ai peur!

3. \_\_\_\_\_ Ouf! J'ai retrouvé mes clefs!

4. \_\_\_\_\_ Pouah! Ce lait est aigre!

a. indifference

b. relief

c. impatience

d. disgust

5. _____ Bof! J'irai demain!  e.  fear

6. _____ Aïe! Je me suis fait mal au doigt!  f.  pain

EXERCICE
4·6

*Write an interjection to respond to these statements. Remember, you need to express your feelings!*

1. Ta voiture a un pneu crevé. _____

2. Tu appelles police-secours pour t'aider. _____

3. L'agent de police remplace ton pneu. _____

4. Ta voiture marche mais la route est mauvaise. _____

5. Tu arrives en retard à ton rendez-vous. _____

6. Tes amis t'attendent toujours. _____

EXERCICE
4·7

*Translate the following sentences into French.*

1. Hush! There is too much noise! _____

_____

2. Heavens! The conference starts at noon! _____

_____

3. Hey! We have arrived! _____

4. Alas! I have no time! _____

5. You (tu) want to win? Let's hope! _____

_____

6. Oh my! This watch is beautiful! _____

_____

# Imperative clauses

·5·

Imperative clauses are used to give orders, commands, and sometimes instructions. This type of clause ends in an exclamation mark and excludes a subject of the verb.

## Word order

The entire clause may consist of a single verb in the imperative mood, or it may consist of the predicate (verb in the imperative mood and complement). The imperative clause does not have an explicit subject. The subject of the verb is implied.

### Imperative clause = verb in imperative mood

Consider the following examples of imperative clauses consisting of a single verb in the imperative mood. Note that the implied subject of each verb is **tu** (*you*) and that the conjugated form of the verb is in the second person of the present indicative (although -**s** has been dropped from the ending for regular -**er** verbs and for the irregular verb **aller**).

| DECLARATIVE CLAUSE | | IMPERATIVE CLAUSE | | VERB GROUP |
|---|---|---|---|---|
| Tu écoutes. | *You listen.* | Écoute! | *Listen!* | -er verb |
| Tu choisis. | *You choose.* | Choisis! | *Choose!* | -ir verb |
| Tu réponds. | *You answer.* | Réponds! | *Answer!* | -re verb |
| Tu prends. | *You take.* | Prends! | *Take!* | irregular verb |
| Tu vas. | *You go.* | Va! | *Go!* | irregular verb and irregular imperative form |

### Imperative clause = verb in imperative mood + complement

Consider the following examples of imperative clauses consisting of a verb in the imperative mood and a complement.

| | |
|---|---|
| Écoute cette nouvelle chanson! | *Listen to this new song!* |
| Choisis ta couleur préférée! | *Choose your favorite color!* |
| Réponds vite à la question! | *Quickly answer the question!* |
| Va à la maison! | *Go home!* |

Note that the negative form of a verb in the imperative mood requires the use of **ne** and **pas** *hugging* the verb.

| | |
|---|---|
| **N'écoute pas** cette nouvelle chanson! | **Do not listen** to this new song! |
| **Ne choisis pas** ta couleur préférée! | **Do not choose** your favorite color! |
| **Ne réponds pas** vite à la question! | **Do not answer** the question quickly! |
| **Ne va pas** à la maison! | **Do not go** home! |

**EXERCICE**

**5·1**

*Change each declarative sentence into an exclamatory imperative clause. Add appropriate punctuation.*

1. Tu regardes un bon film. _____

2. Tu viens à onze heures. _____

3. Tu prends un café. _____

4. Tu vas chez Paul. _____

5. Tu finis cet exercice. _____

6. Tu descends au premier étage. _____

**EXERCICE**

**5·2**

*Answer each question with an affirmative or negative imperative clause.*

1. Je pars maintenant? —Oui, _____ tout de suite!

2. Je fais la vaisselle d'abord? —Non, _____ la vaisselle!

3. Je prends la voiture? —Oui, _____ la voiture!

4. Je téléphone plus tard? —Non, _____ ! Ce n'est pas la peine.

5. Je rentre vers six heures? —Oui, _____ tôt!

## Implied subject of the verb in the imperative clause

In English and French imperative clauses, the subject is implied. However, in the English clause, it may not always be clear whether one person or several persons are targeted in the command, whereas in the French sentence, the form of the verb makes it clear who is targeted in the command.

| | |
|---|---|
| **Va** à la maison! | **Go** home! (*you*, one person) |
| **Cherche** tes lunettes! | **Look** for your glasses! (*you*, one person) |
| **Allez** à la maison! | **Go** home! (*you*, several persons, or *you*, one person in formal address) |
| **Finissez** le diner! | **Finish** dinner! (*you*, several persons, or *you*, one person in formal address) |
| **Allons** à la maison! | **Let's go** home! (*both of us* or *all of us*) |
| **Laissons** nos affaires ici! | **Let's leave** our things here! (*both of us* or *all of us*) |

In an English imperative clause, there are two possible subjects that are implied:

- *You*, talking to one person or several people
- *We*, talking to at least one other person while including oneself

In a French imperative clause, however, there can be three implied subjects:

- **Tu**, talking to one person in a familiar situation
- **Vous**, talking to one person in a formal situation or talking to several people
- **Nous**, talking to at least one other person while including oneself

Imperative clauses in which a third person is the subject of the verb are presented in Unit 8.

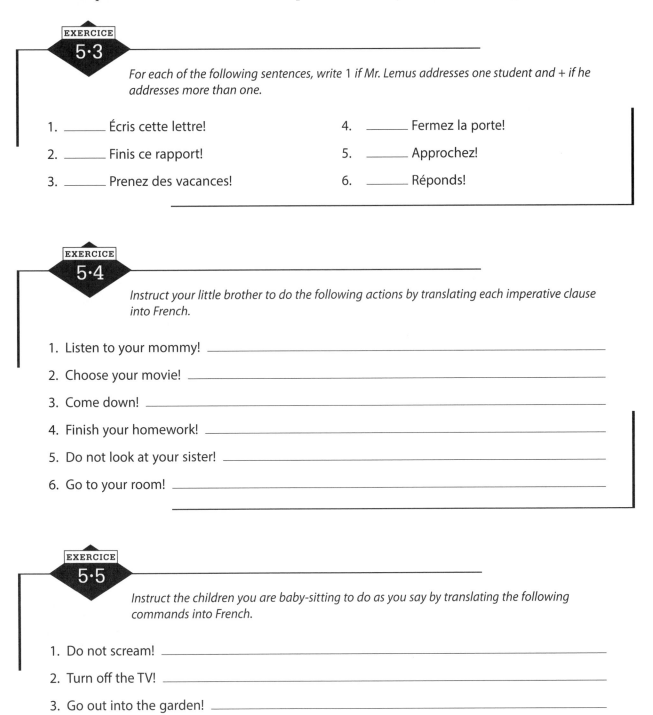

EXERCICE
5·3

*For each of the following sentences, write 1 if Mr. Lemus addresses one student and + if he addresses more than one.*

1. _____ Écris cette lettre!

2. _____ Finis ce rapport!

3. _____ Prenez des vacances!

4. _____ Fermez la porte!

5. _____ Approchez!

6. _____ Réponds!

EXERCICE
5·4

*Instruct your little brother to do the following actions by translating each imperative clause into French.*

1. Listen to your mommy! _____

2. Choose your movie! _____

3. Come down! _____

4. Finish your homework! _____

5. Do not look at your sister! _____

6. Go to your room! _____

EXERCICE
5·5

*Instruct the children you are baby-sitting to do as you say by translating the following commands into French.*

1. Do not scream! _____

2. Turn off the TV! _____

3. Go out into the garden! _____

4. Do not soil the couch! _____

5. Give me this towel! _____

6. Stay in your room! _____

*You are among friends and make suggestions for weekend activities. Translate the following suggestions into French.*

1. Let's eat at the restaurant! _____

2. Let's invite Jeanine! _____

3. Let's check the movie times! _____

4. Let's go! _____

5. Let's take a cab! _____

# Independent clauses

Any structural group organized around a verbal nucleus is a clause. There are two types of clauses in English and in French: independent clauses and dependent clauses. If a clause can stand alone as a sentence—if it has at least a subject and a verb and expresses a complete thought—then it is an independent clause. In this unit, we will see examples of independent clauses that exist by and for themselves (simple independent clauses) as well as independent clauses that give support to dependent clauses.

## Simple independent clauses

Simple independent clauses constitute sentences. Their structure can be affirmative, negative, interrogative, or imperative. They express complete thoughts. They are made up of a subject and a verb, but can also include an adverb, a prepositional phrase, or various objects.

**subject + verb (+ complement) → independent clause**

## Simple affirmative clauses

This type of clause is classified as simple because no other clause depends on it. And the clause is affirmative because it does not include any negative terms such as **pas**, **plus**, **jamais**, **personne**, **rien**, **aucun**, or **nul**. A simple affirmative clause is also independent as it expresses a complete thought and includes a subject as well as a verb. Here is an example of a simple affirmative independent clause:

> Les Roberts sont à l'hôtel aujourd'hui. *The Roberts are at the hotel today.*

In this clause, we can identify the following elements:

- ◆ A subject: **les Roberts**
- ◆ A predicate: **sont à l'hôtel aujourd'hui**

The predicate in this clause includes:

- ◆ The verb: **sont**
- ◆ A prepositional phrase: **à l'hôtel**
- ◆ An adverb: **aujourd'hui**

Additional characteristics of this clause are:

- ◆ The clause is simple: No other clause depends on it.
- ◆ The structure of the clause is affirmative: Look at the verb **sont**.
- ◆ The clause is independent: It expresses a complete thought and includes the structural elements of subject and verb.

# Simple negative clauses

This type of clause is considered simple because no other clause depends on it. The clause is negative because it includes a negative term such as **pas**, **plus**, **jamais**, **personne**, **rien**, **aucun**, or **nul**. (To review negative structures, see Unit 1.) The clause is also independent because it expresses a complete thought and includes a subject as well as a verb. Here is an example of a simple negative independent clause:

<table>
<tr><td>Les Roberts ne sont pas à la maison actuellement.</td><td>The Roberts are not currently at home.</td></tr>
</table>

In this clause, we can identify the same elements and characteristics as in the example of the simple affirmative clause in the previous section. The only difference in this clause is the negative structure of the verb. Here we can identify:

- A subject: **les Roberts**
- A predicate: **ne sont pas à la maison**

The predicate in this clause includes:

- The verb: **ne sont pas**
- A prepositional phrase: **à la maison**
- An adverb: **actuellement**

Other characteristics of this clause to note are:

- The clause is simple: No other clause depends on it.
- The structure of the clause is negative: **ne sont pas**.
- The clause is independent: It expresses a complete thought and includes the structural elements of subject and verb.

Consider another example of a simple independent clause featuring a negative structure:

<table>
<tr><td>Je ne mange rien.</td><td>I am not eating anything.</td></tr>
</table>

Note once again that this clause expresses a complete thought and includes the necessary structural elements of an independent clause even though the clause is very short and includes nothing but the essential elements of a clause: the subject **Je** and the verb **mange**.

Consider a few more examples of simple negative independent clauses and note that these are all independent clauses including a subject and a verb:

<table>
<tr><td>Mon chat ne mange jamais de souris.</td><td>My cat never eats any mice.</td></tr>
<tr><td>Il ne les attrape plus.</td><td>He no longer catches them.</td></tr>
<tr><td>Je n'aime aucun de ces desserts.</td><td>I do not like any of these desserts.</td></tr>
<tr><td>Papa n'a nulle envie de faire la cuisine.</td><td>Dad has no desire to do the cooking.</td></tr>
<tr><td>Je n'ai invité personne ce weekend.</td><td>I did not invite anyone this weekend.</td></tr>
</table>

**EXERCICE**

**6·1**

*Build simple affirmative clauses using the sentence fragments provided. Be sure to punctuate your sentences.*

1. Jean / ce soir / va arriver

_____

2. préparons / nous / un bon repas

_____

3. content / tout le monde / est

_____

4. était / absent / longtemps / il

_____

5. il / dans sa chambre / va dormir

_____

*With these sentence fragments, build simple negative clauses in the present tense using the negations provided and using proper punctuation.*

1. Brigitte / dort / ne pas bien

_____

2. Ginette / aime les gâteaux / ne plus

_____

3. nous / voulons / ne rien / boire

_____

4. vous / pouvez / ne pas / lire tout le roman

_____

5. elles / ont / ne rien / à dire

_____

6. vous / avez / ne pas encore / vingt ans

_____

## Simple interrogative clauses

This type of clause is simple because no other clause depends on it. The clause is interrogative because it asks a question. And the clause is independent because it expresses a complete thought and includes a subject as well as a verb. Now consider the following examples of simple independent clauses featuring an interrogative structure:

**subject + verb + ? → interrogative structure (using pitch of voice in oral expression)**

Elle mange?                                    *Does she eat?*

**est-ce que + subject + verb + ? → interrogative structure**

Est-ce qu'elle mange?                          *Does she eat?*

**verb + subject + ? → interrogative structure**

Mange-t-elle?                                  *Does she eat?*

Although the interrogative structure varies from one sentence to another, each of these clauses expresses a complete thought and includes the necessary structural elements of an independent clause: the subject **elle** and the verb **mange**.

Now consider the following examples of simple interrogative clauses featuring the various interrogative structures and note that they are all independent clauses including a subject and a verb. (To review complex interrogative structures, see Unit 3.)

| | |
|---|---|
| **On va** au cinéma ce soir? | *Do we go to the movies tonight?* |
| Est-ce que **Marie-Claude veut** venir avec nous? | *Does Marie-Claude want to come with us?* |
| **Est-elle** à la maison en ce moment? | *Is she home at this moment?* |

In addition, note that a verbal structure can be interrogative and negative at the same time, as shown in the following sentences. But as long as there is a subject and a verb and the sentence makes sense on its own, you are still building independent clauses.

| | |
|---|---|
| **Le cinéma des Arts n'est-il pas** juste au coin? | *Isn't the Cinéma des Arts just around the corner?* |
| **Est-ce qu'il n'a pas plu** aujourd'hui? | *Did it not rain today?* |
| **Tu n'as pas** la monnaie exacte pour les billets? | *Don't you have the exact change for the tickets?* |
| **Est-ce qu'ils ne coûtent pas** trop cher? | *Don't they cost too much?* |

EXERCICE
6·3

*Change each statement into a question, building simple interrogative clauses using the phrase **est-ce que**. Use proper punctuation.*

EXAMPLE:    Les fleurs poussent bien.    Est-ce que les fleurs poussent bien?

1. Le ciel est bleu. _____

2. Les oiseaux chantent. _____

3. Le chien court derriere moi. _____

4. Je vais au parc. _____

5. Tu viens avec moi. _____

## Simple imperative clauses

This type of clause is simple because no other clause depends on it. The clause is imperative because it serves to give commands, orders, or instructions. And the clause is independent because it expresses a complete thought and includes an *implicit* subject as well as a verb. This type of clause differs from previously mentioned independent clauses, because it lacks the explicit mention of the subject. In an imperative clause, the omitted and implied subject is *you* or *we*. (To review imperative structures, see Unit 5.)

| verb (+ complement) → simple imperative clause | |
|---|---|
| **Rentre** chez toi! (tu) | *Go home!* |
| **Répondez** à la question! (vous) | *Answer the question!* |
| **N'ignorons pas** la vérité! (nous) | *Let's not ignore the truth!* |
| **Conduis** ta sœur au cinéma! (tu) | *Drive your sister to the movie theater!* |

*Build simple affirmative imperative clauses using the words in parentheses. Use the familiar* **tu** *command only.*

1. Decorate your room! (décorer ta chambre)

_____

2. Paint the walls! (peindre les murs)

_____

3. Organize the closet! (organizer le placard)

_____

4. Change the curtains! (changer les rideaux)

_____

5. Hang some paintings! (accrocher des tableaux)

_____

6. Move the bed! (déplacer le lit)

_____

# Main clauses

The examples of the previous section show us that an independent clause can be a complete sentence. Remember the definition of a sentence as a group of words including a subject and a predicate, and compare the following definitions of a sentence and an independent clause:

> **subject + predicate → sentence**
> **subject + predicate → independent clause**

You will notice that they are the same. One might then wonder why it is necessary to use the terminology *independent clause*. Why not simply call any structural grouping of a subject and predicate a *sentence*? The answer lies within the fact that a sentence is sometimes but not always limited to an independent clause. However, sometimes a sentence includes both an independent and a dependent clause.

> **sentence = simple independent clause**

or

> **sentence = independent clause + dependent clause**

Examine the following example of a sentence, which comprises both types of clauses: dependent and independent:

> Je mange en attendant ton arrivée.    *I eat while waiting for your arrival.*

In this sentence, one can identify the following clauses:

- ◆ An independent clause: **Je mange**
- ◆ A dependent clause: **en attendant ton arrivée**

We use the term *independent clause* to describe the subject + verb grouping: **Je mange**. It differentiates this type of clause, which can exist by itself and which makes sense by itself, from a dependent clause such as **en attendant ton arrivée**, which only makes sense in conjunction with the independent clause.

In a sentence such as **Je mange en attendant ton arrivée**, which includes both an independent and a dependent clause, the independent clause (the one which can stand alone and makes sense by itself) is also called the *main clause*.

**main clause + dependent clause**
Viens + faire tes devoirs!
Viens faire tes devoirs!
*Come and do your homework!*

Consider the following examples of sentences. They all include a boldfaced main clause and a dependent clause.

| | |
|---|---|
| **Dax rêvait** de devenir pilote. | ***Dax dreamed*** *of becoming a pilot.* |
| **Dara donne des bises** pour nous charmer. | ***Dara gives kisses*** *to charm us.* |
| **Alex n'aime pas** qu'on l'ignore. | ***Alex does not like*** *to be ignored.* |
| **Sasha se fâche** quand on l'ennuie. | ***Sasha gets mad*** *when you bother him.* |
| **Amethyst adore** s'occuper des enfants. | ***Amethyst loves*** *taking care of children.* |
| **Barbara s'amuse** à faire la cuisine. | ***Barbara has fun*** *cooking.* |
| **Veux-tu** que je t'aide? | ***Do you want*** *me to help you?* |

In each of the previous sentences, the main clause is in itself an independent clause and supports a dependent clause. This dependent clause, by itself, does not express a complete thought. It depends on the main clause to provide the premise and the background for what is to be expressed.

| | |
|---|---|
| **Les Roberts sont à l'hôtel** bien que leur famille habite en ville. | ***The Roberts are at the hotel*** *even though their family lives in town.* |

The clause **Les Roberts sont à l'hôtel** is a main clause because it not only makes sense by itself (which makes it an independent clause) but it is also followed by the dependent clause **bien que leur famille habite en ville.** This last part of the sentence—*even though their family lives in town*—makes sense only if you understand the main idea that *the Roberts are at the hotel.*

**EXERCICE**
**6·5**

*Ariane and Arlette are chatting. On the lines provided, write A if the structure of the clause is affirmative, N if it is negative, and IMP if it is imperative.*

1. _____ Tu veux une glace, Arlette?

2. _____ Je ne mange jamais de glace, Ariane.

3. _____ Tu n'aimes pas ça, Arlette?

4. _____ Si, mais ça fait grossir.

5. _____ Oublie un peu ton régime, Arlette!

6. _____ Je suis trop stricte pour ça.

*Find the appropriate dependent clause in the right column for each main clause on the left, and write the letter on the line provided.*

1. C'est très bizarre _____

2. On avait pourtant rendez-vous _____

3. Bon. Je vais me calmer _____

4. Tu finiras bien par appeler _____

5. J'entends la sonnette _____

6. J'avais bien tort _____

a. ou tu arriveras bientôt.

b. donc te voilà!

c. de me faire du souci.

d. que tu n'appelles pas.

e. car on devait aller danser ce soir.

f. et je vais attendre patiemment.

# Compound sentences

A compound sentence includes two independent clauses. These clauses may be combined into a sentence by using punctuation (e.g., a semicolon).

**independent clause + ; + independent clause**
Lili ne mange pas + ; + elle n'a pas faim.
*Lili does not eat; she is not hungry.*

| | |
|---|---|
| Tu pars**;** tu vas au concert. | *You are leaving; you are going to the concert.* |
| Elle joue**;** elle a le temps. | *She is playing; she has the time.* |
| Nous attendons**;** on va nous appeler. | *We are waiting; they are going to call us.* |

More frequently, however, independent clauses are joined together with one of the following coordinating conjunctions: **et** (*and*), **ni** (*nor*), **ou** (*or*), **car** (*for*), **mais** (*but*), and **donc** (*so*).

**independent clause + coordinating conjunction + independent clause**
Je pense + donc + je suis.
*I think therefore I am.*

| | |
|---|---|
| Josette est fatiguée **car** elle a travaillé très dur. | *Josette is tired **for** she worked hard.* |
| Elle n'est pas encore là **mais** elle est en route. | *She is not there yet, **but** she is on the way.* |
| Elle n'est pas encore arrivée **ni** Jean-Marc d'ailleurs. | *She has not yet arrived **nor** has Jean-Marc.* |

In previous units you built *sentences*: affirmative and negative sentences, direct questions, imperatives, and exclamatory sentences. Some were similar to the examples below:

| | |
|---|---|
| Je me réveille vers sept heures. | *I get up around seven o'clock.* |
| Je ne travaille pas le weekend. | *I do not work on weekends.* |
| Je fais des achats. | *I am going shopping.* |
| Je rentrerai vers midi. | *I will get back around noon.* |
| Je veux un nouveau pantalon. | *I want new pants.* |
| Je n'ai pas beaucoup d'argent. | *I do not have a lot of money.* |
| Donne-moi un peu d'argent. | *Give me a little money.* |
| Je ne pourrai pas l'acheter. | *I will not be able to buy it.* |

In the next examples, see how the *coordinating conjunctions* join the simple sentences you just read.

| | | | |
|---|---|---|---|
| Je me réveille vers sept heures **mais** je ne travaille pas le weekend. | | *I get up around seven o'clock, but I do not work on weekends.* | |
| Je fais des achats **et** je rentrerai vers midi. | | *I am going shopping, and I will get back around noon.* | |
| Je veux un nouveau pantalon **mais** je n'ai pas beaucoup d'argent. | | *I want new pants, but I do not have a lot of money.* | |
| Donne-moi un peu d'argent **sinon** je ne pourrai pas l'acheter. | | *Give me a little money otherwise I will not be able to buy it.* | |

Commonly used coordinating conjunctions are:

| | | | |
|---|---|---|---|
| et | *and* | ou | *or* |
| soit...soit | *either . . . or* | ni | *nor* |
| ni...ni | *neither . . . nor* | mais | *but* |
| sinon | *otherwise* | | |

**EXERCICE**
**6·7**

*Build new sentences by combining the two sentences provided with one of the conjunctions in parentheses as appropriate.*

1. Toute la journée Mimi était chez ses grands-parents. Elle jouait avec leur chien Médor. (et, ni)

   _____

2. Je voulais déjeuner avec elle. Elle avait rendez-vous chez le dentiste. (et, mais)

   _____

3. Elle a dû aller à son rendez-vous. Elle n'aime pas aller chez le dentiste. (sinon, mais)

   _____

4. Mimi n'a pas mangé toute la journée. Elle n'a pas mangé le soir. (ou, ni)

   _____

5. Aujourd'hui elle doit se sentir mieux. Elle doit retourner chez le dentiste. (ni, sinon)

   _____

6. Mimi est très gentille. Elle est aussi très indécise. (et, mais)

   _____

# Omitting the subject and the verb in the second clause

In French, when the subject of the first and second clause is identical, it is frequently omitted. In English it can be omitted, too.

| | |
|---|---|
| Beatrice a fermé les yeux et n'a pas vu l'accident. | *Beatrice closed her eyes and did not see the accident.* |
| Les détectives ont fait leur rapport et sont partis. | *The detectives made their report and left.* |

It is also possible to omit the verb of the second clause for different reasons: for the sake of brevity, a balanced combination of sentences, or a simple matter of style.

Il n'a ni travail ni argent.　　　　　*He does not have a job nor money.*
Je vais préparer une omelette ou une salade.　　*I will prepare an omelet or a salad.*

EXERCICE
6·8

*In each of the following sentences, identify the subject and verb that can be omitted, and then rewrite the sentence using a coordinating conjunction.*

1. Mes parents restent à la maison le samedi et ils restent à la maison le dimanche.

_____

2. Papa ne mange pas la viande de bœuf et il ne mange pas le poulet.

_____

3. Maman prépare la salade et elle prépare la vinaigrette.

_____

4. Nous allons manger vers six heures ou nous allons manger vers sept heures.

_____

5. Avant le dîner, nous buvons un verre de vin ou nous buvons un apéritif.

_____

6. Après le dîner, nous faisons du thé ou nous faisons du café.

_____

# Coordinating conjunctions and their functions

Getting acquainted with coordinating conjunctions and focusing on the purpose each one communicates will help you choose the correct conjunction and build sentences in French.

| CONJUNCTION | PURPOSE |
|---|---|
| **et, ni**<br>Marise chante **et** moi, je danse. | **adding a fact**<br>*Marise sings **and** I dance.* |
| **ou, soit...soit**<br>J'irai **soit** à la piscine **soit** à la plage. | **choosing one over another**<br>*I will go **either** to the pool **or** to the beach.* |
| **donc**<br>Il pleut **donc** nous ne sortons pas. | **expressing real consequences**<br>*It is raining, **so** we are not going out.* |
| **mais**<br>Je suis fatigué **mais** je vais faire ce devoir. | **expressing opposition/contrast**<br>*I am tired, **but** I am going to do this assignment.* |
| **sinon**<br>Fais-le **sinon** ce sera trop tard! | **expressing a possible consequence**<br>*Do it, **otherwise** it will be too late!* |
| **ni**<br>Je ne fume **ni** bois. | **adding two negative actions (verbs)**<br>*I neither smoke **nor** drink.* |
| **ni...ni**<br>Tu n'as **ni** patience **ni** indulgence. | **ni appears before both nouns**<br>*You have **neither** patience **nor** indulgence.* |

EXERCICE

6·9

*Write complete and logical sentences using the sentence fragments provided.*

1. d'écrire un roman / j'ai envie / au bureau / je vais / donc

   _____

2. le premier chapitre / j'écris / je ne l'aime pas / mais

   _____

3. le premier chapitre / je dois / récrire / la fin / sera / sinon / impossible

   _____

4. le début / changer / je peux / ou / la fin / du chapitre

   _____

5. donc / d'idées / je n'ai pas / je vais / me promener

   _____

6. dans un café / j'entre / je commande un express / et

   _____

EXERCICE

6·10

*Combine each of the sentence pairs given, using a coordinating conjunction. There may be more than one possible answer.*

1. Tu écris bien. Tu parles encore mieux.

   _____

2. Le pauvre n'entend pas. Il ne parle pas.

   _____

3. Tu es en retard. Dépêche-toi!

   _____

4. Tu arrives. Tu repars.

   _____

5. Ce manteau est cher. J'ai assez d'argent pour l'acheter.

   _____

6. Le magasin ne ferme pas à six heures. Il ne ferme pas à sept heures non plus.

   _____

# Punctuation of sentences with more than two independent clauses

In French a comma is usually not needed with **et**, **mais**, **donc**, and **sinon**. However, when a sentence includes *more* than two independent clauses, the coordinating conjunction usually precedes the last sentence and a comma separates the other previous sentences.

**independent clause 1 + , + independent clause 2 + conjunction + independent clause 3 → sentence**

Nous prenons le petit déjeuner, allons au travail et rentrons.
*We eat breakfast, go to work, and come back.*

Je cours, je fais du vélo et de la natation.
*I run, ride the bike, and swim.*

Note, in the following examples, that the expressions **ni...ni** and **soit...soit** do not require any punctuation:

Je ne veux **ni** soda **ni** jus.
*I want **neither** soda **nor** juice.*

J'irai au cinéma **soit** samedi **soit** dimanche.
*I will go to the movies **either** on Saturday **or** on Sunday.*

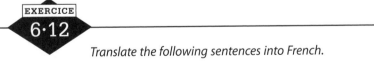

**EXERCICE 6·11**

*Build sentences with the fragments provided, and use the correct punctuation.*

1. s'habille / Zoe / se lève / se maquille / et

   _____

2. elle / ferme la porte à clef / sort / prend son sac / et

   _____

3. le métro / le bus / elle prend le vélo / ou

   _____

4. elle boit un verre de jus / ni thé / ni café / elle ne boit / mais

   _____

5. il fait de l'orage / elle se dépêche / et / il pleut fort / donc

   _____

**EXERCICE 6·12**

*Translate the following sentences into French.*

1. Sometimes I like to stay home and read a good book.

   _____

2. There are days when I do not want to go out nor talk to anybody.

   _____

3. I do answer the phone but only if it is family.

_____

4. I can see my caller's name, so I know who calls.

_____

5. I have neither scruples nor regrets.

_____

# Dependent clauses and the indicative mood

·7·

A dependent clause cannot stand alone as a sentence and does not, by itself, express a complete thought. It depends on the rest of the sentence for its meaning and must always be attached to a main clause that completes its meaning. In addition, the verb in the main clause sometimes governs the mood required for the verb in the dependent clause. In some cases, the indicative mood in the dependent clause is governed by an idea of objectivity and probability in the main clause:

| | |
|---|---|
| Je remarque **qu'il a plu.** | *I notice **that it rained.*** |

In other cases, the indicative mood in the dependent clause is governed by the interrogative adverb, prepositional phrase, or adverbial conjunction introducing the clause:

| | |
|---|---|
| Je ne sais pas **pourquoi tout est mouillé.** | *I do not know **why everything is wet.*** |

## Indicative mood in the dependent clause governed by the verb or adjective in the main clause

When there is a verb or an adjective phrase in the main clause that states a fact, a certainty, or a probability, then the verb in the dependent clause is in the indicative mood.

**que + subject + verb in indicative mood → dependent clause**

In the following examples, the dependent clause completes the idea of the main clause. Since the verb of the main clause suggests certainty or probability, the verb in the dependent clause introduced by the conjunction **que** is in the indicative mood. Note that the verb in the dependent clause can be in various tenses of the indicative mood as appropriate in the context.

| | |
|---|---|
| Je sais **que la terre est ronde.** | *I know **that the earth is round.*** |
| On annonce **qu'elle est arrivée saine et sauve.** | *They announce **that she arrived safe and sound.*** |
| Le prof dit **que nous parlons bien français.** | *The teacher says **that we speak French well.*** |
| Il n'a jamais douté **qu'elle l'aimait.** | *He never doubted **that she loved him.*** |
| Je l'ai convaincue **qu'il faut s'entraider.** | *I convinced her **that we have to help each other.*** |

In the next examples, note that the verbs in the main clauses (**penser**, **croire**, **espérer**) are less suggestive of certainty than verbs such as **savoir**, **annoncer**, **dire**,

**51**

**ne pas douter**, or **convaincre** that were used in the previous example sentences. However, when used in the affirmative form in the main clause, these verbs still require the indicative mood in the dependent clause.

| | |
|---|---|
| Elle pense **qu'elle pourra venir bientôt.** | *She thinks (**that**) she will be able to come soon.* |
| Je crois **qu'il fera beau aujourd'hui.** | *I believe/think (**that**) it will be nice today.* |
| Nous espérons **que l'avion atterrira à 14 h.** | *We hope the plane will land at 2 P.M.* |

In the following examples, it is the adjective phrase of the main clause that suggests certainty or probability. Therefore, the verb in the dependent clause introduced by the conjunction **que** is again in the indicative mood.

| | |
|---|---|
| Je suis sûr **qu'ils ont atteint le sommet.** | *I am sure **they have reached the top.*** |
| Il est certain **que le soleil se lèvera.** | *It is certain **that the sun will rise.*** |
| Il est probable **que l'avion va arriver à l'heure.** | *It is probable **that the plane is going to arrive on time.*** |
| Elles sont sûres **que nous avons gagné un prix.** | *They are sure **that we won a prize.*** |

**EXERCICE 7·1**

*Identify the verb or verb phrase in the main clause of each sentence that conveys certainty or probability. Write the word(s) on the line provided and translate it into English.*

1. Le président affirme que l'économie s'améliorera.

   _____ = _____

2. Nous nous rendons compte qu'il faut absolument participer aux élections.

   _____ = _____

3. Tu sais que j'ai un candidat favori.

   _____ = _____

4. Il est probable que beaucoup de gens voteront comme moi.

   _____ = _____

5. On dit que le nombre d'électeurs battra tous les records.

   _____ = _____

6. Les journalistes constatent que les candidats aux élections sont tous populaires.

   _____ = _____

**EXERCICE 7·2**

*Complete each main clause with the suggested answer in parentheses. Write the appropriate completions in French on the lines provided.*

1. Zut! On annonce... (*that there is going to be a snowstorm*).

   _____

2. Mon mari dit... (*that it already snowed a lot during the night*).

   _____

3. Je sais... (*that in winter this happens*).

   _____

4. Mais j'espère... (*that we will be able to drive to the mountains*).

   _____

5. Je pense… (*that it will be a good day for skiing*).

   _____

6. Voilà une autre annonce météo. Justement ce que je pensais. Je n'ai jamais vraiment douté... (*that it was going to be a beautiful day*).

   _____

# Indicative mood in the dependent clause governed by an interrogative adverb or prepositional phrase

A dependent clause is sometimes introduced by an interrogative adverb or by a prepositional phrase that governs the indicative mood.

## Interrogative adverbs

The following interrogative adverbs require the use of the indicative mood in the dependent clause they introduce: **pourquoi** (*why*), **combien** (*how much/many*), **quand** (*when*), **où** (*where*), **qui** (*who/whom*), or **si** (*if/whether*).

**interrogative adverb + subject + verb in indicative mood → dependent clause**

In the following examples, the boldface dependent clause is introduced by an interrogative adverb and the verb in the dependent clause is in the indicative mood. Note that the verb can be in various tenses as appropriate in the context.

| | |
|---|---|
| Je me demande **s'il va pleuvoir.** | *I wonder **whether it is going to rain.*** |
| Tu savais **pourquoi j'étais là.** | *You knew **why I was there.*** |
| Je me demande **combien tu m'aimes.** | *I wonder **how much you love me.*** |
| Demande-lui **quand il va partir.** | *Ask him **when he is going to leave.*** |
| J'aimerais savoir **où il est allé.** | *I would like to know **where he went.*** |
| Dis-moi **qui c'est.** | *Tell me **who it is.*** |
| Je ne sais pas **quoi/que faire.** | *I do not know **what to do.*** |

## Prepositional phrases

Dependent clauses can be introduced by a prepositional phrase such as **à quelle heure** (*at what time*) or **pour quelle raison** (*for what reason*) or **à quoi** (*for what*). These phrases require the use of the indicative mood in the clauses they introduce.

**interrogative prepositional phrase + subject + verb in indicative mood → dependent clause**

Consider the following sentences in which the dependent clause is introduced by a prepositional phrase bearing an interrogative function and note that the verb can be in various tenses of the indicative mood:

Sais-tu **à quelle heure le spectacle commence?**    *Do you know **at what time the show starts?***

Elle veut savoir **pour quelle raison tu as fait ça.**    *She wants to know **for what reason you did that.***

Je me demande **à quoi ça servira.**    *I wonder **what this will be used for.***

---

**EXERCICE**
**7·3**

*Complete each sentence by choosing the appropriate interrogative adverb or prepositional phrase from the following list.*

que / où / qui / si / comment / à quelle heure / pourquoi / quand

1. Je me demande _____ est cette nouvelle étudiante.

2. J'aimerais savoir _____ elle s'appelle.

3. Je me demande aussi _____ elle arrive au cours avec deux semaines de retard.

4. Je suis un peu timide et je ne sais pas toujours _____ dire dans une situation nouvelle.

5. Je pourrais lui demander _____ elle a besoin de mon aide.

6. Si elle dit que oui, je lui demanderai _____ elle voudrait étudier avec moi. Peut-être demain.

---

**EXERCICE**
**7·4**

*Match a main clause on the left with the most logical dependent clause on the right, and write the corresponding letter on the line provided.*

1. Dis donc, Thomas, tu sais _____

2. Non, Virginie, mais tu peux chercher sur l'Internet _____

3. Ah Thomas! Je me demande _____

4. Au fait, je me demande _____

5. Ah oui, tu te demandes _____

a. si elle est ou n'est pas fermée pour congés de vacances, n'est-ce pas?

b. pourquoi je n'ai pas pensé à cela.

c. si les magasins sont ouverts en août.

d. à quelle heure notre pharmacie ferme le soir?

e. quand elle ferme.

---

**EXERCICE**
**7·5**

*Complete each sentence by filling in the blank with the French translation of the English phrase provided.*

1. Je me demande _____ . (*if the weather will be nice*)

2. Et j'aimerais savoir _____ . (*how we can go to the beach*)

3. Sais-tu _____? (where we can catch a bus)

4. As-tu la moindre idée _____? (where the beach is)

5. Evidemment il faut aussi savoir _____. (at what time buses pass by)

# Relative clauses and indicative mood

A great number of dependent clauses are introduced by a relative pronoun. (See Unit 9 for more on relative pronouns.) These are called relative clauses. The verb in a relative clause can be in the indicative or subjunctive mood depending on whether the main clause suggests certainty or uncertainty.

## What is a relative clause?

A relative clause is a dependent clause introduced by a relative pronoun such as **qui** (*who/which/ that*), **que** (*whom/which/that*), **dont** (*whose/of which*), and **où** (*where*).

**relative pronoun + predicate → relative clause**

| | |
|---|---|
| J'ai vu la personne **qui devait nous livrer le colis.** | *I saw the person **who was supposed to deliver the package to us**.* |
| Elle a perdu la bague **que je lui ai achetée.** | *She lost the ring **I bought her**.* |
| Elle a acheté la robe **dont elle avait envie.** | *She bought the dress **she wanted**.* |
| Je me rappelle **où elle l'a achetée.** | *I remember **where she bought it**.* |

Note that in the following two examples the relative pronoun has no antecedent in the main clause. Therefore it is preceded by **ce** (which has no translation in English).

**ce + relative pronoun + predicate → relative clause**

| | |
|---|---|
| Voilà **ce dont je parlais.** | *That **is what I was talking about**.* |
| Dis-moi **ce que tu veux.** | *Tell me **what you want**.* |

A relative clause sometimes performs as the subject of the main verb, and when this is the case, it precedes the main clause in French and in English. Consider the following examples:

| | |
|---|---|
| **Ce que tu racontes** me paraît bizarre. | ***What you are describing** seems bizarre to me.* |
| **Ce qui s'est passé** restera gravé dans ma mémoire. | ***What happened** will remain engraved in my memory.* |

A relative clause can also be introduced by a preposition followed by the relative pronoun **qui** (*whom*) or a form of the pronoun **lequel** (*which*).

**preposition + qui/lequel + predicate → relative clause**

In this situation, use **qui** when the antecedent is a person. Use the appropriate form of **lequel** in sentences where the antecedent is a thing. Remember that the form of the pronoun **lequel** changes according to the gender and number of its antecedent (the noun it replaces). Consider the following sentences in which the relative clauses are introduced by the preposition **avec**. Note that the relative clauses follow the main clause in English and in French alike. Also note that the verb in the relative clause can be in various tenses of the indicative mood.

| | |
|---|---|
| Voilà la serveuse **avec qui j'ai longtemps bavardé.** | *There is the waitress **with whom I spoke for a long time**.* |
| Je vais te montrer l'appareil **avec lequel je prends mes photos.** | *I am going to show you the camera **with which I take my photos**.* |

*Identify the antecedent of the boldface relative pronoun in each main clause by underlining it.*

1. Le monsieur pour **qui** je travaille s'appelle M. René.

2. C'est la personne avec **qui** je m'entends le mieux au travail.

3. C'est l'ambiance à mon travail **que** j'apprécie beaucoup.

4. C'est mon patron **qui** m'inspire à travailler dur.

5. La seule chose **que** je n'aime pas, c'est le fait qu'on travaille le samedi.

6. Le temps libre **dont** nous avons tous besoin est précieux.

7. Tiens! Voilà une photo de la collègue **dont** je te parlais.

8. Et voilà le bureau dans **lequel** je passe tout mon temps.

*Find the relative clause on the right that will best complete each main clause on the left and write the corresponding letter on the line provided.*

| | |
|---|---|
| 1. Je vais à un pique-nique avec Marc _____ | a. avec qui tu sors, toi? |
| 2. Marc est le genre de gars _____ | b. dont toutes les filles rêvent. |
| 3. Mais dis donc, où est le copain _____ | c. dans lequel il y a deux lacs. |
| 4. On ira à ton parc, là _____ | d. qui vient de m'inviter. |
| 5. C'est le parc _____ | e. où tu vas faire ton jogging. |
| 6. C'est celui _____ | f. où on était la semaine dernière. |

# What governs the indicative mood in a relative clause?

The indicative mood in the dependent relative clause is governed by two elements: 1) the verb in the main clause must express a fact, a certainty, or a probability; and 2) the existence of the antecedent of the relative pronoun must be certain. If these two conditions are met, then the verb in the relative clause is in the indicative mood.

> **relative pronoun + subject + verb in indicative mood → dependent clause**
> J'ai un chien **qui s'appelle Kozi.**  *I have a dog **who is named Kozi.***

In the previous example, the main clause is **J'ai un chien** and the relative clause is **qui s'appelle Kozi**. The antecedent of the relative pronoun **qui** is the noun (**un chien**) in the main clause—which is what is being replaced by the relative pronoun **qui** in the dependent clause. In this sentence, the antecedent exists, therefore it is *certain*. The verb in the main clause is a form of the verb **avoir**. This verb expresses the *fact* of ownership. The conditions leading to the use of the indicative mood in the relative clause have been met.

In the following sentences, note that the verb in the relative clause can be in various tenses of the indicative mood as appropriate in the context, because the verb in the main clause expresses a fact.

| | |
|---|---|
| C'est l'histoire du Petit Prince **qui nous touche le plus**. | It is the story of the Little Prince **that touches us the most**. |
| Regarde le joli ballon **que j'ai acheté**. | Look at the pretty balloon **(that) I bought**. |
| Achetons la maison **dont nous avions toujours rêvé**. | Let's buy the house **we had always dreamed of**. |
| Je vais te montrer la ville **où mes enfants grandiront**. | I am going to show you the city **where my children will grow up**. |

Looking back at the previous sentences, it is clear that the relative pronoun replaced a noun in the main clause. For example, in the first sentence the relative pronoun **qui** replaces the noun phrase **Petit Prince**. Now consider these other sentences, which include a main clause and a relative clause:

| | |
|---|---|
| J'ai trouvé **ce que tu cherchais**. | I found **what you were looking for**. |
| Je sais **ce qui est arrivé**. | I know **what happened**. |

In these sentences, the relative pronoun is preceded by **ce**, which functions as its antecedent since *what I found* or *what happened* is not explicitly stated.

**EXERCICE**
**7·8**

*Following the example, identify the relative pronoun and tell which word it replaces.*

EXAMPLE:   C'est l'homme que j'aime.

que *replaces* l'homme

1. Rends-moi le stylo que je t'ai prêté!

_____ replaces _____

2. Passe-moi le livre qui est sur le bureau!

_____ replaces _____

3. Elle m'a raconté l'histoire dont tout le monde parle.

_____ replaces _____

4. Nous invitons les amis que nous préférons.

_____ replaces _____

5. Tiens! C'est le restaurant où nous avons dîné hier soir.

_____ replaces _____

**EXERCICE**
**7·9**

*If the verb in the main clause expresses a fact, a certainty, or a probability, write **Vrai**. If it does not, write **Faux**.*

1. _____ Je **connais** la dame qui habite ici.

2. _____ Il **sait** tout ce que je lui ai appris.

3. _____ Vous vous **rappelez** bien ce dont nous avons envie.

4. _____ Je **doute** pouvoir trouver un autre chien qui soit aussi mignon.

5. _____ Je **réponds** au client qui téléphone.

6. _____ Je **rêve d'** un collier qui ressemble au collier de Sophia Loren.

EXERCICE
7·10

*Translate into English the relative clause of each sentence in Exercice 7-9.*

1. I know the lady _____ .

2. He knows everything _____ .

3. You remember well _____ .

4. I doubt I can find another dog _____ .

5. I am answering the client _____ .

6. I dream about a necklace _____ .

EXERCICE
7·11

*Choose the appropriate relative clause on the right for each sentence on the left.*

1. La force _____ est incroyable.              a.  qui a fait cela.

2. J'ai aperçu le cyclone _____                 b.  ce que je te raconte.

3. Je vais te décrire _____                     c.  avec laquelle l'arbre a été arraché

4. Tu auras du mal à croire _____               d.  ce que j'ai vu.

5. Je n'oublierai jamais le jour _____          e.  où cela est arrivé.

EXERCICE
7·12

*Translate the following sentences into French.*

1. I am looking for a hat that fits me.

_____

2. But I do not see what I need.

_____

3. I do not see anything (that) I like.

_____

4. Can you (tu) recommend a store that you like?

   _____

5. You (tu) know what I want, right?

   _____

6. Let's go to the store where you (tu) bought your hat!

   _____

# Indicative mood in adverbial clauses

An adverbial clause is a clause that functions as an adverb in modifying another clause. Such a clause is introduced by a subordinating conjunction. Some subordinating conjunctions require the use of the indicative mood in the dependent clauses they introduce while others require the use of the subjunctive mood.

## What is an adverbial clause?

This type of dependent clause may at first appear to express a complete thought but is in fact dependent upon a main clause for its meaning.

| | |
|---|---|
| Les Roberts passent deux jours dans l'hôtel **pendant qu'on rénove leur cuisine**. | *The Roberts are spending two days at the hotel while they renovate their kitchen.* |

In this example, although the adverbial clause **pendant qu'on rénove leur cuisine** seems to make sense by itself, it is nothing but an additional detail to the main clause **Les Roberts passent deux jours à l'hôtel**. It gives us information regarding *when* the Roberts are at the hotel and implies *why* they are at the hotel. It is not a complete thought, because, without the support of the main clause, we wonder what is happening while the kitchen is being renovated.

## Types of adverbial clauses

The adverbial clause modifies and expands the meaning of the main clause by giving information as to *when* (time), *why* (cause or purpose), *if* (condition), and *where* (place) something happens, and in some cases *why it is unexpected* or *restricted* (concession). The type of subordinating conjunction that introduces the adverbial clause is essential as it indicates the nature of the relationship between the main clause and the dependent clause. The following subordinating conjunctions require the use of the indicative mood in the clauses they introduce, because they establish factual relationships of *time* (e.g. **quand**), *cause/effect* (e.g. **parce que**), *condition* (**si**), and *place* (**où**).

| TEMPS (TIME) | CAUSE/EFFET (CAUSE/EFFECT) | CONDITION (CONDITION) | LIEU (PLACE) |
|---|---|---|---|
| **quand** (*when*) | **parce que** (*because*) | **si** (*if*) | **où** (*where*) |
| **lorsque** (*when*) | **puisque** (*since/because*) | | |
| **dès que** (*as soon as*) | **comme** (*as/since*) | | |
| **aussitôt que** (*as soon as*) | | | |
| **après que** (*after*) | | | |
| **pendant que** (*while*) | | | |
| **tandis que** (*while*) | | | |
| **depuis que** (*since*) | | | |

Consider the following sentences in which the dependent clause is in boldface and note that the adverbial clause is an incomplete thought and answers the questions when, why, if, or where.

**conjunction + predicate (verb in indicative mood)**

quand + il arrivera (future indicative)

| | |
|---|---|
| Je serai rassurée **quand il arrivera**. | *I will be reassured **when he arrives**.* |
| J'irai au lit **après que tu auras terminé tes devoirs**. | *I will go to bed **after you have finished your homework**.* |
| Tu étudies **depuis que tu es rentrée**. | *You have been studying **since you came home**.* |
| J'ai mangé **parce que je mourais de faim**. | *I ate **because I was starving**.* |
| Je laisse la lumière allumée **puisque tu travailles encore**. | *I am leaving the light on **since you are still working**.* |
| On se demande **si tu as presque fini**. | *We are wondering **if you have almost finished**.* |
| Je ne sais pas **où il laisse toujours ses clefs**. | *I do not know **where he always leaves his keys**.* |

Consider the following sentences, which include a main clause and an adverbial clause. Note that the adverbial clause may follow or precede the main clause in English and French alike. The verb in the adverbial clause can be in a variety of tenses in the indicative mood.

**main clause + adverbial clause → sentence**

or

**adverbial clause + main clause → sentence**

| | |
|---|---|
| Elle était si heureuse **quand il est arrivé**. | *She was so happy **when he arrived**.* |
| **Quand il est arrivé**, elle était si heureuse. | ***When he arrived**, she was so happy.* |
| Je travaille mieux **depuis que tu es là**. | *I work better **since you are here**.* |
| **Depuis que tu es là**, je travaille mieux. | ***Since you are here**, I work better.* |

## Adverbial clauses establishing a time relationship

As previously stated, the conjunctions **quand/lorsque** (*when*), **après que** (*after*), **dès que/aussitôt que** (*as soon as*), **pendant que/tandis que** (*while*), and **depuis que** (*since*) establish a *time relationship* between the two clauses of the sentences. Consider the following sentences and note that the dependent clause may precede or follow the main clause. Also note the variety of tenses in the adverbial clauses.

| | |
|---|---|
| Je lisais **pendant que tu regardais la télé**. | *I was reading **while you were watching TV**.* |
| **Quand il reçoit son chèque**, il va directement à la banque. | ***When he gets his check**, he goes directly to the bank.* |
| **Dès qu'il est parti**, j'ai téléphoné à ma copine. | ***As soon as he left**, I called my girlfriend.* |
| Moi, je lave la vaisselle **tandis que toi, tu finis ton verre de vin**. | *I do the dishes **while you finish your glass of wine**.* |
| **Depuis qu'il s'est arrêté de fumer**, il ne tousse plus. | ***Since he stopped smoking**, he no longer coughs.* |

When the action in a dependent clause introduced by one of the conjunctions of time (**quand, lorsque, dès que, aussitôt que,** and **après que**) is in the future tense, then correct French grammar requires you to use the future or the past future tense for the verb in that dependent clause. Consider the following sentences and note the use of these future tenses in the dependent clauses:

| | |
|---|---|
| Jeannot pourra regarder la télé **après que tu lui auras donné son bain**. | *Jeannot will be able to watch TV **after you have given him his bath**. (**auras donné** = past future tense)* |
| **Dès qu'il cessera de neiger**, nous déblaierons la neige sur le trottoir. | ***As soon as it stops snowing**, we will clear away the snow on the sidewalk. (**cessera** = future tense)* |

## Adverbial clauses establishing a cause-and-effect relationship

These conjunctions establish a cause-and-effect relationship between the main and dependent clauses of a sentence: **parce que** (*because*), **comme** (*as*), and **puisque** (*since*). Consider the following sentences, which include an adverbial clause introduced by one of these conjunctions. Note that the dependent clause may again follow or precede the main clause in English and French alike.

| | |
|---|---|
| Téléphone plus tard **parce que je suis trop occupée en ce moment**. | *Call later **because I am too busy at the moment**.* |
| **Comme tu vois**, je suis bien bronzée. | ***As you see**, I am quite tanned.* |
| **Puisque tu étais là**, tu aurais pu me donner un coup de main! | ***Since you were here**, you could have given me a hand!* |
| Achète cette robe **puisque tu en meurs d'envie**! | *Buy this dress **since you are dying to do it**!* |

## Adverbial clauses establishing a condition

This type of dependent clause is always introduced by the conjunction **si** (*if*). It is commonly known as a conditional clause because it establishes a premise or condition that must be realized before a result can be obtained. The main clause contains the result.

| | |
|---|---|
| **Si tu es d'accord**, on ira au cinéma. | ***If you agree**, we will go to the movies.* |
| **Si tu voulais**, tu pourrais. | ***If you wanted**, you could.* |
| **S'il avait pris son parapluie**, il n'aurait pas été trempé. | ***If he had taken his umbrella**, he would not have been drenched.* |

The verb in a dependent clause introduced by **si** can be in the present, imperfect, or pluperfect tense of the indicative. The tense used for the verb in the main clause (also called the result clause) depends on the tense of the verb in the dependent **si** clause.

**si + present indicative → main verb (present/future indicative mood or imperative mood)**
**si + imperfect indicative → main verb (conditional mood)**
**si + pluperfect indicative → main verb (past conditional mood)**

Consider the following conditional sentences and note that the dependent **si** clause may precede or follow the main clause in English and in French alike. Also note the tenses of the indicative mood used in the **si** clauses.

| | |
|---|---|
| **Si tu es d'accord**, on ira au cinéma. | ***If you agree**, we will go to the movies.* |
| On ira au cinéma **si tu es d'accord**. | *We will go to the movies **if you agree**.* |
| **S'il pleuvait**, on resterait à la maison. | ***If it rained**, we would stay at home.* |
| On resterait à la maison **s'il pleuvait**. | *We would stay at home **if it rained**.* |
| Nous serions allés à la plage **s'il avait fait beau**. | *We would have gone to the beach **if it had been nice**.* |
| **S'il avait fait beau**, nous serions allés à la plage. | ***If it had been nice**, we would have gone to the beach.* |

## Adverbial clauses establishing a place or a location

This type of dependent clause is introduced by the *conjunction* **où** (*where*). It is different from a relative clause introduced by the *relative pronoun* **où** only because the entire clause refers to a place and **où** does not replace a specific noun or pronoun.

| | |
|---|---|
| Ils sont tous allés exactement **où** ils devaient aller. | *They all went exactly **where** they were supposed to go.* |
| Nous étions **où** on avait emprisonné Marie Antoinette. | *We were **where** they had imprisoned Marie Antoinette.* |

**EXERCICE**
**7·13**

*Use subordinating conjunctions such as **pendant que**, **dès que**, and so on to complete the following sentences.*

1. _____ Sasha regardait la télé, Barbara faisait la cuisine.

2. _____ elle avait suivi un cours de cuisine, elle se passionnait pour cela.

3. Elle faisait des petits plats délicieux _____ son mari se reposait.

4. _____ c'était elle qui insistait à tout faire, lui, n'avait rien à faire.

5. _____ elle finissait à la cuisine, Sasha nettoyait tous les plats.

6. _____ ce travail était terminé, ils dégustaient!

**EXERCICE**
**7·14**

*Determine which synonymous conjunction could replace each underlined conjunction and write it on the line provided.*

1. _____ Lorsque Ludovic arrive à l'aéroport, il y a une longue queue à la sécurité.

2. _____ Comme il est pressé, il demande aux passagers de le laisser passer.

3. _____ Puisqu'il est très poli, on le laisse passer. Quelle chance!

4. _____ Dès qu'il arrive à la porte d'embarquement, il fait la queue pour embarquer.

5. _____ Son cellulaire sonne juste au moment où il embarque dans l'avion.

**EXERCICE**
**7·15**

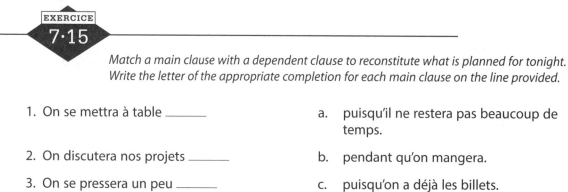

*Match a main clause with a dependent clause to reconstitute what is planned for tonight. Write the letter of the appropriate completion for each main clause on the line provided.*

1. On se mettra à table _____      a. puisqu'il ne restera pas beaucoup de temps.

2. On discutera nos projets _____      b. pendant qu'on mangera.

3. On se pressera un peu _____      c. puisqu'on a déjà les billets.

4. On partira immédiatement _____      d. après qu'on aura terminé le dîner.

5. On n'attendra pas au guichet _____

6. Nous nous amuserons bien _____

e.  comme nous le faisons toujours.

f.  aussitôt qu'il arrivera.

*Complete each thought with the suggested conditional clause. Since all the main clause verbs are in the future tense, use the present tense in the **si** clauses.*

1. Je gagnerai assez d'argent _____ . (*if I work*)

2. J'irai en France _____ . (*if I have time*)

3. Je m'amuserai bien _____ . (*if you* [tu] *come with me*)

4. Je resterai plus de deux semaines _____ . (*if you* [tu] *stay with me*)

5. Je regretterai beaucoup _____ . (*if you* [tu] *decide not to come*)

6. Je resterai plus longtemps _____ . (*if we find an inexpensive hotel*)

7. Je partirai plus tôt _____ . (*if I have no more money*)

8. J'y retournerai bientôt _____ . (*if all goes well*)

# Dependent clauses and the subjunctive mood

Dependent clauses may include a verb in the subjunctive mood for several reasons: A verb, an adjective, an impersonal expression in the main clause, and a subordinating conjunction introducing the dependent clause may all require the subjunctive mood. All of these dependent clauses are introduced by the simple conjunction **que** or by a complex conjunction that includes **que**.

## A verb or adjective in the main clause governs the subjunctive mood in a dependent clause

The verbs or adjectives that govern the subjunctive mood convey a meaning of subjectivity, uncertainty, or improbability.

### Verbs of want, desire, feeling, emotion, and doubt govern the subjunctive mood

Three categories of verbs, whenever found in the main clause, require the subjunctive mood in the dependent clause as long as the dependent verb is different from the main verb. These three verb categories are those that express want or desire, feelings and emotions, or doubt. Here are some commonly used verbs that require the subjunctive mood in the dependent clause:

| WANT/DESIRE | | FEELING/EMOTION | | DOUBT | |
|---|---|---|---|---|---|
| défendre | *to forbid* | adorer | *to adore* | douter | *to doubt* |
| demander | *to ask* | aimer | *to like/love* | nier | *to deny* |
| désirer | *to desire* | craindre | *to fear* | sembler | *to seem* |
| exiger | *to demand* | déplorer | *to deplore* | | |
| interdire | *to forbid* | détester | *to detest/hate* | | |
| ordonner | *to order* | s'étonner | *to be surprised* | | |
| permettre | *to allow* | se lamenter | *to deplore* | | |
| préférer | *to prefer* | regretter | *to regret* | | |
| souhaiter | *to wish* | | | | |
| vouloir | *to want* | | | | |

J'**exige** qu'elle fasse ses devoirs. — *I **demand** that she do her homework.*

Il **déteste** que nous arrivions en retard. — *He **hates** that we arrive late.*

Tu **voudrais** que je vienne te chercher? — ***Would** you **like** me to come and get you?*

Nous **doutons** qu'ils aient perdu le match de tennis. — *We **doubt** that they lost the tennis match.*

| Ils **permettent** que nous sortions. | *They **allow** us to go out.* |
| J'**aimerais** que vous chantiez. | *I **would like** you to sing.* |
| Tu **crains** que je ne puisse te rejoindre! | *You **fear** that I may not be able to join you.* |

Beware that the verb **douter** in the affirmative form is followed by the subjunctive, but in the negative form (**Je ne doute pas**), it conveys certainty and therefore is followed by the indicative.

| Je **doute** que l'avion atterrisse à l'heure. | *I **doubt** that the plane will land on time.* |
| Je **ne doute pas** que l'avion atterrira à l'heure. | *I **do not doubt** that the plane will land on time.* |

On the other hand, note that in the following sentences, the verbs **penser**, **croire**, and **espérer** are followed by the subjunctive only when they are in the negative or interrogative forms. This is because in the negative and interrogative forms, these verbs express uncertainty.

| Je **crois** qu'il **ment**. | *I **believe** that he **is lying**.* |
| Je **ne crois pas** qu'il **mente**. | *I **do not believe** he **is lying**.* |
| **Crois-tu** qu'il **soit** malade? | *Do you think that he **is** sick?* |
| | |
| Je **pense** que c'est là. | *I **think** it is here.* |
| Je **ne pense pas** qu'on **ait annulé** le vol. | *I **do not think** that they **cancelled** the flight.* |
| **Vous ne pensez pas** que j'en **sois** capable? | *Don't you think I **am** capable of it?* |

Note that, in each of the previous examples, the French dependent clause is introduced by the conjunction **que**. In English this conjunction is translated as *that* but may be omitted (note that it has been omitted in the some of the English example sentences).

In addition, because English makes very little use of the subjunctive mood, it is often inadvisable to translate literally a French dependent clause that includes the subjunctive. Note how, in the following examples, the French sentences consist of a main clause followed by a dependent clause including the subjunctive, while the English uses a main clause followed by an infinitive:

| L'agent défend **que nous nous garions** ici. | *The policeman forbids **us to park** here.* |
| Je souhaite **que tu ailles** à l'école. | *I would like **you to go** to school.* |

Now consider the following sentences and note that if the subjects of the two verbs are the same, in English and in French sentences alike, the infinitive replaces the subjunctive. (For more on infinitive clauses, see Unit 10.)

| Il veut **partir**. | *He wants **to leave**.* |
| Nous souhaitons **rester** un peu. | *We wish **to stay** a little.* |
| Elle aimerait **dormir**. | *She would like **to sleep**.* |

**EXERCICE**

**8·1**

*Write the letter of the word that best fits each blank to see what Joanne's problem is. You may use an answer more than once.*

a. doute / b. défend / c. voudrais / d. souhaite / e. permet

1. Je _____ me servir de mon ordinateur pour chatter en ligne.

2. Mais ma mère _____ que je m'en serve en son absence.

3. Elle _____ quand même que je fasse des recherches pour mes devoirs sur l'ordinateur.

4. Moi, je _____ que ma mère me fasse un peu plus confiance.

5. Est-ce qu'elle _____ que je sois assez mature pour savoir ce qu'on peut ou ne peut pas faire en ligne?

6. Je _____ qu'elle me donne un peu plus de liberté!

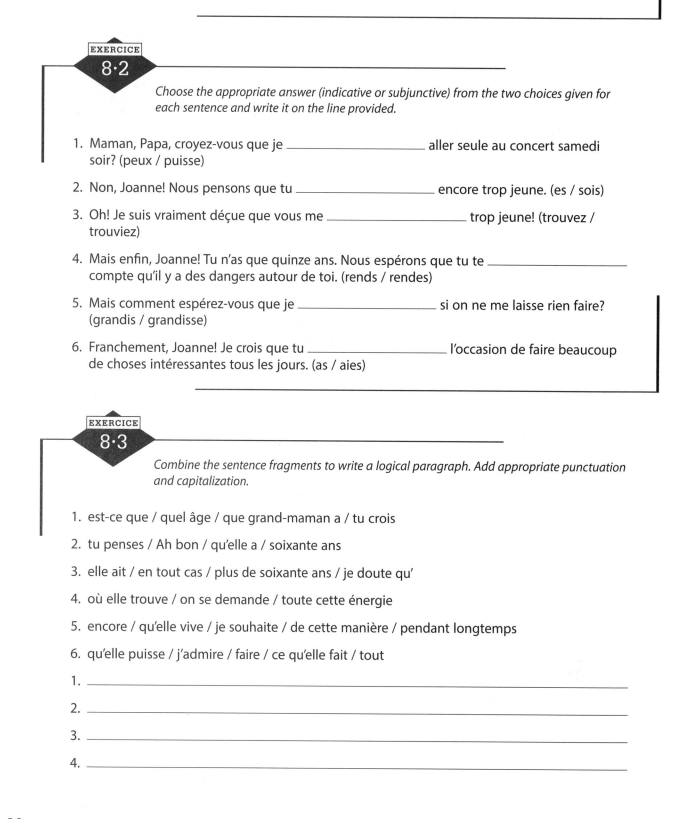

**EXERCICE**
**8·2**

*Choose the appropriate answer (indicative or subjunctive) from the two choices given for each sentence and write it on the line provided.*

1. Maman, Papa, croyez-vous que je _____ aller seule au concert samedi soir? (peux / puisse)

2. Non, Joanne! Nous pensons que tu _____ encore trop jeune. (es / sois)

3. Oh! Je suis vraiment déçue que vous me _____ trop jeune! (trouvez / trouviez)

4. Mais enfin, Joanne! Tu n'as que quinze ans. Nous espérons que tu te _____ compte qu'il y a des dangers autour de toi. (rends / rendes)

5. Mais comment espérez-vous que je _____ si on ne me laisse rien faire? (grandis / grandisse)

6. Franchement, Joanne! Je crois que tu _____ l'occasion de faire beaucoup de choses intéressantes tous les jours. (as / aies)

**EXERCICE**
**8·3**

*Combine the sentence fragments to write a logical paragraph. Add appropriate punctuation and capitalization.*

1. est-ce que / quel âge / que grand-maman a / tu crois

2. tu penses / Ah bon / qu'elle a / soixante ans

3. elle ait / en tout cas / plus de soixante ans / je doute qu'

4. où elle trouve / on se demande / toute cette énergie

5. encore / qu'elle vive / je souhaite / de cette manière / pendant longtemps

6. qu'elle puisse / j'admire / faire / ce qu'elle fait / tout

1. _____

2. _____

3. _____

4. _____

5. _____

6. _____

## Third person imperative clauses require the subjunctive mood

These dependent clauses serve to express a wish, an order, or an instruction to a third party. The entire main clause is omitted and implied. If there were a main clause, it would include one of the verbs expressing want, desire, order, need, and permission previously mentioned.

| | |
|---|---|
| Qu'ils viennent! | *Let them come!* or *They may come in.* |
| Qu'ils s'asseyent! | *Let them sit down!* or *They may sit down.* |
| Qu'elle fasse un effort! | *Let her make an effort!* or *I want her to make an effort.* |
| Qu'il obéisse! | *Let him obey!* or *I want him to obey.* |
| Qu'on m'apporte à manger! | *Let someone bring me food!* or *I need food.* |

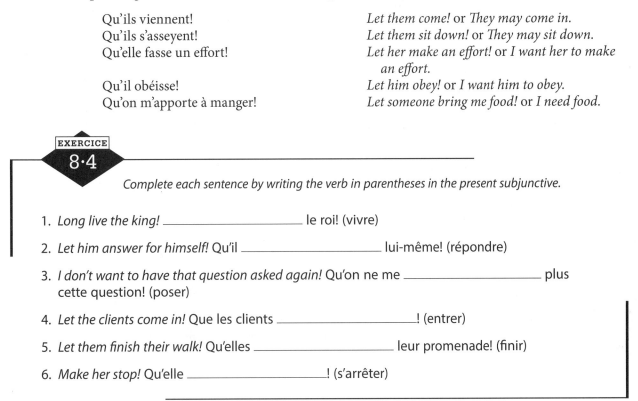

**EXERCICE 8·4**

*Complete each sentence by writing the verb in parentheses in the present subjunctive.*

1. *Long live the king!* _____ le roi! (vivre)

2. *Let him answer for himself!* Qu'il _____ lui-même! (répondre)

3. *I don't want to have that question asked again!* Qu'on ne me _____ plus cette question! (poser)

4. *Let the clients come in!* Que les clients _____! (entrer)

5. *Let them finish their walk!* Qu'elles _____ leur promenade! (finir)

6. *Make her stop!* Qu'elle _____! (s'arrêter)

## Adjectives of feeling and emotion govern the subjunctive in a dependent clause

There are many adjectives that express emotions and feelings such as fear, happiness, anger, regret, and surprise. These are intrinsically subjective as they are personal by nature. Adjectives that are used in their superlative form (e.g. the nicest, the best) also tend to be subjective because they are based on a personal judgment. These adjectives require or suggest the use of the subjunctive mood in the dependent clause.

### Simple adjectives of emotion and feeling

Adjectives expressing feelings or emotions such as **triste** (*sad*), **ému** (*moved*), or **ravi** (*delighted*), whenever they are found in the main clause, require the use of the subjunctive in a dependent clause if the subject of the dependent verb is different from the main verb.

| | |
|---|---|
| Le prof est **ravi** qu'ils **aient** tous **réussi**. | *The teacher is **delighted** that they all **passed**.* |
| La jeune fille est **émue** qu'on la **félicite**. | *The young girl is **moved** that we **congratulate** her.* |
| Mon chien est **malheureux** que je **sois sorti** sans lui. | *My dog is **unhappy** that I **went out** without him.* |
| Je suis **choqué** qu'elle lui **ait menti**. | *I am **shocked** that she **lied** to him.* |

In the following examples, note once again that, in French and English alike, if the subjects of the two verbs are the same, the infinitive verb (in the following examples: **partir**, **rentrer**, **voir**, and **trouver**) replaces the subjunctive. Also note that, in this case, the preposition **de** precedes the French infinitive verb.

| | |
|---|---|
| Il est content **de partir**. | *He is happy **to leave**.* |
| Ils sont enchantés **de rentrer**. | *They are delighted **to go back home**.* |
| Elles seront furieuses **de voir cela**. | *They will be furious **to see that**.* |
| Ils sont étonnés **de me trouver ici**. | *They are surprised **to find me here**.* |

Now consider the following similar examples. The French dependent clause still includes an infinitive (**voir**, **ne pas pouvoir**) or past infinitive (**avoir fait**, **avoir perdu**) instead of a verb in the subjunctive because the subjects of the two verbs in the main and dependent clauses are the same. However, the English dependent clause repeats the subject from the main clause and includes a conjugated verb.

| | |
|---|---|
| **Elle** était émue **de le voir**. | *She was moved when **she saw him**.* |
| **Nous** sommes désolés **de ne pas pouvoir** finir l'examen. | *We are sorry **we cannot finish** the exam.* |
| **Elle** est furieuse **d'avoir fait tant de fautes**. | *She is furious that **she made so many mistakes**.* |
| **Je** suis triste **d'avoir perdu mon bracelet**. | *I am sad **I lost my bracelet**.* |

**EXERCICE**
**8·5**

*Translate each sentence into English to find out what Monique tells her husband.*

1. Je suis si heureuse que tu sois là, Jean.

_____

2. Je m'inquiétais que tu ne puisses pas venir.

_____

3. Je craignais que ton patron ne veuille pas te donner congé.

_____

4. Tu es impressionné qu'il ait été si généreux, n'est-ce pas?

_____

5. En tout cas, il vaut mieux que nous profitions bien de ce weekend.

_____

6. Je doute que cela se reproduise!

_____

*Complete the sentences by translating into French the words in parentheses to find out what Monique's husband is saying.*

1. Le patron est content _____ prendre congé. (*to see me*)

2. Il était quelquefois inquiet _____ au travail jour et nuit. (*to find me*)

3. Il avait peur _____ trop de travail. (*to give me*)

4. Alors, Monique, tu es étonnée _____ cela, n'est-ce pas? (*to hear*)

5. Je suis ravi _____ passer le weekend chez tes parents. (*to be able*)

## Superlative adjectives

Adjectives in the superlative form such as **le meilleur/la meilleure** (*the best*) or **le plus beau/la plus belle** (*the most beautiful*) as well as adjectives that convey a superlative meaning, such as **seul** (*only*), **unique** (*unique*), **dernier** (*last*), **premier** (*first*), whenever they are found in the main clause, may require the subjunctive mood in the relative clause. The mood you choose for the verb in your dependent clause will convey to your interlocutor that you are certain or not certain about your statement.

| | |
|---|---|
| Cette glace-ci est **la meilleure** de toutes les glaces que **j'ai goûtées**. | *This ice cream is **the best** one of all the ice cream **I tasted**.* |

In this first example sentence, the verb in the dependent clause is in the indicative to convey the idea that I am quite sure that this is the best ice cream I ever ate.

| | |
|---|---|
| **La meilleure** glace que j'aie **jamais goûtée**, c'est celle-là. | *The best ice cream **I ever ate** is that one.* |

In this second sentence, the verb in the dependent clause is in the subjunctive to convey the idea that this *may be* the best ice cream I ever ate (but I cannot be absolutely sure).

Both sentences included a superlative adjective (**meilleure**). In English the two sentences had the same translation. In the French sentences, however, you notice that either the indicative or the subjunctive was used in the dependent clause depending on whether the speaker wanted to convey certainty (indicative mood) or uncertainty (subjunctive mood).

In this example I am making a firm assertion:

| | |
|---|---|
| C'est **le seul** endroit où **je peux** me détendre. | *This is **the only** place where **I can** relax.* |

In this second sentence I am hinting that this *may be* the only place where I can relax:

| | |
|---|---|
| C'est **le seul** endroit où **je puisse** me détendre. | *This is **the only** place where **I may** relax.* |

In this example I am making an assertion about the cat. I am quite sure there is no prettier one than this one:

| | |
|---|---|
| Voilà **le plus joli** chat que **j'ai jamais vu**. | *There is **the prettiest** cat **I have ever seen**.* |

In this second sentence, I am merely stating my opinion that this *may be* the prettiest cat I have ever seen:

| | |
|---|---|
| Voilà **le plus joli** chat que **j'aie jamais vu**. | *There may be **the prettiest** cat **I have ever seen**.* |

**EXERCICE**
**8·7**

*Write* C *for* certain *or* U *for* uncertain *on the lines provided, depending on whether the speaker is certain or uncertain about each statement.*

1. _____ C'est la première fois que j'irai en Martinique cet été.

2. _____ Je me demande si c'est une île aux Antilles qui vaille d'être visitée.

3. _____ Je crois que ce sera une expérience mémorable.

4. _____ Le meilleur plat antillais que je connaisse c'est les boulettes de farine.

5. _____ Je dois dire que la plus belle des trois îles antillaises que j'ai vues jusqu'à présent, c'est la Guadeloupe.

6. _____ Et les plus belles des fleurs que j'ai jamais vues, c'étaient vraiment celles que j'ai vues là-bas.

**EXERCICE**
**8·8**

*Put the verbs within parentheses in the subjunctive or the indicative according to whether what Mariette says is a fact or an opinion.*

1. Hier soir, c'est la première fois que je _____ à un ballet. (aller)

2. La ballerine-étoile était la plus jolie danseuse que vous _____ imaginer. (pouvoir)

3. La seule ville où je _____ vivre, c'est Paris. (vouloir)

4. C'est la plus belle de toutes les villes que j' _____ visitées. (avoir)

5. Je pense que la Tour Eiffel est la plus haute tour qu'on _____ jamais construite. (avoir)

## Impersonal expressions govern the subjunctive mood in the dependent clause

Impersonal expressions conveying necessity such as **Il faut** (*It is necessary*), opinions or value judgments such as **Il est juste** (*It is just*), expressions of possibility or improbability such as **Il se peut** (*It is possible*), whenever they are found in the main clause, will require the use of the subjunctive in the dependent clause. Here is a list of such commonly used expressions:

| NECESSITY/JUDGMENT | | POSSIBILITY/IMPROBABILITY | |
| --- | --- | --- | --- |
| Il faut | *It is necessary* | Il se peut | *It is possible* |
| Il est indispensable | *It is indispensable* | Il est possible | *It is possible* |
| Il est utile | *It is useful* | Il est impossible | *It is impossible* |
| Il est nécessaire | *It is necessary* | Il n'est pas probable | *It is not probable* |
| Il est préférable | *It is preferable* | Il est rare | *It is rare* |
| Il est important | *It is important* | Il semble | *It seems* |
| Il est urgent | *It is urgent* | Il n'est pas sûr | *It is not sure* |
| Il est juste | *It is just* | Il n'est pas certain | *It is not certain* |
| Il est bon | *It is good* | | |
| Il est impératif | *It is imperative* | | |
| Il est regrettable | *It is regrettable* | | |

| | |
|---|---|
| Il faut qu'on **soit** à l'heure au rendez-vous. | *We have **to be** on time for the appointment.* |
| Il est juste que les enfant **se partagent** les jouets. | *It is right that the children **share** the toys.* |
| Il est rare que les papillons **vivent** longtemps. | *It is rare that butterflies **live** a long time.* |
| Il est possible que nous **augmentions** le prix de l'essence. | *It is possible that we **increase** the price of gas.* |
| Il est bon que tu n'**ailles** plus au bar. | *It is good that you do not **go** to the bar anymore.* |

Some expressions or verbs, when in the affirmative, require the indicative in the dependent clause because they express certainty or probability. However, when they are in the negative or interrogative form, they express uncertainty and therefore require the subjunctive. Some of these verbs and expressions are as follows:

| | |
|---|---|
| Il est certain/être certain | *It is certain/to be certain* |
| Il est sûr/être sûr | *It is sure/to be sure* |
| Il est clair | *It is clear* |
| Il est évident | *It is evident* |
| Il est vrai | *It is true* |
| Il est probable | *It is probable* |

Note that in the following sentences, there is certainty, therefore the verbs in the dependent clauses are in the indicative mood.

| | |
|---|---|
| **Il est sûr** que cet homme **est** cultivé. | ***It is sure** that this man **is** educated.* |
| **Il est vrai** que nous **travaillons** beaucoup. | ***It is true** that we **work** a lot.* |

Now consider the following sentences, which express doubt or uncertainty. Note that the verbs in the independent clauses are in the subjunctive mood.

| | |
|---|---|
| **Es-tu sûr** que nous **soyons** sur la bonne route? | ***Are you sure** we **are** on the right road?* |
| **Il n'est pas évident** que nous **ayons** l'adresse correcte. | ***It is not evident** that we **have** the correct address.* |

Now consider the next examples and note that the word order in the English sentences is quite different from the word order in the French sentences. Also note that the translation from French into English is not literal. This is due to the fact that impersonal expressions such as **Il faut** (*It is necessary*) and **Il vaudrait mieux** (*It would be better*), which are commonly used in French, are awkward when translated literally into English.

| | |
|---|---|
| **Il vaut mieux** que tu fasses attention. | *You **better** watch out.* |
| **Il faudra** que nous nous amusions ce soir. | *We **have** to have fun tonight.* |
| **Il est urgent** qu'on l'opère. | *He must be operated on **urgently**.* |
| **Il était rare** qu'elle ne veuille pas manger. | ***It was rare** for her not to want to eat.* |
| **Il n'est pas certain** qu'il pleuve. | ***It is not certain** that it will rain.* |

If the subject of the verbs in the dependent clause is indefinite as in the following examples, you may use the preposition **de** and an infinitive verb instead of the subjunctive.

| | |
|---|---|
| Il serait bon **qu'on parte** tout de suite. | *We should **leave** right away.* |
| Il serait bon **de partir tout de suite.** | *It would be good **to leave** right away.* |

**EXERCICE**

**8·9**

*Translate the following sentences into English.*

1. Il vaut mieux qu'on jouisse de la vie.

   _____

2. Il faudra qu'on sauve la planète.

   _____

3. Il semble qu'on vive avec de plus en plus de technologie.

_____

4. Il est naturel qu'on veuille être heureux.

_____

5. Il est rare qu'on n'ait pas de désastre naturel quelque part.

_____

6. Il est urgent qu'on ralentisse la pollution.

_____

7. Il est possible qu'on invente de nouvelles technologies.

_____

8. Il n'est pas possible qu'on puisse faire cela en un jour.

_____

EXERCICE

8·10

*Rewrite the sentences from Exercice 8-9 using infinitive verbs instead of the subjunctive. Follow the example.*

EXAMPLE:      1. Il vaut mieux jouir de la vie.

2. _____

3. _____

4. _____

5. _____

6. _____

7. _____

8. _____

## Subordinating conjunctions govern the subjunctive mood in the dependent clause

Dependent clauses can be introduced by a variety of subordinating conjunctions. These establish a relationship based on restriction, opposition, purpose, fear, or time between the main and dependent clauses. The following is a list of commonly used subordinating conjunctions:

| | | | |
|---|---|---|---|
| à condition que | *provided that* | à moins que | *unless* |
| afin que | *so that* | avant que | *before* |
| bien que | *although* | de crainte que | *for fear that* |
| de peur que | *for fear that* | de sorte que | *so that* |
| en attendant que | *while waiting that* | jusqu'à ce que | *until* |

| | | | |
|---|---|---|---|
| malgré que | *although* | pour que | *so that* |
| pourvu que | *provided that* | quoique | *although* |
| sans que | *without* | | |

| | |
|---|---|
| C'est **pour qu'il soit gentil** que je lui donne un bonbon. | *It is **to have him be nice** that I give him a candy.* |
| Restons à la maison **en attendant que tout le monde soit là**. | *Let's stay at home **while waiting for everybody to be here**.* |
| Fais un bonhomme de neige **avant que la neige ne fonde**. | *Make a snowman **before the snow melts**.* |
| Je souffle la bougie **de peur que tu ne te brûles**. | *I am blowing out the candle **for fear that you could burn yourself**.* |
| On se souvient de lui **bien qu'il n'ait pas vécu longtemps**. | *He is remembered **although he did not live long**.* |

Note that in the last few examples, the expletive **ne/n'** precedes the verb in the dependent clause. The word *expletive* comes from the Latin verb *explere* (*to fill*). This **ne** is not to be interpreted as a negative term but rather as an extension of conjunctions such as **de peur que**, **avant que**, **bien que**. Many French subordinating conjunctions are accompanied by this expletive. It has no translation in English.

## Indefinite conjunctions govern the subjunctive mood in the dependent clause

A number of indefinite conjunctions or phrases require the subjunctive in the clauses they introduce. Consider the following examples:

| | |
|---|---|
| **Quelque sage qu'il soit**, il est un peu rebelle. | ***No matter how well behaved he is**, he is a little rebellious.* |
| **Quelles que soient ses qualités**, j'espère qu'il restera humble. | ***Regardless of his qualities**, I hope he will stay humble.* |
| **Qui que ce soit qui te raconte ces sornettes**, ne les crois pas! | ***Whoever the person is who tells you this nonsense**, do not believe it!* |
| **Quoi qu'on fasse cet été**, j'apprécierai mon repos. | ***Whatever we do this summer**, I will appreciate my rest.* |
| **Où qu'on aille en vacances**, je sais qu'on s'amusera. | ***Wherever we go on vacation**, I know that we will have fun.* |

**EXERCICE**
**8·11**

*Use a conjunction to complete each sentence.*

1. Marie paie des leçons particulières à son fils _____ il réussisse en mathématiques.

2. Elle préfère l'aider maintenant _____ il ne soit trop tard.

3. Elle a embauché un jeune homme très intelligent _____ il lui coûte très cher.

4. Elle veut bien payer très cher _____ son fils fasse des progrès.

5. Son fils travaille très dur _____ sa mère ne soit pas déçue.

6. Il va continuer de faire des efforts _____ les résultats soient meilleurs.

*Complete each sentence with **quelque**, **quoi**, **qui**, or **où**. Then translate the sentence into English.*

1. _____ que tu fasses, sois honnête!

   _____

2. _____ soit ta faute, tu peux toujours te faire pardonner!

   _____

3. _____ que ce soit à la porte, laisse la personne entrer!

   _____

4. _____ que tu ailles, n'oublie pas de téléphoner!

   _____

5. _____ fatigué que tu sois, mange quelque chose avant de te coucher!

   _____

## Some verbs, pronouns, and adjectives govern the subjunctive mood in the relative clause

We have previously seen dependent clauses introduced by the relative pronouns **qui**, **que**, **dont**, and **où**. The verb in those dependent clauses was in various tenses of the indicative mood. However, in some cases, the verb in the dependent relative clause must be in the subjunctive mood because of the type of verb found in the main clause.

### Verbs expressing will, want, need, and advice in the main clause

Verbs such as **chercher** (*to look for*), **vouloir** (*to want*), and **avoir besoin de** (*to need*) as well as the verb **connaître** (*to know*) in the interrogative form, and the expression **y a-t-il** (*is there/are there*), whenever they introduce relative clauses, may require the use of the subjunctive mood in the relative clause because of the uncertain outcome they predict.

| | |
|---|---|
| Je **cherche** une voiture qui **soit** rapide mais ne **consomme** pas d'essence. | *I **am looking for** a car that **is** fast but does not **use** any gas.* |
| Elle **veut** des employés qui **soient d'accord** pour ne jamais prendre de vacances. | *She **wants** employees who **agree** to never go on vacation.* |
| Tu **as besoin d'**un emploi qui n'**ait** pas d'heures fixes. | *You **need** a job that does not **have** fixed hours.* |
| Je **voudrais** un mari qui **fasse la cuisine** comme un professionnel. | *I **would like** a husband who **cooks** like a professional.* |
| **Connais**-tu un DJ qui **connaisse** bien la musique des années 60? | ***Do** you **know** a DJ who **knows** the music from the 60s well?* |
| **Y a-t-il** quelqu'un ici qui **sache** quelle heure il est? | ***Is there** somebody here who **knows** what time it is?* |

Compare the previous sentences to the following ones. You will notice that in the previous set of sentences, the speaker feels and conveys that expectations may or may not be met. In the following sentences, however, the speaker is confident that expectations are realistic and can be met.

| | |
|---|---|
| Je **cherche** une voiture qui ne **coûte** pas trop cher. | *I **am looking for** a car that does not **cost** too much.* |
| Elle **veut** des employés qui **arriveront** à l'heure. | *She **wants** employees who **will arrive** on time.* |
| Tu **as besoin** d'un emploi où tu **auras** des heures fixes. | *You **need** a job where you **will have** steady hours.* |

## Negative indefinite pronouns and adjectives govern the subjunctive mood in a relative clause

Negative pronouns such as **personne** (*nobody*) and **rien** (*nothing*) as well as indefinite pronouns or adjectives such as **aucun/nul** (*no*) tend to indicate uncertainty about whether the noun exists. Therefore the subjunctive may be needed in the dependent clause.

| | |
|---|---|
| Je n'ai trouvé **personne qui veuille m'accompagner**. | *I did not find **anybody who was willing to accompany me**.* |
| Je ne me rappelle **rien qui me fasse rougir**. | *I do not remember **anything that would make me blush**.* |
| Il n'y a **aucune chose ici qui me plaise**. | *There is **nothing here that I like**.* |
| Un nouveau collier? Je n'en vois **aucun qui me plaise**. | *A new necklace? I do not see **any that I like**.* |

EXERCICE
8·13

*Translate the underlined main clause of each sentence into French.*

1. Un coucher du soleil à Key West, _____ qui puisse y résister.

   (*A sunset in Key West, <u>I do not know anyone</u> who can resist it.*)

2. _____ qui soit plus beau que cela.

   (*<u>I cannot imagine anything</u> that is more beautiful than that.*)

3. _____ qui ait aimé cet endroit plus qu'Hemingway.

   (*<u>I do not know any writer</u> who loved this place more than Hemingway.*)

4. _____ qui veuille bien m'emmener en bateau.

   (*<u>I am looking for someone</u> who is willing to take me out on his boat.*)

# Relative clauses

Relative clauses are a special type of dependent clause. They follow a main clause or are sometimes embedded in the main clause, and they are always introduced by a relative pronoun such as **qui** (*who/that*) or **que** (*whom/that*). A relative pronoun refers to someone or something previously mentioned or understood by those who are communicating. That someone or something can be a noun or another pronoun.

## Relative clauses

Remember that a dependent clause needs a main clause to communicate its whole meaning. Relative pronouns serve as links to create longer, complex sentences. Consider the following sentence, which includes a main clause and a relative clause. Note that in the English sentence the relative pronoun may be implied, whereas in the French sentence it must be expressed.

| | |
|---|---|
| Le gâteau **que** je prépare s'appelle Kougelhopf. | *The cake (**that**) I am preparing is called Kougelhopf.* |

The main clause of this sentence (the one that would make sense by itself) is:

| | |
|---|---|
| Le gâteau s'appelle Kougelhopf. | *The cake is called Kougelhopf.* |

In this main clause, you can identify:

- The subject: **le gâteau** (also the antecedent of the relative pronoun **que**)
- The verb: **s'appelle**
- The attribute of the noun **gâteau**: Kougelhopf

Just as in English, a French relative pronoun links a *dependent relative clause* (a clause that cannot stand alone) to a *main clause*. In the previous example sentence, the dependent relative clause is:

| | |
|---|---|
| que je prépare | *(which/that) I am preparing* |

In this dependent relative clause, you can identify:

- The relative pronoun: **que**
- The subject of the verb in the dependent relative clause: **je**
- The verb: **prépare**

*Underline the relative clause in each of the following sentences and then translate the entire sentence into English.*

1. La moto qui est garée là est à moi.

   _____

2. La voiture que je veux acheter est chère.

   _____

3. Le vendeur qui m'a fait la démonstration est super sympa.

   _____

4. Les clients qu'il a aidés sont satisfaits.

   _____

5. La couleur que je préférerais est le rouge.

   _____

6. Les options que j'aimerais sont le lecteur de CD et le toit décapotable.

   _____

# Relative clauses introduced by **qui** or **que**

A relative pronoun always introduces a dependent clause called a relative clause. Within that clause, the pronoun performs a variety of functions such as subject, object of the verb, and object of a preposition. According to its function, the relative pronoun will take on different forms. The most frequently used relative pronouns in French are **que** and **qui**. Their English equivalents can be *who*, *whom*, *that*, and *which*.

## Using the relative pronoun **qui**

This relative pronoun performs the function of subject regardless of whether it stands for a person or a thing. When **qui** refers to a person, it is translated as *who*. When **qui** refers to a thing, it is translated as *that* or *which*. The word that the relative pronoun relates or connects to is called the *antecedent*. Consider the following examples. Note that in each sentence, the relative pronoun **qui** is the subject of the dependent verb.

> **main clause + relative clause**
> Je connais les gens + qui habitent ici.
> *I know the people who live here.*

In this sentence, **les gens** is the direct object of the main verb **connais**. It is replaced by the relative pronoun **qui** in the relative clause that follows it.

> Il cherche la balle **qui est tombée par ici**.     *He looks for the ball **that fell around here**.*

In this sentence, **la balle** is the direct object of the main verb **cherche**. It is replaced by the relative pronoun **qui** in the relative clause that follows it.

Similarly, in the following sentences, the relative pronoun **qui** replaces the direct object of the main clause (**légumes verts/René/portable**, respectively) and **qui** is the subject of the verb in the relative clause. Remember that **qui** may replace a thing or a person.

| | |
|---|---|
| J'achète des légumes verts **qui** sont bons pour la santé. | *I buy green vegetables, **which** are good for your health.* |
| Regarde René **qui** se dépêche! | *Look at René **who** is hurrying up!* |
| Tu as acheté le portable **qui** est si cher? | *Did you buy the portable **that** is so expensive?* |

In the following examples, the subject of the main clause is the antecedent of the relative pronoun. In this case, the relative clause does not follow the main clause; it is embedded in the main clause.

**subject of main clause + relative clause + predicate of main clause**
L'avion + qui vient d'atterrir + est en retard.
The plane that just landed is late.

In this sentence, it is **L'avion**, subject of the main verb **est**, that is being elaborated upon in the relative clause. The relative clause introduced by **qui** is therefore embedded in the main clause.

Similarly, in the following sentences, the relative clauses introduced by **qui** are embedded in their respective main clauses because they elaborate on the subject in the main clause:

| | |
|---|---|
| La comète **qui passe dans le ciel** est jolie. | *The comet, **which passes in the sky**, is pretty.* |
| L'élève **qui vient d'arriver** s'appelle Zina. | *The student **who just arrived** is called Zina.* |
| La voiture **qui est garée là** est à moi. | *The car **that is parked here** belongs to me.* |
| Les gens **qui mentent** sont malhonnêtes. | *People **who lie** are dishonest.* |

EXERCICE
**9·2**

*On the lines provided, write the letter of the relative clause that best completes each sentence.*

1. Le travail _____ c'est l'enseignement.
2. Les étudiants _____ sont ceux qui travaillent.
3. Les professeurs _____ sont le plus populaire.
4. Les devoirs _____ sont ennuyeux.
5. Les notes _____ sont bonnes.
6. J'aime les directeurs d'école _____.
7. Je trouve toujours la réponse _____.
8. Passe-moi le livre _____.

a. qui ont de bonnes notes
b. qui me plaît le plus
c. qui convient
d. qui se soucient des étudiants
e. A et B
f. qui est sur le bureau
g. qui sont trop longs
h. qui sont indulgents

## Using the relative pronoun **que**

The relative pronoun that performs the function of direct object regardless of whether it refers to a person or thing is **que**. When **que** refers to a person, it is translated as *whom*. When it refers to a thing, it is translated as *that* or *which*. Whether it refers to a person or an object, it may be implied and omitted in the English sentence but never in the French sentence. Consider the following sentences. Note that in each sentence the relative pronoun is the direct object of the dependent verb. As noted in the previous section, the relative clause may follow the main clause or be embedded within the main clause.

**main clause + relative clause**
Je vois la dame + que j'ai rencontrée ce matin.
*I see the lady (whom) I met this morning.*

In the previous example, the main clause contains the antecedent of the relative pronoun **que**. The antecedent of the relative pronoun is the *what* or the *who* being replaced by **que** in the relative clause—in this case **la dame** is the antecedent.

In the next example, the relative pronoun **que** replaces its antecedent **le film**.

Je regarde le film **que** tu as vu hier.    *I am watching the movie (**that**) you saw yesterday.*

Similarly, in each of the following sentences, the relative pronoun **que** replaces its antecedent regardless of whether it is a thing or a person (**amis/cadeaux/chat**). Note also that **que** is the direct object of the verb in the relative clause.

Invite les amis **que** tu préfères!    *Invite the friends (**that**) you prefer!*
Où sont les cadeaux **qu'**on a achetés?    *Where are the gifts (**that**) we bought?*
Viens voir le joli chat **que** j'ai adopté!    *Come and see the pretty cat (**that**) I adopted!*

In the following examples, the *subject* of the main clause is the antecedent of the relative pronoun. In this case, the relative clause does not follow the main clause; it is embedded in the main clause.

**subject of main clause + relative clause + predicate of main clause**
L'assistante + que le professeur a demandée + est arrivée.
*The assistant (that) the teacher asked for has arrived.*

In the previous sentence, **l'assistante** is the subject of the main verb **est arrivée**. It is that subject that is being elaborated upon in the relative clause introduced by **que**. Therefore the relative clause is embedded in the main clause.

Similarly, in the next example, **le cahier** is the subject of the main verb **est**. **Le cahier** is the antecedent of the relative pronoun, the *what* or the *who* being replaced in the relative clause. Note that the relative pronoun **que** is the direct object of the verb **as oublié**.

Le cahier **que tu as oublié** est dans mon sac.    *The notebook (**that**) **you forgot** is in my bag.*

Now consider the following sentences. Once again the relative clauses are embedded in the main clauses because they elaborate upon the subject of the main verb. In addition, note that the relative pronoun **que** is the direct object of the verb in the relative clause.

Les arbres **que tu as plantés** poussent bien.    *The trees (**that**) **you planted** grow well.*
Les serveuses **que j'engage** sont polies.    *The waitresses (**whom**) **I hire** are polite.*
La maison **que vous décorez** est belle.    *The house (**that**) **you are decorating** is beautiful.*

**EXERCICE**
**9·3**

*On the lines provided, write the letter of the relative clause that best completes each sentence.*

1. J'ai trouvé le pantalon _____.

2. Tu portes déjà la chemise _____?

3. Si tu veux, ce soir, tu peux mettre la chemise bleue _____.

a. qu'on rencontrera

b. que je voudrais rencontrer

c. qu'on a acheté hier

4. Moi, je préfère que tu portes le complet bleu _____.

d. que tu veux impressionner

5. Les personnes _____ seront là.

e. que tu dois me présenter en premier

6. La personne _____, c'est ton patron.

f. que tu as achetée hier

7. Une autre personne _____, c'est la femme du patron.

g. que tu cherchais

8. Les gens _____ à la soirée sont tous des collègues.

h. que ta mère t'a offerte pour Noël

*Fill in the blanks with* **qui** *or* **que/qu'** *to complete each sentence.*

1. La carte _____ vient d'arriver est une invitation de mariage.

2. C'est Monique _____ nous a envoyé l'invitation.

3. L'adresse _____ est sur l'enveloppe n'est pas tout à fait correcte.

4. La réponse _____ je vais donner dépend de toi.

5. La soirée _____ nous avons ratée était super.

6. On m'a dit que la musique _____ on y jouait était merveilleuse.

*Translate the following sentences into French.*

1. Here is the gift I want.

_____

2. It is the bike that is in the window.

_____

3. Look! The salesman who was there yesterday!

_____

4. He is the one who showed me this bike.

_____

5. It is really the gift I would like.

_____

6. It is even the color that I love.

_____

# Using ce qui or ce que

**Ce qui** and **ce que/ce qu'** are used to refer to ideas, concepts, or a clause. They translate as *what* (*that which*), and refer to an *idea* not specifically mentioned in the sentence.

Je ne sais pas **ce qui** s'est passé dans la classe.   *I do not know **what** happened in the class.*

In this example, we do not have an antecedent for **ce qui**. The *what* being referred to could be an accident, an altercation, a special activity, a lecture, and so on. Note that the same is true in the following sentences: Without context, we do not know exactly what is being refered to.

| | |
|---|---|
| Fais attention à **ce qui** se passe sur la route! | *Watch **what** happens on the road!* |
| Il peut me dire **ce qu'**il veut. | *He can tell me **what** he wants.* |
| Dis-moi **ce que** tu penses. | *Tell me **what** you think.* |

A relative clause with **ce qui** or **ce que** is sometimes the subject of the verb in the main clause. In that case, it precedes the main clause in French and in English.

| | |
|---|---|
| **Ce qui** me gêne me fâche. | ***What** bothers me makes me mad.* |
| **Ce qui** amuse peut aussi instruire. | ***What** is fun can also be instructive.* |
| **Ce que** tu fais est ton affaire. | ***What** you do is your business.* |
| **Ce que** tu dis est vraiment bizarre. | ***What** you are saying is really weird.* |

The reverse order is sometimes used for emphasis. This is a more familiar structure. In this case, a comma separates the two clauses because the usual order of the elements of the sentence is now inverted.

| | |
|---|---|
| C'est ton affaire, **ce que tu fais**. | *It is your business, **what you do**.* |
| C'est vraiment bizarre, **ce que tu me dis**. | *It is really weird, **what you are saying**.* |

**EXERCICE**

**9·6**

*Combine and rewrite each pair of sentences using one of the relative pronouns in parentheses.*

1. Voilà les billets. Je les ai achetés hier. (que, ce que)

   _____

2. J'admire les artistes. Ils vont nous divertir. (qui, ce qui)

   _____

3. Cela m'étonne. C'est que nos amis ne sont pas encore arrivés. (qui, ce qui)

   _____

4. J'ai le temps de boire ce café. J'ai préparé le café. (que, ce que)

   _____

5. Ah! J'entends une voiture. Elle s'arrête devant chez nous. (qui, que)

   _____

6. Ce sont nos amis. Ils arrivent. (qui, que)

   _____

# Using the relative pronouns **qui** and **lequel** after prepositions

Some dependent relative clauses are introduced by a preposition. (For more on prepositions, see Unit 15). In this case the relative pronoun is the object of the preposition. Use either **qui** or **lequel** after a preposition introducing a dependent clause. The choice of which relative pronoun to use will depend upon whether the antecedent of the pronoun (the *what* or the *who* being referred to) is a person or a thing.

## Relative clauses introduced by a preposition and **qui**

When the antecedent of a relative pronoun introduced by a preposition is a *person*, the pronoun **qui** (*whom*) is used.

> **main clause + preposition + relative clause**
> Regarde la personne + **à côté de** + **qui** il s'assied.
> *Look at the person next to **whom** he is sitting.*

In this sentence, the relative clause is introduced by **à côté de qui**. The pronoun **qui** replaces the noun **la personne**, which is the direct object of the main verb.

> **subject of the main verb + preposition + relative clause + main verb**
> L'ami + **avec** + **qui** je travaille + est parti.
> *The friend **with whom** I work left.*

In this sentence, the relative clause is introduced by **avec qui**. The pronoun **qui** replaces the noun **L'ami**, which is the subject of the main verb. Note that the relative clause is embedded in the main clause because it elaborates on the subject of the main clause.

In the following sentences, note that the relative clause may follow the main clause or be embedded in it depending on whether the antecedent of the relative pronoun is the subject or direct object in the main clause.

| | |
|---|---|
| L'employé **sur qui je compte le plus** est Jonas. | *The employee **on whom I count the most** is Jonas.* |
| Les médecins sont les personnes **pour qui j'ai le plus d'admiration.** | *Doctors are the people **for whom I have the most admiration.*** |
| Ma mère **à qui je dois la vie** est super. | *My mother, **to whom I owe my life**, is super.* |

## Relative clauses introduced by a preposition and a form of **lequel**

After a preposition introducing a relative clause, a form of the relative pronoun **lequel** (*which/that*) is used when the antecedent of the relative pronoun is a *thing*. Consider the following sentences and note that the form of the relative pronoun **lequel** changes according to the gender and number of the antecedent:

| | |
|---|---|
| Où est le casier dans **lequel** j'ai mis mes affaires? | *Where is the locker in **which** I put my things?* |
| Voilà les papiers parmi **lesquels** j'ai vu ma carte d'identité. | *There are the papers among **which** I saw my ID card.* |
| La maison devant **laquelle** il s'est garé est grise. | *The house in front of **which** he parked is gray.* |
| Voilà les fleurs pour **lesquelles** j'ai payé une fortune. | *There are the flowers for **which** I paid a fortune.* |

Consider the following relative clauses introduced by prepositions and note that the masculine singular form and both plural forms of the relative pronoun **lequel** contract with the prepositions **à** and **de**.

| | |
|---|---|
| Comment s'appelle la fraternité à **laquelle** il appartient? | *What is the name of the fraternity to **which** he belongs?* |
| Les concerts **auxquels** j'ai assisté étaient sensationnels. | *The concerts (**that**) I attended were sensational.* |
| Le voyage **auquel** je pense est celui de l'an dernier. | *The trip (**that**) I am thinking about is the one from last year.* |
| Voici les villes **desquelles** j'ai le meilleur souvenir. | *Here are the cities of **which** I have the best memories.* |
| C'est le concert au cours **duquel** il y a eu des incidents. | *It is the concert during **which** there have been incidents.* |
| C'est la plage près de **laquelle** j'habite. | *This is the beach near **which** I live.* |

**EXERCICE 9·7**

*Choose the relative pronoun in parentheses that will correctly complete each sentence.*

1. Voici le journal dans _____ j'ai lu l'article sur la crise en Côte d'Ivoire. (qui, lequel)

2. C'est la crise à cause de _____ il y a tant d'orphelins là-bas. (qui, laquelle)

3. J'ai une amie sur _____ je peux toujours compter pour m'informer des affaires africaines. (qui, laquelle)

4. C'est la personne avec _____ je peux discuter de choses sérieuses. (qui, laquelle)

5. Est-ce que les clubs _____ tu appartiens font des œuvres de charité? (à qui, auxquels)

6. C'est la cause humanitaire _____ je m'intéresse le plus. (à qui, à laquelle)

**EXERCICE 9·8**

*Translate the following sentences into French using a preposition followed by **qui** or a form of **lequel** in the relative clauses.*

1. This is the friend for whom I do this.

_____

2. This is the building in which I work.

_____

3. This is the office near to which there is a restaurant.

_____

4. This is the person thanks to whom I have a job.

_____

5. This is the desk on which I put the mail.

_____

6. This is the notebook in which I write appointments.

_____

## Using the relative pronoun **dont**

The pronoun **dont** can be translated as *that, whose, of whom,* or *of which.* This pronoun refers to a person or a thing. Use it whenever the verb in the relative clause is followed by the preposition **de.**

> C'est la ville **dont** je me souviens le mieux.     *This is the city (**that**) I remember best.*

In this sentence, the relative clause is introduced by **dont** because the verb in the relative clause is **se souvenir de.** The preposition **de,** which must follow the verb **se souvenir,** governs the use of **dont.**

> Où est la carte de crédit **dont** j'ai besoin?     *Where is the credit card (**that**) I need?*

In this sentence, the relative clause is introduced by **dont** because the verb in the relative clause is **avoir besoin de.** The preposition **de,** which must follow the phrase **avoir besoin,** governs the use of **dont.**

Similarly, in the following sentences, the verb or phrase in the relative clause (**parler de/être fier de**) governs the use of **dont** because it is followed by the preposition **de.**

> C'est la chanteuse **dont** j'ai parlé.     *This is the singer (**that**) I talked about.*
> Le professeur présente les élèves **dont** il     *The teacher introduces the students **of whom***
>     est le plus fier.     *he is the most proud.*

The relative pronoun **dont** also indicates *possession* or *relationship.* In this case, it is translated as *whose* or *of which.*

> Voici l'élève **dont** les parents ne sont pas     *This is the student **whose** parents are not very*
>     très contents.     *happy.*
> Voici ma copine Françoise **dont** les     *Here is my friend Françoise **whose** cousins are*
>     cousins sont américains.     *American.*
> C'est la fille **dont** le copain est dans l'armée.     *This is the girl **whose** friend is in the army.*
> Regarde la maison **dont** le toit a été arraché.     *Look at the house the roof **of which** was torn*
>     *off.*

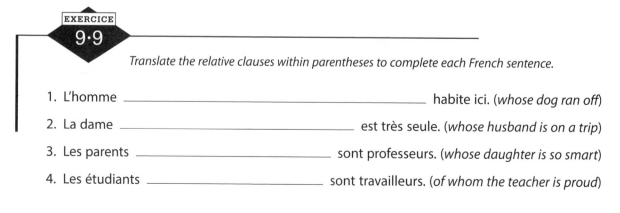

EXERCICE
9·9

*Translate the relative clauses within parentheses to complete each French sentence.*

1. L'homme _____ habite ici. (*whose dog ran off*)

2. La dame _____ est très seule. (*whose husband is on a trip*)

3. Les parents _____ sont professeurs. (*whose daughter is so smart*)

4. Les étudiants _____ sont travailleurs. (*of whom the teacher is proud*)

5. La voiture _____ est au garage. (*the battery of which is dead*)

6. La maison _____ est chère. (*the kitchen of which is renovated*)

# Using the relative pronoun **où**

The relative pronoun **où** refers to both *place* and *time* in French. Therefore it means both *where* and *when* in English.

| | |
|---|---|
| La boulangerie **où** j'ai travaillé est à côté de la banque. | The bakery **where** I worked is next to the bank. (*The bakery [**that**] I worked at . . .*) |
| L'endroit **où** je passe mes vacances n'est pas très connu. | The place **where** I spend my vacation is not very well known. |
| Lundi, c'est le jour **où** nous faisons les achats. | Monday is the day **when** we do our shopping. |
| C'est l'année **où** il a fait le plus chaud. | It is the year **when** it was the hottest. |

**EXERCICE**

**9·10**

*Translate the sentences into French using the phrases in parentheses as guides.*

1. *The year when Sarkozy was born is 1955.* (il est né en 1955)

   _____

2. *The city where he was born is Paris.* (il est né à Paris)

   _____

3. *Carla Bruni is the woman with whom he is married.* (il est marié avec Carla Bruni)

   _____

4. *Politics is what interests him the most.* (il s'intéresse le plus à la politique)

   _____

5. *The palace where French presidents live is called l'Elysée.* (les présidents français habitent le palais de l'Elysée)

   _____

6. *What he is the most proud of is his title of president.* (il est le plus fier de son titre de président)

   _____

# Infinitive and past infinitive clauses

There are numerous infinitive clauses in French and in English. They are dependent clauses in which the verb is not conjugated but rather is left in its infinitive form. Past infinitive clauses, less frequently encountered, are dependent clauses that of course refer to the past and are built around the auxiliary verbs **avoir/être** in their infinitive forms along with the past participle of the verb showing the action.

## Simple infinitive clauses

In French the ending of a verb indicates whether it is in the infinitive form (infinitive endings are **-er, -ir, -re, -oir**). In English the preposition *to* before the verb indicates that it is in the infinitive form. An infinitive clause includes the infinitive verb and the other structural elements found in any other dependent clauses such as objects (direct or indirect), prepositional phrases, and adverbs. Consider the varying structures of infinitive clauses in these examples.

In the following infinitive clause, **un ami** is the direct object of **présenter**:

> **main clause + infinitive clause**
> Je veux + **présenter un ami.**
> *I want **to introduce a friend**.*

In the following infinitive clause, **son copain** is the indirect object of **parler**:

> **infinitive + indirect object**
> Elle aimerait **parler** + **à son copain.**
> *She would like **to speak to her friend**.*

In the following infinitive clause, **le budget** is the direct object of **finir**, and the clause includes an adverb:

> **infinitive + direct object + adverb**
> Il faut **finir** + **le budget** + immédiatement.
> *You have **to finish the budget** immediately.*

EXERCICE
10·1

*Underline the infinitive clause in each sentence.*

1. Ce soir nous allons sortir en famille.

2. Papa va nous emmener dans un restaurant chic.

3. J'espère pouvoir rejoindre mes amis après le dîner.

4. J'aime passer du temps avec ma famille, mais pas trop quand même.

5. Je pourrais peut-être partir au moment du dessert.

6. Si possible, je voudrais finir la soirée en disco.

## Simple infinitive clauses after verbs

Simple infinitive clauses often perform the syntactic role of the direct object of the verb in the main clause and therefore follow the conjugated verb from the main clause. In French, whenever two verbs follow each other, the first verb is conjugated and the second verb is left in its infinitive form. In French as in English, there are many verbs that are directly followed by an infinitive verb.

### Verbs of perception

A simple infinitive clause can be found after a verb of *perception* such as **voir** (*to see*), **écouter** (*to listen*), **entendre** (*to hear*), **regarder** (*to watch*), and **sentir** (*to feel*). Consider the following sentences and note that the word order in the French and English infinitive clauses can be different. There are two possible word orders for the French infinitive clause but only one possible word order in English.

Je vois **le train partir**.
Je vois **partir le train**.

*I see **the train leave**.*

J'entends **des oiseaux gazouiller**.
J'entends **gazouiller des oiseaux**.

*I hear **birds twitter**.*

Note that the infinitive clause **le train partir** performs the role of direct object of the main verb **vois**. Similarly, the infinitive clause **des oiseaux gazouiller** is the direct object of the main verb **entends**.

### Verbs of want, opinion, possibility, necessity, appearance

An infinitive clause can be found after many verbs in these categories. The following lists give some examples of the verbs commonly followed by an infinitive:

| WANT | | OPINION | |
|---|---|---|---|
| désirer | *to desire* | croire | *to believe* |
| préférer | *to prefer* | dire | *to say* |
| souhaiter | *to wish* | penser | *to think* |
| vouloir | *to want* | supposer | *to suppose/assume* |

| POSSIBILITY/NECESSITY | | APPEARANCE | |
|---|---|---|---|
| devoir | *to have to* | paraître | *to appear* |
| falloir | *to be necessary* | sembler | *to seem* |
| pouvoir | *to be able* | | |

Elle préfère **attendre le bus**.
Nous adorons **faire des randonnées**.

*She prefers **to wait for the bus**.*
*We love **to go for hikes**.*

Note that, in the previous example sentences, the subject of the verb in the dependent infinitive clause is the same as the subject in the main clause. In the first example, **elle** is the subject of the main verb **préfère** as well as the subject of the dependent infinitive verb **attendre**. In the second example, **nous** is the subject of the main verb **adorons** as well as the subject of the infinitive dependent verb **faire**.

| | |
|---|---|
| Tu exiges **payer ce soir?** | *You demand **to pay tonight?*** |
| Ils veulent **aller en France.** | *They want **to go to France.*** |
| Je voudrais **maigrir un peu.** | *I would like **to lose a little weight.*** |

In French, it is always better style to use an infinitive clause rather than a subordinate clause whenever the subject is the same in the main and dependent clauses. This is not always the case in English. In the following examples, the dependent clauses in English are subordinate clauses in which the conjunction *that* can be omitted.

| | |
|---|---|
| On croit **tout savoir.** | *One thinks (that) **one knows everything.*** |
| Elle pense **revenir bientôt.** | *She thinks (that) **she will come back soon.*** |
| Nous supposons **être les premiers.** | *We assume (that) **we are first.*** |

In the next two examples, note that in English the preposition *to* is omitted in the infinitive clause because the auxiliary verbs *can* and *must* are used instead.

| | |
|---|---|
| Vous pouvez **finir votre repas maintenant.** | *You can **finish your meal now.*** |
| Nous devons **attendre ici.** | *We must **wait here.*** |

## Verbs of movement

An infinitive clause can be found after verbs of movement such as **aller** (*to go*), **venir** (*to come*), **monter** (*to go up*), **descendre** (*to go down*), and **sortir** (*to go out*).

| | |
|---|---|
| Va **chercher ton frère!** | *Go **get your brother!*** |
| Nous venons **dîner chez toi.** | *We are coming **to eat at your house.*** |
| Je monte **réveiller Papa.** | *I am going up **to wake Dad.*** |
| Nous descendons **voir le défilé.** | *We are going down **to see the parade.*** |
| Sortez **jouer à la balle!** | *Go out **and play ball!*** |

## Causal **faire** structure

An infinitive clause is used after the verb **faire** (*to make/do*) in a variety of tenses to express that someone is having something done by someone else.

| | |
|---|---|
| Il se fait **masser le dos.** | *He is having **his back massaged.*** |
| Nous ferons **construire une piscine.** | *We will have **a pool built.*** |
| Vous avez fait **blanchir vos chemises.** | *You had **your shirts cleaned.*** |
| Cette famille fait **couper le gazon.** | *This family is having **their lawn cut.*** |

An infinitive clause is also used after the verbs **laisser** (*to let/allow*), **oser** (*to dare*), and **faillir** (*to almost . . .*).

| | |
|---|---|
| Ne laisse pas **tomber le gâteau!** | *Do not **drop the cake!*** |
| Il a laissé **brûler les oignons.** | *He let **the onions burn.*** |
| J'ose **dire non.** | *I dare **say no.*** |
| Le boucher a failli **se couper le doigt.** | *The butcher almost **cut his finger.*** |

**EXERCICE**

**10·2**

*Complete each sentence on the left with an appropriate infinitive clause on the right by writing the corresponding letter on the line provided.*

1. Je vais faire _____

2. Ce soir je vais _____

a. réaliser de grands projets comme les miens.

b. avoir une excellente réputation.

3. Je pense _____

4. Je souhaite _____

5. L'architecte semble _____

6. Il adore _____

c. rencontrer l'architecte.

d. accepter sa proposition et ses dessins.

e. habiter bientôt la maison de mes rêves.

f. construire une maison.

EXERCICE
10·3

Write the appropriate infinitive verb from the list to complete each sentence.

faire / tomber / jouer / être / s'amuser / emmener / nager / gronder

1. Dara aime _____ à la poupée.

2. Alex, lui, aime _____ à la piscine.

3. Moi, j'adore les _____ au parc.

4. Là, ils préfèrent _____ avec les autres enfants.

5. Quelquefois ils ne font pas attention et risquent de _____ des balançoires.

6. Alors je leur dis de _____ attention.

EXERCICE
10·4

Translate the following sentences into French.

1. I like to get up late.

_____

2. I hate to hear the clock ring in the morning.

_____

3. I prefer eating breakfast at home.

_____

4. After breakfast, I hurry and get dressed.

_____

5. Then I have to take the bus and go to work.

_____

6. I do not let work become my life.

_____

# Simple infinitive clauses after impersonal expressions

An infinitive clause will be found after impersonal expressions, such as **Il faut** (*It is necessary*), **Il est bon de** (*It is good to*), **Il est important de** (*It is important to*), **Il vaut mieux** (*It is better to*), **Il est juste de** (*It is just to*), in sentences where generalizations are made. Note that most of these impersonal expressions (except for **il faut** and **il vaut mieux**) require the use of the preposition **de** to introduce the infinitive clause.

| | |
|---|---|
| Il est important **de beaucoup boire en s'exerçant.** | *It is important **to drink a lot while exercising.*** |
| Il est bon **de faire du sport.** | *It is good **to do sports.*** |
| Il est juste **de récompenser les enfants sages.** | *It is just **to reward good children.*** |
| Il vaut mieux **ne plus fumer en public.** | *It is better **to no longer smoke in public/ to stop smoking in public.*** |

This type of infinitive clause often replaces a subordinate clause featuring the impersonal pronoun **on** (*one*) and a verb in the subjunctive mood. The generalization is the same in both structures. However, remember that the infinitive clause is usually better style.

Il est important **de beaucoup boire en s'exerçant.** = Il est important **qu'on boive beaucoup en s'exerçant.**

Il est bon **de faire du sport.** = Il est bon **qu'on fasse du sport.**

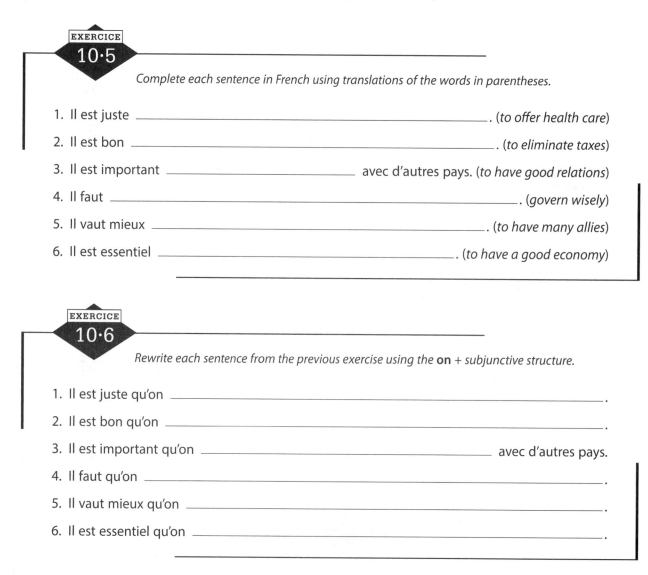

**EXERCICE**
## 10·5

*Complete each sentence in French using translations of the words in parentheses.*

1. Il est juste _____. (*to offer health care*)

2. Il est bon _____. (*to eliminate taxes*)

3. Il est important _____ avec d'autres pays. (*to have good relations*)

4. Il faut _____. (*govern wisely*)

5. Il vaut mieux _____. (*to have many allies*)

6. Il est essentiel _____. (*to have a good economy*)

**EXERCICE**
## 10·6

*Rewrite each sentence from the previous exercise using the **on** + subjunctive structure.*

1. Il est juste qu'on _____.

2. Il est bon qu'on _____.

3. Il est important qu'on _____ avec d'autres pays.

4. Il faut qu'on _____.

5. Il vaut mieux qu'on _____.

6. Il est essentiel qu'on _____.

## Simple infinitive clauses after adjectives of emotion

An infinitive clause will also be found after adjectives of emotion such as **content/heureux** (*happy*), **triste** (*sad*), **fâché** (*angry*), **désolé** (*sorry*), **surpris** (*surprised*), **honteux** (*ashamed*), and **fier** (*proud*) whenever the subject of the main verb and of the infinitive verb is the same. The preposition **de** must then introduce the infinitive clause.

| | |
|---|---|
| Elle est heureuse **de revoir sa maison d'enfance.** | *She is happy **to see her childhood house again.*** |
| Elle est surprise **de constater les changements.** | *She is surprised **to see the changes.*** |
| Nous sommes fiers **de pouvoir parler français.** | *We are proud **we can speak French.*** |
| Vous êtes triste **de ne pas savoir d'autre langue.** | *You are sad **you do not know any other language.*** |

**EXERCICE**

**10·7**

*Complete each sentence with one of the choices in parentheses to determine what makes a good vacation for you, personally.*

1. Je veux _____. (avoir du calme / être entouré(e) de gens)

2. Je suis heureux _____. (de me bronzer sur la plage / de faire des activités nautiques)

3. Je suis content _____. (de rencontrer des étrangers / de ne rencontrer personne)

4. J'adore _____. (dîner dans les restaurants / manger dans les cafés)

5. Je suis triste _____. (de ne pas aller au musée / d'aller en ville)

6. Je souhaite _____. (faire beaucoup d'excursions / rester à un seul endroit)

## Infinitive clauses after prepositions

We just saw that infinitive clauses can be introduced by the preposition **de** when there is an expression of opinion or an adjective of emotion in the main clause. An infinitive clause will also be found after simple and complex prepositions, such as **pour/afin de** (*in order to*), **avant de** (*before*), **au lieu de** (*instead of*), **sans** (*without*), **à condition de** (*provided that/as long as*), and **de crainte de/de peur de** (*for fear that*), whenever the subject in the main and infinitive clauses is the same.

| | |
|---|---|
| Je vais à la piscine **pour faire une heure de nage.** | *I am going to the pool **to swim for an hour.*** |
| Amusons-nous **au lieu de travailler.** | *Let's have fun **instead of working.*** |
| **Afin de s'amuser**, il faut se détendre. | ***In order to have fun**, you have to relax.* |
| Prépare-toi **à répondre!** | *Get ready **to answer!*** |
| Amuse-toi **au lieu de travailler!** | *Have fun **instead of working!*** |
| J'ai hâte **de voir la Tour Eiffel.** | *I am anxious **to see the Eiffel Tower.*** |

Consider the following examples and note that the negative structure of the infinitive clause requires both negative terms **ne** and **pas** *to precede* the infinitive verb:

| | |
|---|---|
| Levons-nous tôt afin **de ne pas être en retard.** | *Let's get up early **so as not to be late.*** |
| Je suis d'accord **à condition de ne pas payer.** | *I agree **as long as I do not have to pay.*** |

An infinitive clause introduced by a preposition can precede or follow the main clause. When it precedes the main clause, it ends in a comma.

| | |
|---|---|
| Lavons-nous les mains **avant de manger**! | *Let's wash our hands **before eating**!* |
| **Avant de manger**, lavons-nous les mains! | ***Before eating**, let's wash our hands!* |

An infinitive clause will be found after verbs that require the prepositions **à** or **de**. There are many such verbs. Here are some examples:

| | |
|---|---|
| Le petit garçon apprend **à lire en français**. | *The little boy learns **to read in French**.* |
| Je m'intéresse **à apprendre le français**. | *I am interested **in learning French**.* |
| J'encourage mes amis **à persévérer**. | *I encourage my friends **to persevere**.* |
| Il cesse **de neiger**. | *It stops **snowing**.* |
| Elle regrette **de ne pas savoir skier**. | *She regrets **not knowing how to ski**.* |
| Ils nous ont dit **de revenir plus tard**. | *They told us **to come back later**.* |

Note: *Do not* use the simple infinitive form after the prepositions **en** or **après**. The preposition **en** is followed by a gerund (see Unit 16) and the preposition **après** is followed by a past infinitive.

### EXERCICE 10·8

*Fill in the blanks with a preposition to best complete each sentence.*

1. Mon professeur m'encourage _____ continuer mes études de français.

2. Moi, je veux bien mais j'ai peur _____ avoir beaucoup de mal l'an prochain.

3. _____ blaguer, je trouve le français un peu facile.

4. Généralement je réussis à tout ce que je fais _____ faire d'efforts.

5. J'ai appris _____ travailler dur dans tous mes cours.

6. Il faut toujours persévérer et s'intéresser _____ son travail.

7. Il est important _____ finir tout ce qu'on fait.

8. _____ m'inscrire, je vais réfléchir.

9. Je regrette _____ ne pas m'inscrire immédiatement.

10. Je vais dire au professeur _____ me donner un peu de temps.

### EXERCICE 10·9

*Write the letter of the infinitive clause on the right that best completes each main clause on the left.*

| | | |
|---|---|---|
| 1. Fais du sport _____ | a. | à vérifier les ingrédients dans les plats. |
| 2. Mange ce que tu veux _____ | b. | de suivre ces conseils. |
| 3. Apprends _____ | c. | au lieu de regarder la télé. |
| 4. Cesse _____ | d. | avant de dîner. |
| 5. Intéresse-toi _____ | e. | afin de rester en forme. |

6. Promène-toi _____

7. Fais du jogging _____

8. Essaie _____

f. à faire des plats végétariens.

g. d'acheter des pâtisseries.

h. à condition que ce soit sain.

## Special functions of infinitive clauses

You have just seen how to build infinitive clauses that complete the meaning of a main verb or expression. Now you will learn to use infinitive clauses to express the main idea in a sentence.

### Using infinitive clauses as subjects

When an infinitive clause performs the function of subject of the main verb, it is the essential component of that sentence. In this case, it precedes the verb in French and in English.

**infinitive + predicate**
**Lire et écrire** + sont des compétences de base.
*Reading and writing are basic skills.*

The entire clause **Lire et écrire** is the subject of the verb **sont**.

| | |
|---|---|
| **Conduire** trop vite est dangereux. | ***Driving*** *too fast is dangerous.* |
| **Chanter** me fait toujours plaisir. | ***Singing*** *always makes me happy.* |
| **Faire du parachutisme** est une activité grisante. | ***Parachuting*** *is an exhilarating activity.* |
| **Refuser leur invitation** me gêne beaucoup. | ***Refusing*** *their invitation bothers me a lot.* |

### Using infinitive clauses to give commands or instructions

An infinitive clause can serve as a command or instruction just like a verb in the imperative mood. However, infinitive clauses are preferred and consistently found in food recipes, in assembly instructions, and in public warnings.

| IMPERATIVE MOOD | | INFINITIVE CLAUSE | |
|---|---|---|---|
| Ne fumez pas! | *Do not smoke!* | Ne pas fumer. | *Do not smoke!* |
| | | Bouillir à petit feu. | *Simmer.* |
| | | Ajouter de l'huile. | *Add some oil.* |
| | | Laisser refroidir. | *Allow to cool off.* |
| | | Conserver au frais. | *Keep refrigerated.* |
| | | Agiter le flacon. | *Shake the bottle.* |
| | | Serrer la vis. | *Tighten the screw.* |
| | | Aligner les deux flèches. | *Align the two arrows.* |
| | | Ne pas marcher sur le gazon. | *No walking on the grass.* |

### Using infinitive clauses as interrogatives

Infinitive clauses are sometimes used as interrogative clauses to express hesitation or reflection. These clauses are introduced by an interrogative word and may be preceded by a main clause.

**main clause + interrogative word + infinitive clause**
Je cherche un endroit + où + garer ma voiture.
*I am looking for a place where I can park my car.*

| | |
|---|---|
| Je me demande **que faire maintenant**. | *I am wondering **what to do now**.* |
| Je ne sais pas **comment y aller**. | *I do not know **how to go there**.* |

The following infinitive clauses are introduced by an interrogative word and are not preceded by a main clause:

**interrogative word + infinitive clause**
Que + faire ce soir?
*What should I/we do tonight?*

| | |
|---|---|
| Que dire à tout cela? | *What can one say to all that?* |
| Où aller aujourd'hui? | *Where should I/we go today?* |
| Comment répondre à cette insulte? | *How should I/we respond to this insult?* |

**EXERCICE**
**10·10**

*Combine the sentence fragments to create warnings.*

1. toucher / ne pas / aux allumettes _____

2. garer / sur le gazon / ne pas / les voitures _____

3. la limite de vitesse / respecter _____

4. sévèrement puni / voler / est _____

5. ne pas / du feu / s'approcher _____

6. au frigo / les aliments frais / conserver _____

**EXERCICE**
**10·11**

*Complete each sentence by translating the infinitive clause within parentheses into French.*

1. J'aime beaucoup _____. (*travel by train*)

2. Je compte _____ (*take the TGV*) _____
(*to go*) à Nice.

3. Je me réjouis déjà de _____. (*be able to sunbathe*)

4. De plus, _____ est un plaisir. (*swimming in the sea*)

5. Il est essentiel de _____ (*take a vacation*) de temps en temps.

6. Il est bon de _____. (*rest*)

**EXERCICE**
**10·12**

*Choose the most logical follow-up on the right to each statement given on the left and write the corresponding letter on the line provided.*

1. Il ne faut pas allumer de cigarette. _____     a. Que faire?

2. C'est encore très chaud. _____     b. Que dire?

3. Allons-y alors! _____     c. Laisser refroidir.

4. J'hésite. Je ne sais pas. _____

5. J'ai perdu la parole. _____

6. Il a dit des choses insultantes. _____

d. Ne pas fumer.

e. Comment lui répondre?

f. Il faut aller à la fête.

# Past infinitive clauses

A past infinitive clause includes an auxiliary verb in its infinitive form (**avoir/être**) and a past participle. In the following examples, note that the English auxiliary verb is always *to have*. However, in French it can be **avoir** (*to have*) or **être** (*to be*).

Il voudrait **avoir voyagé davantage**.    *He would like **to have traveled more**.*
Il regrette de **ne pas être retourné là-bas**.    *He regrets **not having gone back there**.*

## Past infinitives

A past infinitive structure in French includes the auxiliary verb **avoir/être** in the infinitive form and a past participle.

**avoir** or **être** + past participle → past infinitive

Most verbs in French belong to the regular -**er** verb group. The past participle of these verbs is obtained by replacing the -**er** infinitive ending with **é**.

| INFINITIVE VERB | | | PAST PARTICIPLE | |
| --- | --- | --- | --- | --- |
| aim**er** | *to like* | → | aim**é** | *liked* |
| apport**er** | *to bring* | → | apport**é** | *brought* |
| cherch**er** | *to look for* | → | cherch**é** | *looked for* |
| écout**er** | *to listen* | → | écout**é** | *listened* |
| regard**er** | *to watch/look at* | → | regard**é** | *watched/looked at* |
| rest**er** | *to stay* | → | rest**é** | *stayed* |

Some verbs in French belong to the regular -**ir** verb group. The past participle of these verbs is obtained by replacing the -**ir** infinitive ending with **i**.

| INFINITIVE VERB | | | PAST PARTICIPLE | |
| --- | --- | --- | --- | --- |
| applaud**ir** | *to applaud* | → | applaud**i** | *applauded* |
| chois**ir** | *to choose* | → | chois**i** | *chosen* |
| fin**ir** | *to finish* | → | fin**i** | *finished* |
| grand**ir** | *to grow* | → | grand**i** | *grown* |
| réuss**ir** | *to succeed* | → | réuss**i** | *succeeded* |

Some verbs in French belong to the regular -**re** verb group. The past participle of these verbs is obtained by replacing the -**re** infinitive ending with **u**.

| INFINITIVE VERB | | | PAST PARTICIPLE | |
| --- | --- | --- | --- | --- |
| défend**re** | *to defend/forbid* | → | défend**u** | *defended/forbidden* |
| descend**re** | *to go down* | → | descend**u** | *went down* |
| perd**re** | *to lose* | → | perd**u** | *lost* |
| rend**re** | *to return* | → | rend**u** | *returned* |
| répond**re** | *to answer* | → | répond**u** | *answered* |

Irregular verbs have unpredictable past participle forms. Here are a few examples:

| INFINITIVE VERB | | | PAST PARTICIPLE | |
| --- | --- | --- | --- | --- |
| avoir | *to have* | → | eu | *had* |
| être | *to be* | → | été | *been* |
| mettre | *to put/put on* | → | mis | *put* |
| partir | *to leave* | → | parti | *left* |
| prendre | *to take* | → | pris | *taken* |

Most French verbs use **avoir** as an auxiliary verb in the past infinitive structure (as well as in compound tenses such as the passé composé). Here are a few examples:

| | |
| --- | --- |
| avoir cherché | *having searched* |
| avoir donné | *having given* |
| avoir été | *having been* |
| avoir eu | *having had* |
| avoir pris | *having taken* |
| avoir répondu | *having answered* |
| avoir réussi | *having succeeded* |
| avoir vendu | *having sold* |

However, some French verbs use **être** as a helping verb. This is mostly the case for verbs of movement and for reflexive verbs. Remember that a past participle that follows the auxiliary verb **être** must have the same gender and number as the subject of the verb. Here are a few examples:

| | |
| --- | --- |
| être allé/allée/allés/allées | *having gone* |
| être monté/montée/montés/montées | *having gone up* |
| être descendu/descendue/descendus/ descendues | *having gone down* |
| être revenu/revenue/revenus/revenues | *having come back* |
| être parti/partie/partis/parties | *having left* |
| être né/née/nés/nées | *having been born* |

Just like a simple infinitive, a past infinitive structure may follow a verb such as **souhaiter** (*to wish*), an impersonal expression such as **Il est important de** (*It is important*), or a preposition such as **sans** (*without*). However, the past infinitive structure is used whenever the action of the infinitive clause precedes the action in the main clause.

| | |
| --- | --- |
| Je souhaite **avoir fait plus études**. | *I wish **I had done more studies**.* |

Note that the studying would have been done in the past while the wishing takes place right now.

| | |
| --- | --- |
| Il est important **d'avoir fini ses devoirs**. | *It is important **to have finished one's homework**.* |

Note that the homework was finished before the statement of importance was made.

| | |
| --- | --- |
| Il part sans **n'avoir rien dit**. | *He is leaving without **having said anything**.* |

Note that the failure to say something preceded the action of leaving.

Remember that in clauses where the auxiliary verb is **être**, the French past participle must reflect the gender and number of the subject in the main clause.

| | |
| --- | --- |
| Elle souhaiterait **être née à une autre époque**. | *She wished **she had been born in another time**.* |

In this sentence, the past participle **née** is in the feminine form because the subject of the dependent clause is **elle**.

**Après être rentrés**, ils ont ouvert les valises.    *After coming back home, (After having come back home,) they opened the suitcases.*

In this sentence, the past participle **rentrés** is in the plural form because the subject of the dependent verb is **ils**.

## Past infinitive clauses after verbs and expressions of opinion and emotion

The past infinitive structure can follow a variety of verbs and expressions of opinion and emotion including some verbs that require the preposition **de** or **à**, as previously seen with simple infinitive clauses. As also previously seen with the simple infinitive clauses, the past infinitive clause may include structural elements found in any other dependent clauses such as objects (direct or indirect), prepositions, prepositional phrases, adverbs, and adverbial phrases. Consider the structure of the following sentence:

**main clause + avoir/être + past participle**
Je croyais + avoir + répondu à la question.
*I thought I had answered the question.*

In this sentence, the main clause **Je croyais** is followed by a dependent clause that includes:

- ◆ A past infinitive structure: **avoir répondu**
- ◆ A prepositional phrase: **à la question**

| | |
|---|---|
| Il vaut mieux **ne pas avoir fait de fautes**. | *I hope **we did not make any mistakes**.* |
| Le prof nous félicite d'**avoir si bien réussi**. | *The teacher congratulates us **for having done so well**.* |
| Elle regrette d'**être rentrée si tard**. | *She is sorry **she came home so late**.* |
| Nous craignons de **nous être trompés de route**. | *We fear **we took the wrong road**.* |
| Je promets à tous de **ne pas avoir triché**. | *I promise everybody **I did not cheat**.* |
| On apprend à **toujours se protéger**. | *We learn to **always protect ourselves**.* |

As previously seen, an infinitive clause could be replaced by a subordinate clause. Consider the following sentence in which the past infinitive clause **avoir répondu à la question** and the subordinate clause **que j'avais répondu à la question** have the exact same meaning:

Je croyais **que j'avais répondu à la question**.    *I thought **I had answered the question**.*
= Je croyais **avoir répondu à la question**.

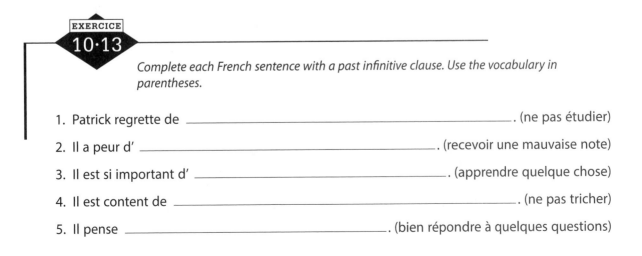

**EXERCICE**
**10·13**

*Complete each French sentence with a past infinitive clause. Use the vocabulary in parentheses.*

1. Patrick regrette de _____. (ne pas étudier)

2. Il a peur d' _____. (recevoir une mauvaise note)

3. Il est si important d' _____. (apprendre quelque chose)

4. Il est content de _____. (ne pas tricher)

5. Il pense _____. (bien répondre à quelques questions)

6. Il serait triste d' _____. (échouer)

7. Il se rappelle _____. (aller souvent à la bibliothèque)

8. Il se rappelle aussi _____. (y rester pendant des heures)

EXERCICE
10·14

*Write the simple or past infinitive form of the verbs in parentheses on the lines provided as deemed appropriate.*

Nanette habitait à la campagne loin de tout quand elle était petite. Maintenant elle souffre de ne pas 1. _____ (avoir) d'amis quand elle était petite. Ses parents, eux aussi, regrettent de ne pas 2. _____ (fréquenter) plus de monde à l'époque. Maintenant ils habitent en ville où ils commencent à se 3. _____ (faire) des amis. Maintenant la petite Nanette a l'occasion de 4. _____ (voir) des jeunes de son âge et elle apprend à se 5. _____ (comporter) dans ce milieu d'adolescents.

## Past infinitive clauses after prepositions

The past infinitive is used only when the action in the dependent clause precedes the action in the main clause. Therefore the same prepositions used in simple infinitive clauses are sometimes followed by a past infinitive, but only when it is necessary to make that distinction in time frames.

| main clause | + | preposition | + | avoir/être | + | past participle |
|---|---|---|---|---|---|---|
| J'ai relu | + | de peur d' | + | avoir | + | fait + des fautes. |

*I read again for fear I might have made some mistakes.*

Consider and compare the following sentences:

| | |
|---|---|
| Je te rendrai ton livre **à condition de ne pas l'avoir perdu**. | *I will return your book **provided I did not lose it**.* |
| Je te rendrai le livre **à condition de ne pas le perdre**. | *I will return the book to you **provided I do not lose it**.* |

In the first sentence, the past infinitive **avoir perdu** is used to express that the book may already be lost. In the second sentence, the simple infinitive **perdre** is used to express that the book may get lost in the future. These two sentences convey a very different message.

| | |
|---|---|
| Elle s'est couchée **sans m'avoir téléphoné**. | *She went to bed **without having called me**.* |
| Elle s'est couchée **sans me téléphoner**. | *She went to bed **without calling me**.* |

In the first sentence, the use of the past infinitive **avoir téléphoné** is grammatically correct because it does underline the fact that she should have or could have called *before* going to bed. In the second sentence, the use of the simple infinitive **téléphoner** implies that she could have called at the time when she was going to bed. Both sentences are grammatically correct, but the simple infinitive will more frequently be used in a case such as this because it can seem futile to make a distinction between calling before going to bed or at the very moment of going to bed. Here are some examples of the appropriate use of the past infinitive after a preposition:

| | |
|---|---|
| Tu es partie **sans l'avoir vu**? | *You left **without having seen him**?* |

| | |
|---|---|
| Tu es sorti **avant d'avoir fini**? | *You went out **before having finished**?* |
| Tu seras payé **à condition d'avoir bien travaillé**. | *You will be paid **provided you worked well**.* |
| Il a reçu une médaille **pour avoir sauvé des vies**. | *He received a medal **for having saved lives**.* |

As seen with simple infinitive clauses, a past infinitive clause introduced by a preposition can either precede or follow the main clause. When it precedes the main clause, it ends in a comma.

| | |
|---|---|
| Je te rendrai ton livre **à condition de ne pas l'avoir perdu**. | *I will return your book **provided I did not lose it**.* |
| **À condition de ne pas l'avoir perdu**, je te rendrai ton livre. | ***As long as I have not lost it**, I will return your book.* |

EXERCICE
10·15

*Translate the phrases in parentheses into French to complete each sentence.*

1. J'irai en France _____. (*as long as I have enough money*)

2. Je n'irai pas _____. (*before having finished my studies*)

3. Je me souviens d'y _____ quand j'étais petit. (*to have gone*)

4. Je regrette de ne pas y _____. (*not to have gone back*)

5. Je suis triste de ne pas _____ y aller tout de suite. (*not be able to*)

6. J'ai trouvé un petit boulot de peur de ne pas _____. (*not be able to save money*)

## Past infinitive clauses after the preposition **après**

The preposition **après** (*after*) is different from other prepositions because it cannot be followed by a simple infinitive. It can only be followed by a past infinitive because by definition it introduces a past and completed action.

| | |
|---|---|
| **Après avoir lu le livre**, nous avons écrit un essai. | *After having read the book, we wrote an essay.* |
| **Après nous être lavés les mains**, nous avons mangé. | *After having washed our hands, we ate.* |
| **Après être monté au premier étage**, il a vu le rayon des hommes. | *After having gone up to the first floor, he saw the men's department.* |
| Nous avons mieux compris **après avoir révisé la leçon**. | *We understood better after having reviewed the lesson.* |
| Vous avez choisi la bleue **après avoir essayé plusieurs robes**. | *You chose the blue one after having tried on several dresses.* |

Note, in the first example that follows, that the action of *selling a house* preceded the action of *buying an apartment*. Also note in these examples that each past infinitive clause starts with the preposition **après**. Remember, whereas most prepositions can be followed by a simple or past infinitive, **après** *can only be followed by a past infinitive*.

| | |
|---|---|
| **Après avoir vendu la maison**, nous avons acheté un appartement. | *After we sold the house, we bought an apartment.* |
| **Après être allée en France**, elle a fait des progrès. | *After going to France, she made progress.* |
| **Après avoir pris un TGV**, elle n'a plus voulu voyager en voiture. | *After taking a TGV, she did not want to travel by car anymore.* |
| **Après s'être perdue en route**, elle a loué un système GPS. | *After getting lost on the road, she rented a GPS.* |

When introduced by **après**, the past infinitive clause may precede or follow the main clause. In the previous example, note the comma after the infinitive clause when it precedes the main clause. Note in the following examples that the subject in the main and infinitive clauses is the same: *she* closes the window and *she* feels the wind.

| | |
|---|---|
| Elle a fermé la fenêtre **après avoir senti le vent souffler**. | *She closed the window **after having felt the wind blow**.* |
| **Après avoir senti le vent souffler**, elle a fermé la fenêtre. | *After having felt the wind blow, she closed the window.* |

Past infinitive clauses commonly replace subordinate clauses introduced by the conjunction **après que** whenever the subject of the verbs in the main and dependent clauses is the same. The past infinitive clause is better style and more formal than the subordinate clause. It is used in speaking as well as in writing.

| | |
|---|---|
| après avoir senti le vent souffler = après qu'elle a senti le vent souffler | *after having felt the wind blow* *after she felt the wind blow* |
| après avoir fait les devoirs = après qu'ils ont fait les devoirs | *after having done the homework* *after they did the homework* |

**EXERCICE**
## 10·16

*On the lines provided, write the letter of the best completion for each past infinitive clause.*

1. Après nous être promenés, nous _____

2. Après s'être réveillée, elle _____

3. Après s'être blessé au genou, il _____

4. Après avoir mangé, nous _____

5. Après avoir perdu mon chien, je/j' _____

6. Après avoir reçu mon livre, je/j' _____

7. Après avoir passé de belles vacances, elle _____

8. Après être rentrée, elle _____

a. ai mis des annonces partout.

b. a préparé le dîner.

c. nous sommes reposés.

d. a dû retourner au travail.

e. avons regardé la télé.

f. l'ai lu en un jour.

g. n'a plus joué au foot.

h. s'est lavée.

**EXERCICE**
## 10·17

*Rewrite each subordinate clause as a past infinitive clause.*

1. après qu'il a vu le film _____

2. après que nous avons acheté la maison _____

3. après que je suis monté _____

4. après qu'ils ont fait les achats _____

5. après qu'elles sont arrivées _____

6. après que tu as fini les devoirs _____

*Write the past infinitive form of each verb in parentheses on the lines provided. Beware of making the past participle agree with the feminine direct object (Suzanne) where necessary.*

1. Suzanne, je vous remercie d'_____ à ce rendez-vous. (venir)

2. Après vous _____ chez Colette, je voulais vous revoir. (rencontrer)

3. Sans _____ la chance de bien vous connaître, j'étais pourtant
   impressionné. (avoir)

4. Après vous _____, je me suis demandé si j'étais un peu audacieux.
   (téléphoner)

5. J'espère ne pas vous _____. (surprendre)

6. En tout cas, je suis content de vous _____. (inviter)

# Using nouns

Nouns are used to name persons, animals, places, things, and abstract ideas. A noun is the nucleus of a noun phrase, which may include an article and one or several adjectives.

> **article + noun + adjective**
> un + ciel + magnifique
> Aujourd'hui il y a **un ciel**      *Today there is **a magnificent***
>   **magnifique**.      *sky*.

In this sentence, the noun phrase **un ciel magnifique** includes the article **un**, the noun **ciel**, and the adjective **magnifique** describing the sky.

## Types of nouns

There are many different types of nouns such as proper, common, concrete, abstract, countable, noncountable, and collective nouns.

## Proper and common nouns

Proper nouns are capitalized and used for names of specific places, animals, and people. Any other noun is considered a common noun and is not capitalized.

> La **Seine** traverse la **ville** de **Paris**.      *The **Seine River** crosses the*
>      *city of **Paris**.*

This sentence includes the proper nouns **Seine** and **Paris** as well as the concrete noun **ville**.

> La **beauté** est une **perception**.      ***Beauty** is a **perception**.*

This sentence includes two abstract nouns, **beauté** and **perception**.

> L'**or** brille.      ***Gold** shines.*

This sentence includes the noun **or**, a noncountable entity.

> L'**armée** est disciplinée.      *The **army** is disciplined.*

This sentence includes the collective noun **armée**.

    Except for names of cities, French nouns are generally preceded by a masculine, feminine, or plural article. Remember that you must be able to identify nouns such as **l'image** or **l'arbre** (which are contracted with the definite articles because they start with a vowel sound) as masculine (m.) or feminine (f.), in order to make the adjective describing that noun agree in gender and number with it.

| | | | | |
|---|---|---|---|---|
| l'arbre (m.) | *the tree* | → | un grand arbre | *a big tree* |
| l'image (f.) | *the picture* | → | une jolie image | *a pretty picture* |

Also remember to use the contractions of the preposition **à** or the preposition **de** with the articles **le** and **les** whenever appropriate.

| | |
|---|---|
| à + le = au | de + le = du |
| à + les = aux | de + les = des |

| | |
|---|---|
| Je vais **au tableau**. | *I am going **to the board**.* |
| Ils reviennent **du parc**. | *They are coming back **from the park**.* |

## Noncountable and collective nouns

Noncountable nouns do not have a plural form. In English *fish* and *furniture* are such nouns. Consider the following examples of French noncountable nouns. These are usually not used in the plural form except on very rare occasions as in poetic writings or in comparisons. Here are some such nouns:

| | | | |
|---|---|---|---|
| l'eau | *water* | l'éclairage | *lighting* |
| l'or | *gold* | la beauté | *beauty* |
| la farine | *flour* | la rocaille | *rocks* |
| le communisme | *communism* | | |

| | |
|---|---|
| **Le communisme** est une idéologie. | ***Communism** is an ideology.* |
| **L'éclairage** est mauvais ici. | ***The lighting** is bad here.* |
| **L'or** ne perd pas de sa valeur. | ***Gold** does not lose its value.* |

Compare the following pairs of sentences and notice that these noncountable nouns are sometimes used in the plural form:

| | |
|---|---|
| **L'eau** est essentielle pour survivre dans le désert. | ***Water** is essential to survive in the desert.* |
| **Les eaux** minérales sont toutes bonnes pour la santé. | *Mineral **waters** are all good for your health.* |
| **La farine** blanche n'est pas la meilleure. | *White **flour** is not the best.* |
| Nous analysons **des farines** de différentes origines. | *We are analyzing **flour** of various origins.* |

A collective noun refers to an entity that includes many individual components such as **l'armée** (*the army*) or **le mobilier** (*furniture*). These nouns can have a singular and a plural form.

| | |
|---|---|
| **Son mobilier** est du style Louis XVI. | ***Her furniture** is in the Louis XVI style.* |
| Ce musée expose **des mobiliers** de tous styles. | *This museum exhibits various styles of **furniture**.* |

| | | | |
|---|---|---|---|
| l'armée | *the army* | l'équipe | *the team* |
| le mobilier | *the furniture* | le plancton | *the plankton* |

| | |
|---|---|
| **L'armée** française est une armée de volontaires. | *The French **army** is an army of volunteers.* |
| **L'équipe** de football brésilienne est excellente. | *The Brazilian soccer **team** is excellent.* |

*Underline the common and proper nouns in the following paragraph.*

Un groupe d'étudiants américains suivent un cours de français à la Sorbonne cet été. Leur professeur, M. Maximilien, est un spécialiste de littérature antillaise. Ils vont lire et analyser des écrivains et des poètes tels qu'Aimé Césaire, originaire de la Martinique et Guy Tirolien, originaire de la Guadeloupe. A la fin du cours, tout le monde va se réunir et fêter dans un restaurant antillais très connu par les Parisiens.

*Write the name of the person or place that fits each description.*

1. des montagnes hautes entre la France, la Suisse et l'Italie: _____

2. un empereur d'origine corse: _____

3. l'océan qui sépare la France des États-Unis: _____

4. le président de la république Française en 2008: _____

5. le pays au nord des États-Unis: _____

6. le peintre français qui a peint les jardins de Giverny: _____

*Circle the correct noun in parentheses for each sentence.*

1. (Le Français / Les Français) adorent visiter les différentes régions de leur pays.

2. Que ce soit dans les (alpes / Alpes) ou dans les (pyrénées / Pyrénées), il faut passer des vacances en montagne.

3. Les galets blancs de la Côte d'Azur sont aussi attrayants que (la rocaille / les rocailles) de la (corse / Corse).

4. Qui pourrait résister (à l'eau / aux eaux) bleue de la Méditerranée?

5. Les (bretons / Bretons) vous diraient que la (manche / Manche) n'est pas si mal que ça.

6. (La beauté / les beautés) des plages bretonnes et (la renommée / les renommées) des crêpes bretonnes en font une région très cotée aussi.

*From the following word list, choose a noun that completes each sentence.*

L'institutrice / l'image / pupitre / livre / petite fille / tableau

1. Je me rappelle bien mon école du temps où j'étais une _____.

2. Nous étions deux élèves assis au même _____.

3. Devant la classe, il y avait un grand _____.

4. _____ écrivait souvent au tableau noir.

5. Je me rappelle même mon premier _____ de lecture.

6. Et je me rappelle _____ d'un petit chien sur la couverture.

*Complete each sentence using translations of the words in parentheses. Use the contractions* **au** *and* **du** *whenever necessary.*

1. J'allais _____ tous les jours excepté dimanche. (*to school*)

2. Le dimanche, mon père n'allait pas _____. (*to the office*)

3. Nous passions souvent la journée _____. (*to the park*)

4. Le soir nous rentrions _____ bien fatigués. (*home*)

5. _____, les enfants s'amusaient. (*From morning to evening*)

*Circle the correct noun in parentheses for each sentence.*

1. Lors de la deuxième guerre mondiale, _____ (une armée / des armées) venant de nombreux pays ont participé à la libération de la France.

2. _____ qui participent aux Jeux Olympiques sont les meilleures. (L'équipe / Les équipes)

3. Les enfants jouent dans _____ (le sable / les sables)

4. J'ai mis trop de _____ dans la pâte. (farine / farines)

5. Tu aimes _____ du robinet? (l'eau / les eaux)

6. Tu préfères _____? (l'or / les ors)

*Use the following sentence fragments to build sentences.*

1. conduit / l'antagonisme / à la violence

_____

2. est / le fanatisme / à la paix / un obstacle

_____

3. au 17e siècle / une monarchie absolue / était / la France

_____

4. la pauvreté / à l'origine / est / de beaucoup de problèmes sociaux

_____

5. mauvaise conscience / après avoir menti / nous avons

_____

6. ne s'achète pas / le bonheur

_____

# Function of nouns

A noun can have various functions in a sentence. A noun can be the subject or object of the verb. It can also be the object of a preposition, or the complement/attribute of a noun, of an adjective, or of an adverb. As you learn more about the many functions a noun performs, you will be able to build better French sentences.

## Nouns as the subjects of verbs

A noun (thing, animal, person, or abstract idea) that performs the action of the verb is the subject of the verb. You may review the function of noun-subjects in Unit 1.

| subject + verb (+ adverb or object or prepositional phrase) → sentence | |
|---|---|
| **Cet arbre** grandit vite. | *This tree* is growing fast. |
| **La Seine** traverse Paris. | *The Seine River* crosses Paris. |
| **Le chat** court après la souris. | *The cat* runs after the mouse. |

In a French sentence, the subject is usually at the head of the sentence. In the previous sentences, **cet arbre**, **la Seine**, and **le chat**, respectively, performed the actions of the verb that followed. Occasionally an adverb or adverbial phrase such as **quelquefois** or **chaque matin** precedes the subject of the verb as in the following examples:

| **Quelquefois** Paul préfère rester chez lui. | *Sometimes* Paul prefers staying at home. |
|---|---|
| **Chaque matin,** Nicole va au gymnase. | *Each morning,* Nicole goes to the gymnasium. |

*Complete each sentence with an appropriate noun-subject using translations of the phrases in parentheses.*

1. Jean, _____, est très mignon. (*my girlfriend's brother*)

2. _____ la grondent toujours quand elle est en retard au dîner. (*Her parents*)

3. _____ sont toujours indulgents. (*My parents*)

4. _____ ont des roses magnifiques cette année. (*My garden's beautiful rosebushes*)

5. _____ adorent chasser les souris. (*The big cats*)

6. _____ ont fait leurs nids dans nos arbres. (*Some pretty birds*)

## Nouns as the objects of verbs

There exist several types of noun-objects. Any noun that receives the action of the verb is called a noun-object. To distinguish a direct object from an indirect object, you must first become aware of the presence or absence of a preposition in front of the noun receiving the action. In addition, if the preposition is **à**, then you must also distinguish an object-thing from an object-person.

### Nouns as direct objects

If the noun-object (person or thing) is not preceded by a preposition, then it is a *direct object* of the verb. Consider the following sentences:

Le capitaine donne **les ordres**.        *The captain gives **the orders**.*

In the previous example, the noun phrase **les ordres** (thing) is the direct object of the verb **donne**.

Jean appelle **sa copine**.        *Jean calls **his girlfriend**.*

In this example, the noun phrase **sa copine** (person) is the direct object of the verb **appelle**.
    The direct object noun comes after the verb as in the following examples:

**subject + verb + direct object**
Le chien + avale + **l'os**.
*The dog swallows the bone.*

La serveuse apporte **le menu**.        *The waitress brings **the menu**.*
Jean accompagne **Marie**.        *Jean accompanies **Marie**.*
Nicolas adore **la musique reggae**.        *Nicolas adores **reggae music**.*
Il adore **sa mère**.        *He adores **his mother**.*

### Nouns as indirect objects

When a noun refers *to a person* and receives the action of the verb indirectly while being introduced by the preposition **à**, then that noun is an *indirect object*. Remember that the preposition **à** contracts with the definite articles **le** and **les**; therefore if a noun referring to a person is preceded by the contracted article **au** or **aux**, this noun is an indirect object. The indirect object noun comes after the verb in a sentence.

**subject + verb + à + indirect object**
Dara + répond + à + **Alex**.
*Dara answers Alex.*

L'homme d'affaires téléphone **aux clients**.     *The businessman calls **clients**.*
Le professeur parle **à ses élèves**.     *The teacher talks **to his students**.*

A sentence often includes a direct and an indirect object as in the following sentences. The direct object noun then precedes the indirect object noun as in the following examples:

**subject + verb + direct object + à + indirect object**
Jeanine + donne + **une bise** + à + **sa mère**.
*Jeanine gives her mom a kiss.*

Louis déclare **son amour à Monique**.     *Louis declares **his love to Monique**.*
Laurent envoie **les fleurs à sa tante**.     *Laurent sends **the flowers to his aunt**.*
Nous envoyons **nos poèmes au prof**.     *We send **our poems to the teacher**.*

In the following sentence, note that the indirect object is a noun phrase including the adjective **petit**, which describes the noun **garçon**.

**subject + verb + direct object + contraction + indirect object phrase**
Vous + lancez + la balle + **au** + **petit garçon**.
*You are throwing the ball to the little boy.*

**EXERCICE**
**11·9**

*Choose a logical direct object to complete each sentence. Write the corresponding letter on the line provided.*

1. Les animaux domestiques aiment _____     a. des activités tranquilles.

2. Les animaux sauvages dévorent _____     b. beaucoup d'eau minérale.

3. Les personnes âgées font _____     c. peu d'essence.

4. Les jeunes préfèrent _____     d. peu d'entretien.

5. Les petites voitures consomment _____     e. leur proie.

6. Les bicyclettes exigent _____     f. beaucoup de coca.

7. Les Français boivent _____     g. leurs maîtres.

8. Les Américains boivent _____     h. les sports extrêmes.

**EXERCICE**
**11·10**

*Complete each sentence with a direct and indirect object noun. Use the nouns within parentheses, and remember to insert the proper preposition before the indirect object.*

1. Nanette envoie souvent _____ _____. (e-mails / Jean)

2. Le professeur rend _____ _____. (essais / ses étudiants)

3. La petite fille donne _____ _____. (bises / sa maman)

4. Le journaliste envoie _____ _____. (articles / son journal)

5. Le papa fait _____ _____. (reproches / son petit garçon)

6. Claude dit _____ _____. (mots d'amour / Gigi)

# Nouns as complements

Nouns can be complements of other nouns, adjectives, or adverbs. These complements are often linked to the noun, adjective, or adverb by the prepositions **à**, **de**, or **en**. Although not indispensable to the structure of the sentence, these complements contribute a significant characteristic to the noun, adjective, or adverb they complete. Learning to use them will help you build more complete and more detailed sentences.

## Nouns as complements of nouns

Sometimes a noun is attached to another noun to add to its meaning or to give it description, thereby performing much like an adjective. Unlike adjectives, however, they do not express quality, nor can they be compared as adjectives can. Here are some examples of complements of nouns:

| | |
|---|---|
| une averse **d'été** | a **summer** shower |
| une raison **d'état** | a **state** reason |
| l'écharpe **en laine** | the **woolen** scarf |
| le bouquet **de fleurs** | the bouquet **of flowers** |
| le verre **d'eau** | the glass **of water** |
| la cuillère **à café** | the **coffee** spoon |

Sometimes the complement of a noun is linked to the noun-subject by a hyphen, or it simply follows the noun directly.

| | |
|---|---|
| le wagon-**lit** | the **sleeping** car |
| un thé **citron** | a **lemon** tea |

EXERCICE
**11·11**

*Translate the following sentences into French.*

1. Give me a glass of water! _____

2. I would like a summer dress. _____

3. Pass me that coffee spoon. _____

4. She took a family leave. _____

5. I am going to order a steak with fries. _____

6. Let's look for the dining car! _____

## Nouns as complements of adjectives or adverbs

Nouns can add a characteristic to an adjective by giving an additional detail concerning the quality, the substance, and the nature of the descriptive term. Here are some examples of nouns that are complements of adjectives:

**subject + verb + adjective + de/en/à + noun**
Le toit + est + **couvert** + **de** + **neige**.
*The roof is covered with snow.*

| | |
|---|---|
| Cette date est **écrite en chiffres romains**. | *This date is **written in Roman numerals**.* |
| La bouteille est **remplie de jus**. | *The bottle is **filled with juice**.* |
| Cette place est **réservée aux handicapés**. | *This place is **reserved for the handicapped**.* |
| Elle est **comblée de joie**. | *She is **overwhelmed with joy**.* |

Occasionally a noun can be the complement of an adverb.

**subject + verb + adverb + de/en/à + noun**
Elle + a agi + **contrairement** + **à** + **la loi**.
*She acted against the law.*

EXERCICE
**11·12**

*Translate the phrases in parentheses into French to complete each sentence.*

1. Il a neigé hier soir et la route est _____. (*covered with snow*)

2. Attention! Cette tasse est _____. (*filled with hot coffee*)

3. Elle est _____ à cette triste nouvelle. (*stricken with grief*)

4. Les dates sur ce sarcophage sont _____. (*written in hieroglyphs*)

5. Cette chambre est _____. (*reserved for newlyweds*)

6. Il vaut mieux faire cela _____. (*according to the law*)

## Nouns as objects of a preposition

When a noun (a person or thing) receives the action of the verb and is preceded by a preposition, then it is part of a prepositional phrase. Many noun phrases in French include a preposition such as **à** (*at, in, to*), **de** (*from, of*), **dans** (*in*) or a prepositional phrase such as **loin de** (*far from*), **près de** (*near*), **à côté de** (*next to*). For more information on prepositional phrases, see Unit 15. A noun introduced by a preposition is the object of that preposition. Consider the following examples:

**subject + verb + preposition + object of the preposition**
Elles + arrivent + **à** + **chez Inès**.
*They arrive at Inès' place.*

| | |
|---|---|
| Je parle **avec un copain**. | *I speak **with a friend**.* |
| Nous partons **en voiture**. | *We leave **by car**.* |
| Je serai **de retour**. | *I will be **back**.* |
| Les passagers montent **dans le train**. | *The passengers board **the train**.* |
| Jean est **chez sa copine**. | *Jean is **at his girlfriend's house**.* |
| Ta maison est **près de la mer**. | *Your house is **near the sea**.* |
| Mimi est **à l'école**. | *Mimi is **at school**.* |

Now compare the following sentences, which include the preposition **à** followed by a noun.

| | |
|---|---|
| Jean téléphone **à sa copine**. | *Jean calls **his girlfriend**.* |
| Jean est **à l'appareil**. | *Jean is **on the phone**.* |

Remember that when the noun-object refers to a person and is preceded by the preposition **à**, then the noun-object is called an *indirect object* of the verb. Therefore the noun phrase **à sa copine** is an indirect object of the verb **téléphone** in that example sentence. On the other hand, when the noun-object refers to a thing (**l'appareil**) and is preceded by the preposition **à**, then the noun-object is part of a *prepositional phrase*; it is not called an indirect object.

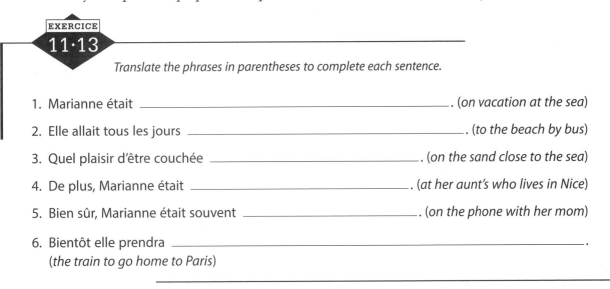

**EXERCICE**

**11·13**

*Translate the phrases in parentheses to complete each sentence.*

1. Marianne était _____. (*on vacation at the sea*)

2. Elle allait tous les jours _____. (*to the beach by bus*)

3. Quel plaisir d'être couchée _____. (*on the sand close to the sea*)

4. De plus, Marianne était _____. (*at her aunt's who lives in Nice*)

5. Bien sûr, Marianne était souvent _____. (*on the phone with her mom*)

6. Bientôt elle prendra _____.
   (*the train to go home to Paris*)

## Nouns as attributes of a noun

The noun-subject usually bears the main informative value in a sentence. The noun-attribute gives secondary information about the noun-subject. The noun-subject and the noun-attribute are often linked by a verb of being rather than by a verb of action. Verbs of being are such verbs as **être** (*to be*), **sembler** (*to seem*), **paraître** (*to appear/seem*), **devenir** (*to become*), and **rester** (*to stay*). Consider the following examples:

> **noun-subject + verb + noun-attribute**
> Cette fille + restera + **enfant**.
> *This girl will remain a child.*

| | |
|---|---|
| Le lézard est **un reptile**. | *The lizard is **a reptile**.* |
| Charlemagne est devenu **empereur**. | *Charlemagne became **emperor**.* |
| Ton frère sera **pilote**? | *Your brother will be **a pilot**?* |

## Noun in apposition to another noun

When a noun completes another noun in a sentence without the intervention of a preposition, it is simply juxtaposed to it, and the two nouns are separated by a comma.

> **noun-subject + noun in apposition + de + complement of noun + predicate**
> Le lion, + **roi** + de + la jungle, + règne sur le monde animal.
> *The lion, **king** of the jungle, rules over the animal world.*

In this example, the noun-subject is **le lion**. But the noun **roi** designates the same subject **le lion**, and completes its function of subject of the verb **règne**. Note that the noun phrase that describes the main noun is tucked in between commas.

| | |
|---|---|
| Victor Hugo, **célèbre écrivain français**, est enterré au Panthéon. | *Victor Hugo, **the famous French writer**, is buried at the Panthéon.* |
| Paris, **ville-lumière**, est inoubliable. | *Paris, **the city of lights**, is unforgettable.* |
| Astérix, **guerrier gaulois**, est invincible. | *Astérix, **Gaul warrior**, is invincible.* |

*Place the sentence fragments in the correct order to make complete sentences. Use correct punctuation.*

1. des Michelin / achetez / pneus durables

_____

2. est connue / «La Vie en rose» / dans le monde entier / chanson d'Édith Piaf

_____

3. région montagneuse / est un endroit très rural / le Massif Central

_____

4. Saint-Tropez / est une ville accueillante / berceau des célébrités françaises

_____

5. ancienne résidence des papes / offre des expositions toute l'année / le palais d'Avignon

_____

6. est le siège / Strasbourg / ville européenne / du Conseil de l'Europe

_____

7. est un chanteur Rap / MC Solar / né à Dakar

_____

8. président de la république française / Sarkozy / en 2007 / a été élu

_____

# Using personal pronouns

Pronouns usually replace a noun but can occasionally replace an adjective or an entire clause. Their role is to avoid repeating the noun, adjective, or clause they replace. There are many different types of pronouns: personal, demonstrative, possessive, interrogative, and relative. This last type of pronoun is covered in Unit 7 on dependent clauses.

Most of the time, a pronoun replaces a noun or noun phrase. A pronoun can be introduced in a conversation only after everybody knows what or who is being referred to. Note how the referent of the pronoun **ils** has to be clarified in the following dialogue:

| | |
|---|---|
| —**Ils** parlent bien anglais. | —**They** speak English well. |
| —Qui? John et Simon? | —Who? John and Simon? |
| —Mais non, mes frères Elan et Joseph. | —No, my brothers Elan and Joseph. |

Consider the following paragraph, which has been divided into individual sentences. Note the repetition of the noun *Madeleine* and of the noun *students* when no pronoun is used.

| | |
|---|---|
| **Madeleine** est institutrice. | *Madeleine is a teacher.* |
| **Madeleine** enseigne une classe primaire. | *Madeleine teaches a primary class.* |
| **Les élèves** adorent **Madeleine**. | *The children love Madeleine.* |
| **Les élèves** donnent un cadeau à **Madeleine**. | *The students give a gift to Madeleine.* |
| **Ses élèves** et **mes élèves** sont gentils. | *Her students and my students are nice.* |

In the following sentences, let's identify which pronouns replace the proper noun **Madeleine** and where they are placed in the sentence. The first sentence establishes who Madeleine is; she is the main referent in the paragraph. Therefore it is not necessary to repeat her name in every subsequent sentence; pronouns may be used in lieu of her name.

| | |
|---|---|
| **Madeleine** est institutrice. | *Madeleine is a teacher.* |

In this first sentence, **Madeleine** is introduced as the main referent.

| | |
|---|---|
| **Elle** enseigne une classe primaire. | *She teaches a primary class.* |

In this second sentence, **Madeleine** (subject of the verb **enseigne** because she *performs* the action of teaching) is replaced with the subject pronoun **elle**.

| | |
|---|---|
| Les élèves l'adorent. | *The children love **her**.* |

In this third sentence, **Madeleine** (direct object of the verb **adorent** because she now *receives* the action of the verb—she is the one *whom* they adore) is replaced with the direct object pronoun **l'** (a substitute for **la** before a vowel sound).

**Ils lui** donnent un cadeau.      *They give **her** a gift.*

In this fourth sentence, **Madeleine** (indirect object of the verb **donnent** because she is the one *to whom* the students give a gift) is replaced by the indirect object **lui**.

Now consider the last three sentences of the paragraph and note how the noun **les élèves** is being replaced after it has been mentioned a first time:

**Les élèves** adorent Madeleine.      ***The children** love Madeleine.*

In this sentence, **les élèves** is being mentioned for the first time.

**Ils** lui donnent un cadeau.      ***They** give her a gift.*

In this sentence, **les élèves** (the referent) is replaced by the subject pronoun **ils**.

Ses élèves et **les miens** sont gentils.      *Her students and **mine** are nice.*

In this sentence, **mes élèves** is replaced by the possessive pronoun **miens**.

These are examples of pronouns, small but powerful words loaded with meaning. Now read the following paragraph of consolidated sentences. Note how the pronouns make sentences less choppy and less redundant, and how the sentences run more smoothly with pronouns than when the same nouns are continually repeated.

**Madeleine** est institutrice. **Elle** enseigne une classe primaire. **Les élèves** l'adorent.      **Ils lui** donnent un cadeau. Ses élèves et **les miens** sont gentils.

# Personal pronouns

Personal pronouns refer to persons or inanimate objects. They can perform the functions of subject, direct object, and indirect object in a sentence.

## Subject pronouns

Subject pronouns perform the action of the verb. They are placed before the verb in declarative sentences and in interrogative sentences except where the inversion structure is used.

**subject pronoun + verb + modifier**
**Tu** + écoutes + bien.
*You listen attentively.*

| | |
|---|---|
| **Nous** travaillons tous les jours. | *We work every day.* |
| **Vous** apportez vos radios? | *Are **you** bringing your radios?* |
| Est-ce qu'**elles** entendent ce que je dis? | *Do **they** hear what I say?* |

### Interrogative/Inverted structure

Subject pronouns (except for **je**) are placed after the verb in interrogative sentences where inversion is used.

**verb + subject pronoun + modifier**
Ecoutes- + **tu** + bien?
*Do you listen attentively?*

| | |
|---|---|
| Sont-**elles** charmantes? | *Are **they** charming?* |
| Travaille-t-**il** dur? | *Does **he** work hard?* |
| Avez-**vous** de l'argent? | *Do **you** have money?* |

The only personal pronoun–subject that is rarely found after the verb even in the inverted structure of the interrogative is the pronoun **je**. Here are a few examples of such rare occurrences:

| | |
|---|---|
| Puis-je? | *May I?* |
| Pourrais-je? | *Could I?* |
| Suis-je? | *Am I?* |
| Ai-je? | *Do I have?* |

| | |
|---|---|
| **Puis-je** me servir? | ***May I** help myself?* |
| **Pourrais-je** vous parler? | ***Could I** speak to you?* |
| **N'ai-je pas** assez de stress? | ***Don't I have** enough stress?* |

**EXERCICE 12·1**

*For each sentence write the appropriate subject pronoun on the line provided.*

1. Où est Gil? _____ est toujours à l'heure!

2. Tu as vu Sarah et Robert? _____ sont si heureux!

3. Toi et moi, allons-_____ à la soirée ensemble?

4. Juliane, _____ est vraiment jolie!

5. Raymond et toi, _____ faites un beau couple.

6. Les penguins? _____ sont très fidèles!

**EXERCICE 12·2**

*Fill in the blanks with the appropriate subject pronoun expressing* you *when addressing the following people.*

1. Docteur Andres, comment allez-_____?

2. Professeur Dumont, je _____ remercie.

3. Cher frère, _____ me manques.

4. Chers parents, je _____ embrasse.

5. Chère madame, je _____ félicite.

6. M. le Directeur, je _____ salue.

## Stress pronouns

These pronouns in French serve to stress personal subject pronouns and can be placed directly in front of the subject pronoun in a sentence; the two pronouns are then separated by a comma.

| | |
|---|---|
| **Moi,** je veux partir. | *I want to leave.* (emphatic *I* ) |
| **Toi,** tu plaisantes toujours. | *You always joke.* (emphatic *you*) |
| **Lui**, il me rappelle mon frère. | *He reminds me of my brother.* (emphatic *he*) |

Stress pronouns can also be placed at the very end of a sentence and are then separated from the rest of the sentence by a comma.

| | |
|---|---|
| Je veux partir, **moi.** | *I want to leave.* (emphatic *I* ) |
| Nous aimons la glace, **nous.** | *We like ice cream.* (emphatic *we* ) |
| Ils savent tout, **eux.** | *They know everything.* (emphatic *they*) |

Stress pronouns are also found after prepositions and prepositional phrases as in the following examples:

| | |
|---|---|
| Tu as envie de diner **avec moi?** | *Do you feel like having dinner **with me**?* |
| Elle est assise **derrière lui**. | *She is seated **behind him**.* |
| Vous êtes **loin de nous**. | *You are **far away from us**.* |

## Impersonal pronoun on

The impersonal pronoun **on** used in a sentence is the subject of the verb, but as its name indicates it does not refer to a specific person. In English it must be translated intuitively as *one, we, people,* or *you* depending on the context.

| | |
|---|---|
| Dax, **on** va à la plage? | *Dax, are **we** going to the beach?* |
| En été, en France, **on** se bronze sur la Côte d'Azur! | *During the summer, in France, **everyone** gets a tan on the Riviera!* |
| **On** ne se met pas le doigt dans le nez en public, mon petit! | *You should not pick your nose in public, my little one!* |

The pronoun **soi** refers to the *impersonal* pronoun **on**. However, it is *not used* to stress the *subject* pronoun **on**. Rather it is found after a preposition as in the following examples:

| | |
|---|---|
| On a souvent honte **de soi.** | *One is often ashamed **of oneself**.* |
| Il ne faut pas tant parler **de soi.** | *One should not talk so much **about oneself**.* |
| On a le droit d'avoir son opinion **à soi.** | *One has the right to **one's own** opinion.* |

---

**EXERCICE**

**12·3**

*Add the appropriate stress pronoun to emphasize the subject pronoun in each sentence.*

1. _____, elles font tout ce qu'elles veulent.

2. _____, vous êtes honnête!

3. Tu parles bien français, _____!

4. Je ne sais pas quoi faire, _____.

5. _____, il était en France l'an dernier.

6. _____, elle est restée chez elle hier soir.

7. Ils se sont bien amusés, _____.

8. _____, nous voulons voyager!

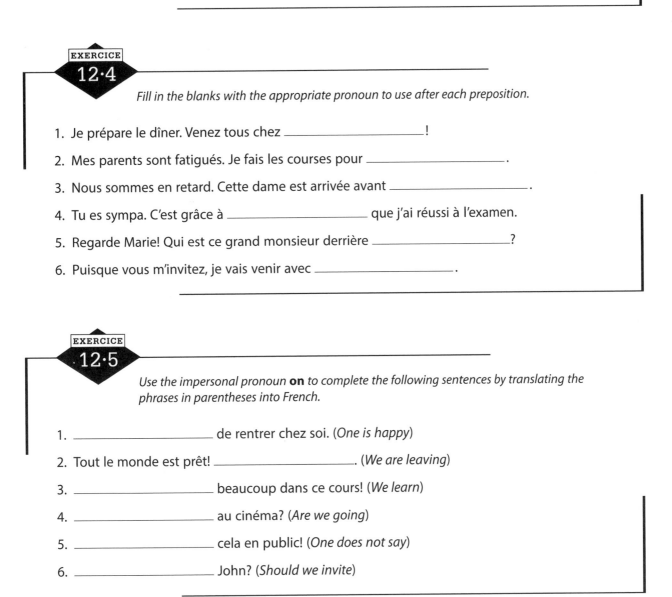

EXERCICE
12·4

*Fill in the blanks with the appropriate pronoun to use after each preposition.*

1. Je prépare le dîner. Venez tous chez _____!

2. Mes parents sont fatigués. Je fais les courses pour _____.

3. Nous sommes en retard. Cette dame est arrivée avant _____.

4. Tu es sympa. C'est grâce à _____ que j'ai réussi à l'examen.

5. Regarde Marie! Qui est ce grand monsieur derrière _____?

6. Puisque vous m'invitez, je vais venir avec _____.

EXERCICE
12·5

*Use the impersonal pronoun **on** to complete the following sentences by translating the phrases in parentheses into French.*

1. _____ de rentrer chez soi. (*One is happy*)

2. Tout le monde est prêt! _____. (*We are leaving*)

3. _____ beaucoup dans ce cours! (*We learn*)

4. _____ au cinéma? (*Are we going*)

5. _____ cela en public! (*One does not say*)

6. _____ John? (*Should we invite*)

## Direct object pronouns in declarative sentences

Direct object pronouns replace nouns or noun phrases that receive the action of the verb directly (they are not introduced by a preposition or prepositional phrase).

Consider the following sentences. In the first sentence, **Jeanette** is the direct object of the verb **cherche** because she receives the action of that verb. She is the *person whom* I (**je**) am looking for. In the second sentence, **Jeanette** has been replaced with the pronoun **la**.

| | |
|---|---|
| Je cherche **Jeanette**. | *I am looking for **Jeanette**.* |
| Je **la** cherche. | *I am looking for **her**.* |

Now consider the next example sentences. In the first sentence, **sa note** is the direct object of the verb **a eu** because it receives the action of that verb. It is *what* she got. In the second sentence, **sa note** has been replaced with the pronoun **la**, which becomes **l'** before the vowel sound of the auxiliary verb **a**.

| | |
|---|---|
| Elle a eu **sa note**. | *She got **her grade**.* |
| Elle **l'**a eue. | *She got **it**.* |

In the next group of examples, **nos CD** is the direct object of the verb **apporterons** in the first sentence because it receives the action of that verb. It is the *what* that we will bring. In the second sentence, **nos CD** has been replaced with the pronoun **les**.

| | |
|---|---|
| Nous apporterons **nos CD**. | *We will bring **our CDs**.* |
| Nous **les** apporterons. | *We will bring **them**.* |

Finally, consider the following sentence. Here **m'** is the direct object of the verb **emmènes** because it receives the action of that verb. It is the *person whom* you are taking along.

| | |
|---|---|
| Tu **m'**emmènes? | *Are you taking **me** along?* |

Based on the previous examples, we see that a direct object:

- ◆ Replaces the noun word for a thing or a person
- ◆ Receives the action of the verb: answers the question **Quoi?** (*What?*) or **Qui?** (*Whom?*)
- ◆ Receives the action of the verb directly: there is no preposition between the verb and the object
- ◆ Is singular or plural to agree with the noun it replaces

The previous examples also show us that there are direct object pronouns that replace *people nouns only*, and direct object pronouns that replace *people or things*.

## Direct object pronouns that replace people nouns

Direct object pronouns that receive the action of the verb directly and refer to people only are the following:

| | |
|---|---|
| me (m') | *me* |
| te (t') | *you* (familiar, singular) |
| nous | *us* |
| vous | *you* (formal, plural) |

| | |
|---|---|
| Tu **me** conduis chez moi? | *Are you driving **me** home?* |
| Je **vous** reconnais, mademoiselle. | *I recognize **you**, miss.* |

Note the position of the pronoun **me** before the verb **conduis** and that of the pronoun **vous** before the verb **reconnais**.

| | |
|---|---|
| Joanne **nous** invitera sûrement. | *Joanne will surely invite **us**.* |

Note the position of the pronoun **nous** before the verb **invitera**.

| | |
|---|---|
| Je **t'**ai vu au concert. | *I saw **you** at the concert.* |

Note the position of the pronoun **t'** before the verb **ai vu**.

| | |
|---|---|
| Ils vont **nous** rejoindre ce soir. | *They are going to join **us** tonight.* |

Note the position of the pronoun **nous** before the infinitive verb **rejoindre**. In this sentence, **nous** is not the object of the conjugated verb **vont**, which is merely a helping verb used to express the near future, but is instead the direct object of the verb **rejoindre**.

Fill in the blanks with the pronouns **me** or **te**.

1. Blandine: Dis donc, Julie, tu veux bien _____ conduire au travail aujourd'hui?

2. Julie: Ta voiture ne marche pas? Bon, bien sûr, je _____ emmènerai.

3. Blandine: Merci. Je _____ dois pour la dernière fois et pour aujourd'hui.

4. Julie: De rien! Il faut s'aider entre sœurs! Tu _____ feras un de tes petits dîners.

5. Blandine: Volontiers! Samedi je _____ ferai une lasagne si tu veux.

Fill in the blanks with the pronouns **nous** or **vous**.

1. Le prof: Aujourd'hui je vais _____ donner un contrôle.

2. Les élèves: Oh monsieur! Si vous _____ donnez un contrôle aujourd'hui, nous allons échouer.

3. Le prof: Mais je _____ ai annoncé ce contrôle la dernière fois.

4. Les élèves: Mais hier soir c'était la remise des prix et le directeur _____ a retenus jusqu'à vingt-deux heures.

5. Le prof: Je comprends. Je _____ donnerai ce contrôle demain.

6. Les élèves: Vous êtes trop sympa! Nous _____ rendrons très fiers de nous!

## Direct object pronouns that replace nouns for people and things

The following direct object pronouns receive the action of the verb directly and answer the questions **Qui?** (*Whom?*) or **Quoi?** (*What?*)

| | |
|---|---|
| le (l') | *him, it* |
| la (l') | *her, it* |
| les | *them* |

Note how in the following sentences, the direct object answers the question **Qui?** or **Quoi?** Also note that the direct object pronoun is **le** when it replaces a masculine person or a thing, it is **la** when it replaces a feminine person or a thing, and it is **les** when it replaces plural persons or things.

| | |
|---|---|
| Paul? Je ne **le** supporte pas. | *Paul? I cannot stand **him**.* |
| Le CD? Je **l'**ai perdu. | *The CD? I lost **it**.* |
| Marie? Je **la** verrai ce weekend. | *Marie? I will see **her** this weekend.* |
| La disco? Je **l'**ai trouvée. | *The disco? I found **it**.* |
| Les magazines? Je **les** apporterai demain. | *The magazines? I will bring **them** tomorrow.* |

EXERCICE
**12·8**

*In each question, underline the noun phrase that can be replaced with a pronoun. Then, to complete each answer, fill in the blanks with the appropriate pronoun (**le, la, l', les**).*

EXAMPLE:     Vous aimez <u>les roses</u>? Oui, nous <u>les</u> adorons.

1. Tu aimes les films psychologiques, Maman? Oui, je _____ adore.

2. Papa va emmener les petits au zoo? Non, il va _____ emmener à la piscine.

3. Vous comptez regarder le dernier film d'Audrey Tatou? Oui, nous allons _____ regarder ce soir.

4. Vous appréciez cette actrice? Oh oui, nous _____ aimons beaucoup.

5. Alors, vous allez voir Audrey aussi aux nouvelles? Bien sûr, nous allons _____ voir à la télé tout à l'heure.

## Position of direct object pronouns in declarative sentences

In affirmative, negative, and interrogative declarative sentences, the French direct object pronoun *precedes* the verb, contrary to English where the pronoun *follows* the verb in a sentence.

**subject + direct object pronoun + verb**
Je + **vous** + rappellerai.
*I will call **you** back.*

Note in this example that the verb is in the simple future tense.

In the following examples, you will note that the position of the direct object pronoun is before:

- The verb in simple tenses such as the present and simple future
- The auxiliary verb in the passé composé
- The infinitive in the near future tense

| | |
|---|---|
| Nos parents **nous** aiment. | *Our parents love **us**.* |
| Les légumes, je ne **les** mangerai pas crus. | *Vegetables, I will not eat **them** raw.* |
| Suzie, je **l'**ai vue hier. | *Suzie, I saw **her** yesterday.* |
| Le DVD, je vais **le** chercher. | *The DVD, I am going to get **it**.* |

Remember that in the passé composé, the object pronoun precedes the auxiliary verb.

**subject + direct object pronoun + auxiliary verb + past participle**
Je + **vous** + ai + appelé.
*I called you.*

Note that the verb in each of the following sentences is in the passé composé and see how the direct object pronouns precede the auxiliary verbs used.

| | |
|---|---|
| Le patron **les** a invités. | *The boss invited **them**.* |
| Pierre **nous** a surpris. | *Peter surprised **us**.* |
| Le sac? Oui, je **l'**ai pris. | *The purse? Yes, I took **it**.* |
| Toi, je **t'**ai entendu rentrer tard. | *You? I heard **you** come home late.* |

Remember that in the near future, the object pronoun precedes the infinitive verb.

**subject + conjugation of aller + direct object pronoun + infinitive verb**

Marie + va + **nous** + retrouver au café.

Each of the following example sentences is in the near future. This tense requires the use of the auxiliary verb **aller** and an infinitive verb. Note that when the verb is negative, the position of the pronoun remains the same as in the affirmative sentence.

| | |
|---|---|
| Marie va **nous** retrouver au café. | *Marie is going to meet **us** at the café.* |
| Marie ne va pas **nous** retrouver au café. | *Marie is not going to meet **us** at the café.* |
| Son père va **la** conduire. | *Her father is going to drive **her**.* |
| Son père ne va pas **la** conduire. | *Her father is not going to drive **her**.* |
| Nous allons **le** remercier. | *We are going to thank **him**.* |
| Nous n'allons pas **le** remercier. | *We are not going to thank **him**.* |

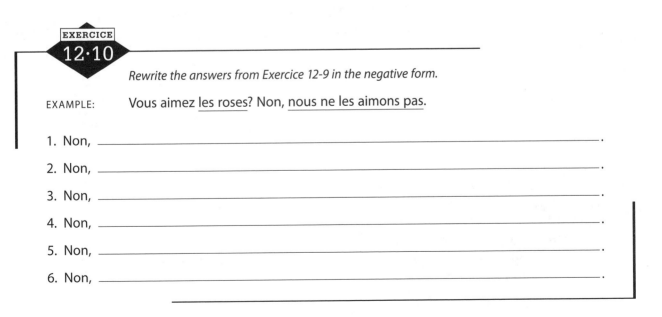

**EXERCICE**

**12·9**

*In each question, underline the noun phrase that can be replaced with a direct object pronoun. Then, answer each question using the appropriate pronoun (**le**, **la**, **l'**, **les**). Be aware of the placement of the pronoun in each answer sentence.*

EXAMPLE: Vous aimez les roses? Oui, nous les adorons.

1. Tu as acheté le journal? Oui, _____.

2. Le vendeur rend la monnaie? Oui, _____.

3. Les clients choisissent le *Times*? Oui, _____.

4. Tu préfères les magazines? Oui, _____.

5. Tu vas lire ces magazines dans l'avion? Oui, _____.

6. Tu vas jeter les magazines à l'arrivée? Oui, _____.

**EXERCICE**

**12·10**

*Rewrite the answers from Exercice 12-9 in the negative form.*

EXAMPLE: Vous aimez les roses? Non, nous ne les aimons pas.

1. Non, _____.

2. Non, _____.

3. Non, _____.

4. Non, _____.

5. Non, _____.

6. Non, _____.

# Indirect object pronouns in declarative sentences

These pronouns replace nouns or noun phrases that receive the action of the verb *indirectly* (because the nouns are preceded by the preposition **à** or **de**). In French there are three types of indirect object pronouns. Consider the following example sentence and note how the noun phrase preceded by **à** or **de** is replaced by a pronoun:

**à/de + noun/noun phrase → indirect object pronoun**

| | |
|---|---|
| Je fais la bise à ma copine. | *I am giving a kiss to my friend.* |
| Je lui fais la bise. | *I give her a kiss.* |

In the following sentence, the preposition **à** followed by a *noun phrase* is implied. The indirect object represents a person who does not need to be named because it is *you.*

| | |
|---|---|
| Je te fais la bise. | *I am giving you a kiss.* |

Now consider the following question and answer. In the answer, note that the pronoun **leur** replaces the preposition **à mes parents**.

| | |
|---|---|
| —Tes parents sont partis? —Oui, je **leur** ai souhaité un bon voyage. | *—Did your parents leave? —Yes, I wished **them** a good trip.* |

Consider the following question and answer. In the answer, note that the pronoun **y** replaces **à Paris**.

| | |
|---|---|
| —Tu vas **à Paris**? —Oui, j'**y** vais demain. | *—Are you going **to Paris**? —Yes, I'm going **there** tomorrow.* |

Consider the following question and answer. In the answer, note that the pronoun **en** replaces **de la limonade**.

| | |
|---|---|
| —Tu veux **de la limonade**? —Oui, j'**en** voudrais un peu. | *—Do you want **some lemonade?** —Yes, I would like **some**.* |

In the previous examples, you have seen indirect object noun phrases replaced by pronouns such as **te, leur, y,** and **en**. Now let's look at the other various types of indirect object pronouns and how to appropriately use them.

## Indirect object pronouns that replace people nouns

These indirect object pronouns answer the question **À qui?** (*To whom?*) The following is a list of these pronouns:

| | |
|---|---|
| me/m' | *to me* |
| te/t' | *to you* |
| nous | *to us* |
| vous | *to you* (*all* familiar or *you* formal) |
| lui | *to him/to her* |
| leur | *to them* |

You have seen the pronouns **me, te, nous,** and **vous,** in a previous section of this chapter, used as direct object pronouns referring to people. You may recall that they answered the question **Qui?** (*Whom?*) The same pronouns can mean *to you* when they answer the question **À qui?** (*To whom?*) In the following sentences, note that the indirect object pronoun always answers the question **À qui?** (*To whom?*) Also note that this pronoun *often* translates into English as *you* instead of *to you, to me,* and so on.

| | |
|---|---|
| Je **t'**envoie des e-mails. | *I am sending **you** e-mails.* |
| Tu voudrais **m'**offrir cette bague? | *Would you like to offer **me** this ring?* |

| | |
|---|---|
| Tu **nous** parleras de ton voyage? | *Will you speak **to us** about your trip?* |
| Je vais **vous** raconter mes aventures. | *I am going to tell **you** my adventures.* |

Similarly, the pronoun **lui** (*to him/to her*) and the pronoun **leur** (*to them*) are indirect object pronouns answering the question **À qui?** (*To whom?*) In the following sentences, note that **lui** can be translated into English as *him/her* instead of *to him/to her* and the pronoun **leur** can be translated into English as *them* instead of *to them*.

| | |
|---|---|
| Elle **lui** a écrit. | *She wrote **to him**.* |
| Nous **leur** avons apporté une bouteille de vin. | *We brought **them** a bottle of wine.* |
| Tu **lui** as donné un baiser? | *You gave **her** a kiss?* |
| Je **leur** ai fait un bon gâteau. | *I made **them** a good cake.* |

## Position of indirect object pronouns

The position of indirect object pronouns in declarative sentences is before the verb.

**subject + indirect object pronoun + verb**
Nous + **vous** + répondons.
*We are answering **you**.*

Consider the following sentences and focus on the position of the indirect object pronoun. You will notice that it is before:

◆ The verb in simple tenses such as the present and the future
◆ The auxiliary verb in compound tenses such as the passé composé
◆ The infinitive verb in the near future

| | |
|---|---|
| On ne **vous** demande pas de partir. | *They do not ask **you** to leave.* |
| Tu **lui as** parlé? | *Did you speak **to him/her**?* |
| Elle **m'**offrira un verre de limonade. | *She will offer **me** a glass of lemonade.* |
| Je ne vais pas **leur** parler! | *I am not going to speak **to them**!* |

The position of indirect object pronouns is before the auxiliary verb in the passé composé.

**subject + indirect object pronoun + auxiliary verb + past participle**
Nous + **vous** + avons + répondu.
*We answered **you**.*

| | |
|---|---|
| Ils **vous** ont enseigné le français. | *They taught **you** French.* |
| Tu **lui** as acheté un bouquet. | *You bought **her** a bouquet.* |
| Je **leur** ai montré la ville. | *I showed **them** the city.* |
| Ils ne **nous** ont pas résisté. | *They did not resist **us**.* |
| Elle **m'**a appris à nager. | *She taught **me** how to swim.* |

When the verb is in the near future tense, the position of the indirect object pronoun is before the infinitive.

**subject + conjugation of aller + indirect object pronoun + verb**
Nous + allons + **leur** + donner des conseils.
*We are going to give **them** advice.*

| | |
|---|---|
| Vous allez **m'**apprendre a utiliser cet appareil. | *You are going to teach **me** to use this camera.* |
| Elles ne vont pas **nous** refuser ce service. | *They are not going to refuse **us** this service.* |

**EXERCICE**

## 12·11

*Look at the sentence below. Underline the phrases in the following sentences that are redundant or could be replaced by indirect object pronouns.*

Ce matin j'ai téléphoné aux candidats qui se sont présentés pour le poste de secrétaire.

1. J'ai donné rendez-vous aux candidats.

2. J'ai demandé aux candidats de fournir un CV à mon patron avant les entretiens.

3. Maintenant je vais décrire chaque candidat à mon patron.

4. Il pourra préparer les questions qu'il posera aux candidats.

**EXERCICE**

## 12·12

*Rewrite the sentences from the previous exercise, replacing the underlined phrases with the appropriate object pronoun **lui** or **leur**.*

1. _____

2. _____

3. _____

4. _____

**EXERCICE**

## 12·13

*Construct sentences by placing the following sentence fragments in the right order.*

1. m' / l'office de tourisme / a appelé

    _____

2. m' / a dit / l'employé / chercher les billets / de venir

    _____

3. je / lui / ai demandé / si / venir / je pouvais / demain

    _____

4. m' / a répondu / il / que oui

    _____

5. nous / l'office de tourisme / les employés de / procurent / toujours / nos billets

    _____

6. leur / exprimer / je vais / ma gratitude

    _____

## Object pronoun **y**

Another type of object pronoun in French is **y**. It refers to *things only* and replaces the preposition **à** followed by an object. Most of the time—not always—it will translate into English as *there* because it often refers to a location.

| | |
|---|---|
| Tu répondras **à ma question**? | *Will you answer **my question**?* |
| Oui, j'**y** répondrai. | *Yes, I will answer **it**.* |
| Tu penses **à tes vacances**? | *You are thinking **about your vacation**?* |
| Non, je n'**y** pense pas. | *No, I am not thinking **about it**.* |
| Tu veux rester **à la maison**? | *Do you want to stay **at home**?* |
| Oui, je veux **y** rester. | *Yes, I want to stay **there**.* |
| Tu as mis la clef **sur le bureau**? | *Did you put the key **on the desk**?* |
| Oui, j'**y** ai mis la clef. | *Yes, I put the key **there**.* |

The pronoun **y** also replaces prepositional phrases that refer to locations such as **en France**, **chez moi**, **devant la table**, **sous le lit**. For more on prepositional phrases, see Unit 15.

## Object pronoun **en**

This is another type of object pronoun. Just like the pronoun **y**, **en** refers to *things only*. However, it replaces the preposition **de** followed by a *noun* or *noun phrase*. This pronoun has a variety of translations in English.

| | |
|---|---|
| Il revient **de Paris**? Oui, il **en** revient. | *Is he coming back **from Paris**? Yes, he is coming back **from there**.* |
| Elle prendra **du dessert**? Oui, elle **en** prendra. | *Will she have **some dessert**? Yes, she will have **some**.* |
| Vous avez bu assez **d'eau**? Oui, nous **en** avons bu beaucoup. | *Did you drink enough **water**? Yes, we drank a lot **of it**.* |

---

### EXERCICE
### 12·14

*In each question, underline the **à** + thing or **de** + thing phrase that can be replaced by the object pronouns **y** and **en**. Then write the appropriate pronoun on the line provided, and answer the question using **y** or **en**.*

EXAMPLE: Tu reviens de France?

Pronom: _____en_____   Réponse: Oui, j'en reviens.

1. Tu iras à Paris?

Pronom: _____   Réponse: _____

2. Tu resteras à Paris?

Pronom: _____   Réponse: _____

3. Tu achèteras des souvenirs?

Pronom: _____   Réponse: _____

4. Tu m'apporteras des bonbons?

Pronom: _____   Réponse: _____

5. Tu boiras du vin tous les jours?

Pronom: _____                     Réponse: _____

6. Tu m'écriras des e-mails?

Pronom: _____                     Réponse: _____

# Order of object pronouns in declarative sentences

Often sentences that include an indirect object pronoun also include a direct object pronoun. In such cases, it is necessary to know the order in which these pronouns appear. Consider the following sentences:

**subject + indirect object pronoun + verb + direct object noun**
Tu + **m'** + achètes + **une glace**?
*Will you buy **me** an ice cream?*

**subject + indirect object pronoun + direct object pronoun + verb**
Tu + **me** + **l'** + achètes?
*Will you buy **it** for **me**?*

| | |
|---|---|
| Nous ne **te** montrerons pas **notre maison**. | *We will not show **you our house**.* |
| Nous ne **te la** montrerons pas. | *We will not show **it to you**.* |
| Je vais **vous** envoyer **le paquet** demain. | *I am going to send **you the package** tomorrow.* |
| Je vais **vous** l'envoyer demain. | *I am going to send **it to you** tomorrow.* |

In these examples, note that the pronouns **me**, **te**, **nous**, and **vous** are placed *before* the direct object pronouns **le**, **la**, **l'**, and **les**. This is true of the indirect object pronouns **lui** and **leur** also, as is shown in the following diagrams:

me, te, nous, vous < le, la, l', les,
me, te, nous, vous < lui, leur

Now consider the following sentences:

| | |
|---|---|
| Je donne **la montre en or à Jean**. | *I am giving **the gold watch to Jean**.* |
| Je **la lui** donne. | *I am giving **it to him**.* |
| Je **leur** ai envoyé **un e-mail**. | *I sent **them an e-mail**/I sent **an e-mail to them**.* |
| Je **le leur** ai envoyé. | *I sent **it to them**.* |

In these examples, note that the direct object pronouns **le**, **la**, **l'**, and **les** are placed *before* the indirect object pronouns **lui** and **leur**.

Now consider these sentences:

| | |
|---|---|
| Il ne **lui** achètera pas **la voiture**. | *He will not buy **her the car**.* |
| Il ne **la lui** achètera pas. | *He will not buy **him/her it**./He will not buy **it for him/her**.* |

In these examples, note that the direct object pronouns **le**, **la**, **l'**, and **les** are placed *before* the indirect object pronouns **lui** and **leur**, as is shown in the following diagram:

le, la, l', les < lui, leur

Now consider this final diagram, which summarizes what we have just learned about the position of a variety of object pronouns in declarative sentences:

me, te, nous, vous < le, la, l', les < lui, leur

*Replace each underlined object noun in the following sentences with an object pronoun and write it/them on the first line. Then rewrite each original sentence, replacing the nouns with those pronouns. Be sure to place the pronouns correctly in the sentences.*

1. Suzanne a rencontré <u>Paul</u> au cours d'anglais.

   Pronom: _____

   _____

2. Elle a prêté son livre <u>à Paul</u>.

   Pronom: _____

   _____

3. Le professeur a demandé <u>à Paul et à Suzanne</u> de faire un projet.

   Pronom: _____

   _____

4. Il a félicité <u>Paul et Suzanne</u> quand ils ont fini <u>leur projet</u>.

   Pronoms: _____

   _____

5. Ils ont remercié <u>le professeur</u>.

   Pronom: _____

   _____

6. À la fin du cours, ils ont organisé une fête pour leurs amis. Ils ont préparé <u>cette fête</u> pendant deux semaines.

   Pronom: _____

   _____

*For each of the following questions, replace each underlined phrase with a pronoun and write it on the first line. Then, answer the question on the second line, placing the pronoun correctly in the sentence.*

1. Rose achète <u>les fleurs</u> <u>chez le fleuriste du coin</u>?

   les fleurs: _____        chez le fleuriste du coin: _____

   Oui, elle _____ _____ achète.

2. Elle va offrir <u>les fleurs</u> <u>à sa mère</u>?

   les fleurs: _____        à sa mère: _____

   Oui, elle va _____ _____ offrir.

3. Le professeur pose beaucoup de questions à ses élèves?

de questions: _____ à ses élèves: _____

Oui, il _____ _____ pose beaucoup.

4. Vous donnez des conseils à vos étudiants?

des conseils: _____ à vos étudiants: _____

Oui, nous _____ _____ donnons.

5. Tu peux prêter ton stylo à ton camarade?

ton stylo: _____ à ton camarade: _____

Oui, je peux _____ _____ prêter.

6. Tu as cherché ton portable dans ta chambre?

ton portable: _____ dans ta chambre: _____

Non, je ne _____ _____ ai pas cherché.

# Order of object pronouns in imperative affirmative sentences

We have previously seen that object pronouns precede the verb in declarative sentences; we have also seen the order in which several pronouns appear together in such sentences. Now observe that, in *imperative affirmative* sentences only, object pronouns follow the verb:

| | |
|---|---|
| Ecoute le professeur! | *Listen to the teacher!* |
| Ecoute-**le**! | *Listen **to him**!* |
| Cherche la radio! | *Look for the radio!* |
| Cherche-**la**! | *Look **for it**!* |
| Mets tes skis! | *Put your skis on!* |
| Mets-**les**! | *Put **them** on!* |
| Réponds aux questions! | *Answer the questions!* |
| Réponds-**y**! | *Answer **them**!* |
| Prends du lait! | *Have some milk!* |
| Prends-**en**! | *Have **some**!* |

Now see how to build imperative affirmative sentences around object pronouns:

| | |
|---|---|
| Donne-nous les réponses! | *Give us the answers!* |
| Donne-**les-nous**! | *Give **them to us**!* |
| Chante-nous cette chanson! | *Sing us this song!* |
| Chante-**la-nous**! | *Sing **it to us**!* |
| Montre-moi ton essai! | *Show me your essay!* |
| Montre-**le-moi**! | *Show **it to me**!* |
| Envoie-lui les tableaux! | *Send him/her the paintings!* |
| Envoie-**les-lui**! | *Send **them to him/her**!* |
| Présente-leur tes félicitations! | *Present your congratulations to them!* |
| Présente-**les-leur**! | *Present **them to them**!* |

In the next examples, note how the pronoun **moi** transforms into **m'** when preceding the pronoun **en**.

Donne-moi de l'argent!          *Give me some money!*
Donne-**m'en**!                 *Give **me some**!*
Prête-moi des livres!           *Lend me some books!*
Prête **m'en**!                 *Lend **me some**!*

**EXERCICE**
**12·17**

*Answer each question with an affirmative command replacing the italicized phrase with the appropriate object pronoun.*

1. Je dois faire *le ménage*? Oui, _____!

2. Je dois prendre *le déjeuner* d'abord? Oui, _____!

3. Je dois sortir *le chien*? Oui, _____!

4. Je dois mettre *mes tennis*? Oui, _____!

5. Je dois *te* montrer *mes devoirs*? Oui, _____!

6. Lise et moi, nous devons jeter *les ordures*? Oui, _____!

**EXERCICE**
**12·18**

*Answer each question with an affirmative command replacing the italicized phrase with the appropriate object pronoun.*

1. Je dois montrer *mon essai à Marie*? Mais oui, _____!

2. Je dois apprendre *la conjugaison à Marie*? Mais oui, _____!

3. Je peux *te* donner *mon adresse*? Ah oui, _____!

4. Je peux *te* demander *des conseils*? Mais oui, _____!

5. Je peux *te* chanter *cette nouvelle chanson*? Bien sûr, _____!

6. Puis-je *te* montrer *mes réponses*? Bien sûr, _____!

## Word order in imperative clauses including object pronouns

The word order in affirmative and negative imperative clauses differs whenever object pronouns are included. Consider the following examples of imperative clauses where the verb is in the affirmative form, and note that, when there is an object pronoun, it is after the verb in the English and French clauses alike:

**verb + direct object noun/pronoun + ! → imperative clause**

| | |
|---|---|
| Fais tes devoirs! | *Do your homework!* |
| Fais-**les**! | *Do **it**!* |
| Faites vos devoirs! | *Do your homework!* |
| Faites-**les**! | *Do **it**!* |
| Faisons nos devoirs! | *Let's do our homework!* |
| Faisons-**les**! | *Let's do **it**!* |

Now consider the following examples of imperative clauses where the verb is in the negative form, and note that the placement of the object pronoun remains *after* the verb in the English clause, but it is now *before* the verb in the French clause:

| **verb + object noun + !** | **Ne + verb + pas + object noun + !** |
|---|---|
| Cherche + tes livres + ! | Ne + cherche + pas + tes livres + ! |
| | |
| AFFIRMATIVE IMPERATIVE CLAUSE | NEGATIVE IMPERATIVE CLAUSE |
| Get your books! | *Do not get your books!* |

| **verb + object pronoun + !** | **Ne + object pronoun + verb + pas + !** |
|---|---|
| Cherche-**les**! | Ne + **les** + cherche + pas + ! |
| | |
| AFFIRMATIVE IMPERATIVE CLAUSE | NEGATIVE IMPERATIVE CLAUSE |
| *Get **them**!* | *Do not get **them**!* |

Consider the following pairs of negative imperative clauses and note the position of the object noun after the verb and the position of the object pronoun before the verb:

| | |
|---|---|
| Ne fais pas **tes devoirs**! | *Don't do **your homework**!* |
| Ne **les** fais pas! | *Don't do **it**!* |
| Ne faites pas **vos devoirs**! | *Don't do **your homework**!* |
| Ne **les** faites pas! | *Don't do **it**!* |
| Ne faisons pas **nos devoirs**! | *Let's not do **our homework**!* |
| Ne **les** faisons pas! | *Let's not do **it**!* |

**EXERCICE**
**12·19**

*Translate each command into French using the words provided in parentheses. Beware of the placement of the pronoun in the imperative clause!*

1. The window? Close it!

   La fenêtre? _____! (la / ferme)

2. Your paper? Do not throw it on the floor!

   Ton papier? _____! (le / ne pas / jette / par terre)

3. The dog? Do not bother him!

   Le chien? _____! (le / ne pas / embête)

4. Your friends? Call them!

   Tes amis? _____! (les / appelle)

*Translate the following sentences into French. Use the familiar **tu** form when needed.*

1. Where is your money? Where did you put it?

   _____

2. I saw a twenty-dollar bill right here. Where is it now?

   _____

3. OK. I am giving you another twenty-dollar bill. Please, do not lose it!

   _____

4. Now let's find the flowers for your grandma! Where are they?

   _____

5. Yes, of course, in the vase. Give them to me, please!

   _____

6. We will give them to her together.

   _____

 # Special uses of pronouns

In Unit 12 we learned how object pronouns allow sentences to flow without redundancy. In this unit, these pronouns are presented from a different perspective. You will see that object pronouns are an essential companion to verbs that require a special structure in French and to verbs called reflexive verbs.

## Special verbs that require an indirect object

The verb **plaire** is frequently used in French instead of the verb **aimer** to express *to like*. However, the sentence structure is very different in French than in English when the verb **plaire** is used.

Consider the word order in the following French and English sentences. Note that in both languages the subject is doing the action of the verb and precedes the verb.

> **subject + verb + complement**
> J' + aime + la musique.
> *I like music.*

Now consider the word order in the following French sentence. Note that the French subject still comes first in the French sentence, but the subject is now *what is pleasing to the person*.

> **subject + indirect object + verb**
> **La musique** + me + plaît.

The literal translation of the previous sentence will help you understand how to build a French sentence around the verb **plaire**. Literally, it is translated as *Music is pleasing to me*. Focusing on the fact that music is pleasing *to me*, note that an indirect object pronoun is used to describe who likes music. The word order around the verb **plaire** is as follows:

> *what/who* **+ indirect object pronoun** (*for whom*) **+ third person plaire**
> Le copain de sa fille + **lui** + plaît.
> *She/He likes her daughter's friend.*

The use of the indirect object pronoun **lui** (*to him/her*) tells you that it is a *he* or a *she* who likes the friend (the friend is pleasing to him/her). Similarly, in the following sentence, the use of the indirect object pronoun **leur** indicates that *they* like this type of house:

> Ce modèle de maison **leur** plaît.      *They like this type of house.*

Other object pronouns used with the verb **plaire** are **me**, **te**, **nous**, and **vous**, as in the following sentences:

| | |
|---|---|
| Cette attitude ne **me** plaît pas. | *I do not like this attitude.* |
| Cette couleur **te** plaît? | *You like this color?* |
| Cette vie **nous** plaît. | *We like/enjoy this life.* |

In the following sentence, note that the conjugated form of the verb *plaire* agrees with the plural subject *ces notes*.

| | |
|---|---|
| Ces notes **vous** plaisent. | *You like these grades.* |

Some other frequently used expressions that require the same sentence structure as the verb **plaire** are:

| | |
|---|---|
| **faire de la peine** (à quelqu'un) | *to cause grief (to someone)* |
| **faire mal** (à quelqu'un) | *to hurt (someone)* |
| **falloir** (à quelqu'un) | *to need (for someone)* |
| **manquer** (à quelqu'un) | *to lack something* or *to miss (someone)* |
| **paraître** (à quelqu'un) | *to seem (to someone)* |
| **rester** (à quelqu'un) | *to be left (for someone)* |
| **suffir** (à quelqu'un) | *to be enough (for someone)* |

| | |
|---|---|
| Il **me** faut une nouvelle radio. | *I need a new radio.* |
| Le courage **lui** a manqué. | *He/She lacked courage.* |
| Ses amis **lui** manquent. | *She misses her friends.* |
| Il **nous** restera une page à lire. | *We will have one page left to read.* |
| Cette nouvelle **nous** paraît fausse. | *We think this news is wrong.* |

EXERCICE
13·1

*From the choices given, choose the appropriate answer for each question and write the corresponding letter on the line provided.*

1. Est-ce que tu as mis assez de sucre dans cette limonade? _____

2. Ça fait deux mois que tu n'as pas vu ta famille? _____

3. Les étudiants pensent que leur prof va prendre la retraite. _____

4. Est-ce que tous les étudiants ont rendu les essais au prof? _____

5. Où sont les serviettes? _____

6. Oh! Qu'est-ce qu'il s'est fait au bras? _____

7. Tu crois qu'ils sont allés dîner? _____

8. Ils ont dépensé tout leur argent. _____

a. Oui, cela leur causera de la peine car ils l'aiment bien.

b. Il ne nous reste que deux blanches.

c. Oui, je crois que ça me suffit.

d. Oui, il leur reste juste assez pour boire un pot.

e. Oui, mes enfants me manquent.

f. Ça me paraît probable.

g. Il s'est fait mal en tombant de son vélo.

h. Non, il lui en manque encore deux.

*Complete each answer with an appropriate object pronoun:* **me**, **lui**, **nous**, *or* **vous**.

1. Mimi a commencé à faire du yoga et cela _____ plaît énormément.

2. Moi, j'ai participé à deux cours de yoga et cela _____ suffit.

3. Nous sommes souvent assis au travail; donc il _____ faut du sport pour rester en forme.

4. Luc, il _____ reste encore deux semaines avant qu'on ne vous laisse partir.

5. Vous êtes anxieux de finir. Alors ces deux semaines vont _____ paraître assez longues, n'est-ce pas?

6. Cela va _____ faire beaucoup de peine, à Mimi et à moi, de ne pas vous voir au bureau.

# Verbs that require reflexive pronouns

Any verb admitting a direct object may also be used with a reflexive pronoun to express that an action is performed by the subject to himself/herself.

## Reflexive action verbs

Reflexive pronouns can be direct or indirect object pronouns depending on the verb that governs them. They are direct objects when they answer the question **Qui?** (*Whom?*) In this case they usually mean *myself, yourself, himself/herself, ourselves, yourselves, themselves.*

—**Qui** est-ce qu'elle lave? —Elle **se** lave.    —*Whom does she wash?* —*She washes **herself**.*

—**Qui** est-ce que nous habillons? —Nous **nous** habillons.    —*Whom do we dress?* —*We dress **ourselves**.*

—**Qui** est-ce qu'ils baignent? —Ils **se** baignent.    —*Whom do they bathe?* —*They bathe **themselves**.*

—**Qui** est-ce que tu sèches? —Je **me** sèche.    —*Whom do you dry?* —*I dry **myself**.*

In the following examples, note that the literal translation of a reflexive verb into English is sometimes awkward and therefore needs to be rephrased in a more natural manner.

—**Qui** est-ce que tu couches? —Je **me** couche.    —*Whom do you put to bed?* —*I am putting **myself** to bed (I am going to bed).*

—**Qui** est-ce que tu appelles Claire? —Je **m'**appelle Claire.    —*Whom do you call Claire?* —*I call myself Claire (My name is Claire).*

Reflexive pronouns are indirect objects when they answer the question **À qui?** (*To whom?*) In this case they usually mean *to myself, to yourself, to himself/herself, to ourselves, to yourselves,* and *to themselves* in the French sentence even though they are not always translated as such in English.

—**À qui** est-ce que tu vas brosser les dents? —Je vais **me** brosser les dents.    —*Whose teeth are you going to brush?* —*I am going to brush **my** teeth.*

—**À qui** est-ce qu'elle sèche les cheveux? —Elle **se** sèche les cheveux.    —*Whose hair does she dry?* —*She dries **her own** hair.*

—**À qui** est-ce que tu limes les ongles? —Je **me** lime les ongles.    —*Whose nails are you filing?* —*I am filing **my own** nails.*

—**À qui** est-ce qu'il a fait mal? —Il **s'**est fait mal.    —*Whom did he hurt?* —*He hurt **himself**.*

You already know reflexive pronouns (except for **se**) because you have studied them as direct and indirect object pronouns in Unit 12. However, reflexive pronouns serve a different purpose. With reflexive verbs, the action of the verb is done by the subject to himself/herself; in other words the subject and the object are the same person.

> **subject + direct object/reflexive pronoun + verb**
> **Marie** + **se** + lève.
> *Marie gets up.*

Observe how the equivalent sentence of **Marie se lève** is built in English. Note the absence of any pronoun. When we say *Marie gets up* in English, we *imply* that she is getting *herself* up.

The following object pronouns can be used as reflexive pronouns:

| | |
|---|---|
| me | *(to) myself* |
| te | *(to) yourself* |
| nous | *(to) ourselves* |
| vous | *(to) yourselves* |
| se | *(to) himself/herself/themselves* |

Although it is not customary in English to express that this action is done to *oneself*, it is necessary in French. Compare the following French and English sentences:

| | |
|---|---|
| Je **me** réveille vers six heures. | *I wake up around six o'clock.* |

In the English sentence, it is implied that I wake *myself* up; in the French sentence the word *myself* has to be stated (**me**). Now consider the following French sentence. In this sentence, I am waking my little sister (direct object). Since the subject (**Je**) is different from the direct object **ma petite sœur**, there is no need for a reflexive pronoun.

| | |
|---|---|
| Je réveille **ma petite sœur**. | *I wake up **my little sister**.* |

Compare the following sentences to better understand why a verb must be accompanied by a reflexive pronoun in French—as opposed to in English where that reflexive pronoun is omitted. Note that when the verb is reflexive, the action of the verb is performed by the subject to himself/herself. However, when the verb is not reflexive, the action performed by the subject is done to someone else.

| | |
|---|---|
| Suzie **se** lave les mains. | *Suzie washes **her** hands.* |
| Suzie lave **son chien**. | *Suzie washes **her dog**.* |
| La maman **se** réveille. | *The mom is waking up.* |
| La maman réveille **ses enfants**. | *The mom wakes **her children**.* |
| Le monsieur **s'**arrête. | *The gentleman stops.* |
| L'agent arrête **la voiture**. | *The policeman stops **the car**.* |

Any verb admitting a direct object (these verbs are called transitive) may be used with or without a reflexive pronoun. Consider the following pairs of sentences and note how a transitive verb can be used with or without a reflexive pronoun:

| | |
|---|---|
| Je **mets** un CD dans le lecteur. | *I **am putting** a CD in the player.* |
| Je **me mets** à sa place. | *I **put myself** in his/her place.* |
| Nous **écoutons** le CD. | *We **are listening** to the CD.* |
| Nous **nous écoutons** sur le CD. | *We **listen to ourselves** on the CD.* |

In French many reflexive verbs refer to daily activities we perform while grooming ourselves. Others refer to getting hurt (hurting ourselves).

| | |
|---|---|
| Je **me** lève tôt. | *I get up early.* |
| Je **me** maquille. | *I put on my makeup.* |
| Je **m'**habille vite. | *I get dressed quickly.* |

| Je **me** dépêche. | *I am hurrying.* |
| Je tombe et je **me** fais mal. | *I fall and get hurt.* |
| Je **m'**égratigne le genou. | *I scrape my knee.* |
| Je **m'**arrête au coin. | *I stop at the corner.* |
| Je **me** rends au travail. | *I go to work.* |
| Nous **nous** promenons au parc. | *We walk in the park.* |
| On **s'**amuse à jouer au Frisbee. | *We have fun playing Frisbee.* |
| Alors nous **nous** en allons. | *Then we go away.* |
| Nous **nous** lavons. | *We wash ourselves.* |
| Nous **nous** couchons. | *We go to bed.* |

Consider the following sentence and note the differences between the French and English wording.

**subject + pronoun + verb + direct object**
Suzie + **se** + lave + les mains.
*Suzie washes her hands.*

Note that, in the French sentence, the use of the reflexive pronoun makes it clear that Suzie is doing something *to herself* (**elle *se* lave**); therefore the use of the possessive article *her* is not necessary before *hands*, so the definite article **les** (not the possessive **ses**) is used before **mains** in this case. As a general rule, use the definite article (**le, la, l', les**) before parts of the body when used in conjunction with a reflexive verb.

| Je **me** brosse **les** dents. | *I am brushing **my** teeth.* |
| Nous **nous** peignons **les** cheveux. | *We comb **our** hair.* |
| Vous **vous** rasez **la** barbe. | *You are shaving **your** beard.* |
| Elles **se** maquillent **le** visage. | *They put makeup on **their** faces.* |
| Il **se** lime **les** ongles. | *He files **his** nails.* |
| Ils **se** lavent **les** pieds. | *They are washing **their** feet.* |

**EXERCICE**
**13·3**

*Complete each sentence with the appropriate reflexive pronoun **se/s'** or **nous**.*

1. Marie et George _____ aiment depuis longtemps.

2. Ils _____ marient aujourd'hui.

3. Nous _____ sommes habillés de façon très chic pour la cérémonie.

4. Nous allons _____ rendre à l'église.

5. Après la cérémonie, tout le monde va _____ amuser.

6. Nous _____ coucherons très tard ce soir.

**EXERCICE**
**13·4**

*Fill in the first blank in each sentence with the appropriate reflexive pronoun and the second blank with the appropriate definite article.*

1. Tu _____ rases _____ jambes?

2. Monique _____ coupe _____ ongles.

3. Jean-Jacques et Paul _____ lavent _____ cheveux.

4. Pascale et moi, nous _____ brossons _____ dents.

5. Vous _____ essuyez _____ figure.

6. Et moi, je _____ sèche _____ mains.

**EXERCICE**

**13·5**

*Complete each sentence with the appropriate reflexive pronoun only when it is necessary.
Place an X on the line when a pronoun is not necessary.*

1. Le matin, Gérard _____ lève à six heures.

2. Il _____ réveille sa femme Véronique.

3. Véronique _____ lave et _____ maquille.

4. Gérard _____ rase.

5. Ensuite Gérard et Véronique _____ habillent.

6. À sept heures, ils _____ réveillent les enfants.

## Reciprocal action verbs

Verbs are also accompanied by a reflexive pronoun when expressing *reciprocal actions* as in people kissing each other, writing to each other, or speaking to each other. Since at least two people are involved in reciprocal actions, only the reflexive pronouns **nous**, **vous**, and **se** will be used in these cases. In the following sentences, note that the phrase *each other* can often be implied and omitted in English:

| | |
|---|---|
| Les deux mariés **s'**embrassent. | *The two married people kiss (**each other**).* |
| Les trois amis **s'**écrivent tous les jours. | *The three friends write **each other** every day.* |
| Nous **nous** parlons souvent. | *We often speak (**to each other**).* |
| Nous **nous** quittons rarement. | *We are rarely apart (**from each other**).* |
| Vous **vous** êtes disputés. | *You quarreled (**with each other**).* |
| Vous **vous** êtes réconciliés? | *Did you reconciliate (**with each other**)?* |
| Elles **se** prêtent beaucoup de choses. | *They lend **each other** many things.* |
| Les hommes **se** serrent la main. | *Men shake hands (**with each other**).* |

**EXERCICE**

**13·6**

*Complete each sentence with the reflexive pronoun **se** only when it is necessary. Place an X
on the line when **se/s'** is not necessary.*

1. Josiane et Richard _____ sont rencontrés à l'université.

2. D'abord ils ne _____ sont pas plu.

3. Mais un jour, Richard _____ a protégé Josiane d'un voleur qui voulait son sac à main.

4. Naturellement Josiane _____ a admiré le courage de Richard.

5. Bientôt Josiane et Richard _____ sont devenus inséparables.

6. Un an plus tard ils _____ sont fiancés.

7. Deux ans plus tard, ils _____ sont mariés.

8. Et depuis ce temps ils _____ sont très heureux.

EXERCICE
13·7

*Complete the following conversation by creating replies to Suzanne's comments and questions. Translate and use the responses in parentheses.*

1. —Dis donc, Marc! Tu ne crois pas qu'on devrait se préparer pour la grande tempête qui s'annonce? —_____ (*Yes, Suzanne! Let's prepare [ourselves]!*)

2. —Je m'inquiète surtout à cause des vents très forts qui risquent de déraciner nos arbres. —_____ (*I know. I, too, am worried. I do not like this weather at all.*)

3. —Bon. Dépêchons-nous de rentrer toutes les chaises-longues! —_____ (*Yes, let's get to work!*)

4. —Oh! Regarde! Je me suis cassé un ongle. Zut alors! —_____ (*All right. We are going to stop for a moment.*)

EXERCICE
13·8

*Write the following short note from Suzanne to Michel in French using the suggested vocabulary.*

My dear Michel, I miss you terribly (**manquer**). When are you coming home (**rentrer**)? It pains me to be without you for so long (**faire de la peine d'être sans toi**). I really need your company to be happy (**falloir ta compagnie d'être heureuse**). Without you, every day is the same: I get up (**se lever**), get dressed (**s'habiller**), go to work (**se rendre au travail**), come home (**rentrer**), and go to sleep (**se coucher**). People who love each other (**s'aimer**) as we do should not be separated (**être séparés**)!

_____

_____

_____

_____

_____

_____

# Using adverbs and adverbial phrases

## Adverbs

Adverbs usually modify the meaning of a verb; they also occasionally modify (or describe) an adjective or another adverb. The most common function of adverbs and adverbial phrases consists in modifying the meaning of a verb by telling how or in what way, how much or to what degree, when or how often, and where something is done.

## Adverbs defining manner, place, and time

Many adverbs help define how, where, or when an action takes place. Here are some of these types of commonly used adverbs:

| COMMENT | HOW | OÙ | WHERE | QUAND | WHEN |
| --- | --- | --- | --- | --- | --- |
| bien | *well* | ailleurs | *elsewhere* | alors | *then* |
| élégamment | *elegantly* | autour | *around* | après | *afterward* |
| ensemble | *together* | dedans | *inside* | aujourd'hui | *today* |
| fortement | *strongly* | dehors | *outside* | autrefois | *formerly* |
| gentiment | *nicely* | derrière | *behind* | déjà | *already* |
| gratuitement | *free* | dessous | *under* | demain | *tomorrow* |
| mal | *badly* | dessus | *above* | enfin | *finally* |
| mieux | *better* | devant | *in front of* | ensuite | *then* |
| patiemment | *patiently* | ici | *here* | fréquemment | *frequently* |
| poliment | *politely* | là | *there* | jamais | *never* |
| puissamment | *powerfully* | là-bas | *over there* | maintenant | *now* |
| seulement | *only* | partout | *everywhere* | rarement | *rarely* |
| silencieusement | *silently* | | | récemment | *recently* |
| vite | *quickly* | | | soudain | *suddenly* |
| | | | | toujours | *always* |

| | |
| --- | --- |
| Il danse **bien**. | *He dances **well**.* |
| Va chercher **ailleurs**! | *Go look **elsewhere**!* |
| Les enfants vont jouer **dehors**. | *The children go play **outside**.* |
| Je reste **ici**. | *I am staying **here**.* |
| Le mardi on va **gratuitement** au musée. | *On Tuesdays people go to the museum **free of charge**.* |
| | |
| Tu as regardé **partout**? | *Did you look **everywhere**?* |
| Nous mangions **seulement** les légumes. | *We used to eat **only** vegetables.* |
| Le vélo? Il est **là**, **devant** la maison. | *The bike? It is **there**, **in front of** the house.* |

**139**

*On the lines provided, write the letter of the adverb in the list on the right that answers each question logically.*

1. Comment parles-tu français? _____        a.   Demain.

2. Comment répond-on au professeur? _____        b.   Hier.

3. Où est le chien? _____        c.   Beaucoup.

4. Où sont les provisions? _____        d.   Poliment.

5. Quand as-tu vu ce film? _____        e.   Maintes fois.

6. Quand mangeras-tu ces croissants? _____        f.   Bien.

7. Combien de fois as-tu essayé cette robe? _____        g.   Dedans, dans le frigo.

8. Combien as-tu dépensé pour ce fichu? _____        h.   Dehors.

*Combine the following sentence fragments to create complete sentences. Be sure to use correct punctuation.*

1. bien / nous chantons / cet hymne

_____

2. l'argile / patiemment / l'artiste / sculpte

_____

3. ce soir / ensemble / dînons

_____

4. jouent / les enfants / silencieusement

_____

5. faire des achats / allons / ailleurs

_____

6. leurs études / rapidement / ils désiraient / finir

_____

## Adverbs defining quantity or intensity

A number of adverbs help define how much or to what degree something is done. The following are some commonly used adverbs of this type:

| assez | *enough* | moins | *less* |
|-------|----------|-------|--------|
| aussi | *as* | peu | *little* |
| autant | *as much* | plus | *more* |
| beaucoup | *much/many/a lot* | si | *so* |
| combien (de) | *how much* | tant | *so (much)* |
| davantage | *more* | tellement | *so much* |
| environ | *about* | trop | *too much* |

| | |
|--|--|
| Tu as **assez** mangé? | *Did you eat **enough**?* |
| J'ai **trop** bu. | *I drank **too much**.* |
| Elles ont **tellement** grandi. | *They grew **so much**.* |
| Marie a grandi tout **autant**. | *Marie grew just **as much**.* |
| On parle **trop** dans cette salle. | *They talk **too much** in this room.* |
| Je désirais **tant** faire ce voyage. | *I **so** wished to go on this trip.* |

## EXERCICE 14·3

*Complete each sentence with one of the adverbs from the following list to find out about Toby.*

moins / trop / si / combien / tellement / davantage / assez

Toby est un petit chien mignon mais un peu (1) _____ gros. Il a toujours faim. Quand on lui donne son dîner, sa portion est (2) _____ grande mais Toby veut (3) _____. Il a (4) _____ grossi ces derniers temps qu'il doit maintenant faire régime. La grande question, c'est (5) _____ il faut lui donner à manger? Oui, je sais bien qu'il faut lui donner (6) _____ qu'avant, mais j'ai (7) _____ peur de l'affamer et de le rendre malade. Oh la la! Quel dilemme!

## EXERCICE 14·4

*Translate the following sentences into French.*

1. Last night I did not sleep enough. _____

_____

2. I had too many things on my mind. _____

_____

3. Yet, I was so tired. _____

4. Today I feel more tired than ever. _____

_____

5. And I have so much to do. _____

6. I will be so happy when the day is over! _____

_____

# Adverbs used in comparative and superlative structures

There are three comparative structures using adverbs; they serve to establish relationships of equality, superiority, or inferiority. The auxiliary adverbs used in comparisons are **plus** (*more*), **moins** (*less*), and **aussi** (*as*).

**auxiliary adverb + adverb + que**
Il répond **plus** + **fréquemment** + **que** moi.
*He answers **more frequently than** me.*

| | |
|---|---|
| Je sors **moins souvent que** ma sœur. | *I go out **less often than** my sister.* |
| Elle s'habille **aussi élégamment que** moi. | *She dresses **as elegantly as** I do.* |
| Le chien courait **aussi vite que** le chat. | *The dog ran **as fast as** the cat.* |
| Nous jouons **aussi bien que** vous. | *We play **as well as** you.* |
| Ils parlent **aussi mal que** toi. | *They speak **as badly as** you.* |

In the following example, note that the irregular comparative form of the adverb **bien** (*well*) is **mieux** (*better*), and that **plus mal** can be expressed as **pis**. However, this irregular form of **pis** is infrequently used in speaking.

| | |
|---|---|
| Joanne se coiffe toujours **mieux que** Céline. | *Joanne always does her hair **better than** Céline.* |
| Céline s'est coiffée **plus mal** (**pis**) **qu'** hier. | *Céline styled her hair **worse than** yesterday.* |

The adverb **bien** as well as its irregular comparative form **mieux** are used idiomatically with the verb **être** (which is normally followed by an adjective).

| | |
|---|---|
| Ce pull rouge **est bien**, mais le vert **est mieux**. | *This red sweater **is fine**, but the green one **is better**.* |
| Le jogging, c'**est bien** mais la nage c'**est mieux**. | *Jogging **is fine**, but swimming **is better**.* |

If the comparison includes a quantitative element, use **autant** rather than **aussi** in front of the noun to express *as*.

| | |
|---|---|
| Il a gagné **autant d'argent que** sa femme. | *He won **as much money as** his wife.* |
| Elle a marqué **autant de buts** aujourd'hui **qu'**hier. | *She made **as many goals** today **as** yesterday.* |
| Je lis **aussi** bien en Anglais **qu'**en Français. | *I read **as well** in English **as** in French.* |

The superlative adverbial structure serves to express the highest degree in which an action can be performed. It uses the adverbs **plus** and **moins** preceded by the masculine form of the definite article (**le**).

| | |
|---|---|
| Yves joue **le moins bien**. | *Yves plays **the worst**. (literally, *the least well*)* |
| Moi, je ris **le moins souvent**. | *I laugh **the least** (often).* |
| Jean court **le plus vite**. | *Jean runs **the fastest**.* |
| Irène écrit **le plus soigneusement**. | *Irène writes **the most carefully**.* |

In the following examples, note the irregular superlative form of the adverb **bien** (**mieux**) as well as that of the adverb **mal** (**pire**). **Le pis** and **le plus mal** are both acceptable superlative forms, although **le pis** is infrequently used in speaking.

| | |
|---|---|
| Ça, c'est bien mais cela **est mieux**! | *This is fine, but that is **better**!* |
| Ça c'est mal, mais cela est **pire**! | *This is bad, but that is **worse**!* |
| Hélène parle **le mieux**. | *Hélène speaks **the best**.* |
| Marc joue **le pis/le plus mal**. | *Marc plays **the worst**.* |

Complete each sentence in French appropriately, using translations of the words in parentheses.

1. Marc aime jouer aux cartes _____ que Luc. (*as much*)

2. Luc joue _____ fréquemment que Marc car il a plus de temps que lui. (*more*)

3. Aujourd'hui ils ont joué _____ l'un que l'autre mais c'est Luc qui a eu le plus de chance. (*as seriously*)

4. Luc a fait des fautes, mais _____ souvent que Marc. (*less*)

5. Marc n'a pas joué _____ que Luc. (*as well*)

6. Ils avaient décidé que celui qui aura joué _____ paiera le dîner. (*the worst*)

7. Marc s'habille _____ que Luc. (*better*)

8. Alors c'est lui qui attire l'attention des femmes _____. (*the most*)

9. Luc gagne _____ aux cartes mais Marc a du succès avec les femmes. (*the most often*)

10. Qu'est-ce qui est _____? (*better*)

# Adverbs used in assertions

Some adverbs are used to assert, confirm, or agree. Here are some that are commonly used in this way:

| | | | |
|---|---|---|---|
| assurément | *for sure* | si | *yes* |
| certainement | *certainly* | soit | *all right* |
| oui | *yes* | volontiers | *gladly* |

—Tu n'as pas froid? —**Si**, j'ai froid.　　—*Are you not cold?* —***Yes, I am cold.***
—Tu veux boire un pot? —**Volontiers**.　　—*Do you want a drink?* —***Gladly.***
—Tu voudrais venir?—**Assurément**!　　—*Would you like to come?* —***For sure!***

# Adverbs used in negations

Some adverbs are used to make negative statements. The adverb **ne** (**n'** before a vowel sound) must be present to make a verb negative and is often accompanied by a negative auxiliary word that may be an adverb such as **pas** (*not*). Here are a few such auxiliary adverbs:

| | | | |
|---|---|---|---|
| aucunement | *not at all/in no way* | nullement | *not at all* |
| guère (*formal*) | *not much* | pas | *not* |
| jamais | *never* | plus | *no longer/no more* |
| ni...ni | *neither . . . nor* | point (*formal*) | *not* |

Je n'ai **plus** de patience.
Ils **ne** font **aucunement** attention.
Tu **ne** veux **ni** café **ni** thé?

*I have **no** patience **left**.*
*They **do not** pay **any** attention.*
*You want **neither** coffee **nor** tea?*

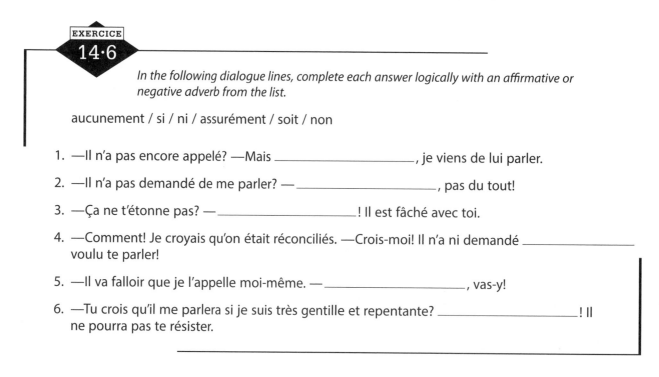

**EXERCICE**
**14·6**

*In the following dialogue lines, complete each answer logically with an affirmative or negative adverb from the list.*

aucunement / si / ni / assurément / soit / non

1. —Il n'a pas encore appelé? —Mais _____, je viens de lui parler.

2. —Il n'a pas demandé de me parler? —_____, pas du tout!

3. —Ça ne t'étonne pas? —_____! Il est fâché avec toi.

4. —Comment! Je croyais qu'on était réconciliés. —Crois-moi! Il n'a ni demandé _____ voulu te parler!

5. —Il va falloir que je l'appelle moi-même. —_____, vas-y!

6. —Tu crois qu'il me parlera si je suis très gentille et repentante? _____! Il ne pourra pas te résister.

## Placement of adverbs

Adverbs have various positions in a sentence depending on the intended emphasis on the adverb, the length of the adverb, and whether the verb it modifies is in a simple or compound tense.

### Adverbs of time as transitional words

Adverbs of time such as **hier** (*yesterday*) or **ensuite** (*then*) usually appear at the beginning of a sentence in both English and French because they act as transitional words. However, when the emphasis is on the action rather than on the time factor, they may appear at the end of a sentence.

| | |
|---|---|
| **D'abord** tu manges. **Ensuite** tu te reposes. **Après** tu vas en classe. | ***First*** *you eat.* ***Then*** *you rest.* ***Afterward*** *you go to class.* |
| Tu manges **d'abord**. Tu te reposes **ensuite**. Tu vas en classe **après**. | *You eat **first**. You **then** rest. You go to class **afterward**.* |
| **Hier** elle est rentrée de France. **Aujourd'hui** elle défait ses valises. **Demain** elle ira au bureau. | ***Yesterday*** *she came back from France.* ***Today*** *she is emptying her bags.* ***Tomorrow*** *she will go to the office.* |
| Elle est rentrée de France **hier**. Elle défait ses valises **aujourd'hui**. Elle ira au bureau **demain**. | *She came back from France **yesterday**. She is emptying her bags **today**. She will go to the office **tomorrow**.* |

*Translate the italicized English adverbs into French to complete each sentence.*

1. *First*, I review my notes. *Then*, I do my exercises. *Finally*, I work on the computer.

   _____ je révise mes notes. _____ je fais mes exercices. _____ je travaille à l'ordinateur.

2. I went to the airport *this morning*. *Now* I am waiting for the plane. *Soon* I will leave for Canada.

   Je suis allé à l'aéroport _____. _____ j'attends l'avion. _____ je partirai pour le Canada.

3. *Last night*, I was exhausted. *Today* I feel better. *Tonight* I will go to bed *early*.

   _____ soir, j'étais épuisé. _____ je me sens mieux. _____ je me coucherai _____.

4. Last year I used to be *late* to class *every day*. This year I improved a lot. *Currently* I am hardly *ever* late.

   L'année dernière j'étais _____ au cours _____. Cette année j'ai fait beaucoup de progrès. _____ je ne suis presque _____ en retard.

## Adverbs as modifiers of verbs in simple tenses

Short adverbs (no more than two syllables) are usually placed *after the verb* when the sentence features a verb in a *simple tense* (present, future, imperfect, imperative forms). This is quite different from English. In an English sentence, the adverb is usually placed *before* the verb. Note the differing positions of the adverb in the following French and English sentences:

> **French:** subject + verb + adverb + (complement)
> **English:** subject + adverb + verb + (complement)
> Tu parleras **souvent** français.      *You will **often** speak French.*
> Elle enseigne **aussi** l'anglais.      *She **also** teaches English.*
> Tu comprenais **déjà** le français.      *You **already** understood French.*
> Fais **vite** tes devoirs!      ***Hurry** to do your homework!*

In the previous examples, the short adverb was consistently placed after the verb in the French sentences while placed before the verb in the English sentences. Now consider the following examples. Note that the French adverb continues to follow the verb while the English adverb is now at the end of the sentence and after the complement.

> **French:** subject + verb +adverb (+ complement)
> **English:** subject + verb (+ complement) + adverb
> Tu aimes **beaucoup** le français.      *You like French **a lot**.*
> Nous connaissons **bien** Paris.      *We know Paris **well**.*

Consider the following sentences and note that the short French adverb is still consistently placed after the verb it modifies. In these sentences, however, the English adverb also follows the verb.

| | |
|---|---|
| Il courra **vite**. | *He will run **fast**.* |
| Tu es **déjà** en retard. | *You are **already** late.* |
| Elle écrit **mal**. | *She writes **badly**.* |
| Je chantais **bien**. | *I used to sing **well**.* |
| Nous étions **là**. | *We were **there**.* |

Long adverbs (more than two syllables) can be placed at the beginning of a sentence (for emphasis), after the verb it modifies, or at the end of a sentence:

**adverb + subject + verb**

or

**subject + verb + adverb + complement**

or

**subject + verb + complement + adverb**

| | |
|---|---|
| **Silencieusement**, ils partent. | ***Silently**, they leave.* (emphasis on *silently*) |
| Ils partent **silencieusement** de la maison. | *They **silently** leave the house.* |
| Ils partent de la maison **silencieusement**. | *They leave the house **silently**.* |
| **Gentiment**, elle lui prendra la main. | ***Gently**, she will take his hand.* (emphasis on *gently*) |
| Elle lui prendra **gentiment** la main. | *She will **gently** take his hand.* |
| Elle lui prendra la main **gentiment**. | *She will take his hand **gently**.* |

**EXERCICE**

**14·8**

*Make complete sentences by reconstructing the sentence fragments, placing each adverb in the only possible position.*

1. sait / le petit garçon / déjà / parler

_____

2. mal / parle / sa petite sœur

_____

Now reconstruct each sentence in two different ways by placing the adverb in two different positions.

3. parle / le professeur / aux élèves / intelligemment

_____

_____

4. prépareront / leurs collègues / soigneusement / les conférenciers

_____

_____

5. assistaient / les spectateurs / aux concerts / régulièrement

_____

_____

6. les acteurs / la pièce / patiemment / répètent

_____

_____

## Adverbs as modifiers of verbs in compound tenses

In French sentences featuring a *compound tense*, such as the passé composé or the pluperfect, which require a helping verb and a past participle, short adverbs are found *between* the auxiliary verb **avoir** or **être** and the past participle.

**subject + auxiliary verb + adverb + past participle + complement**
Elle + **a** + **déjà** + **fait** + ses exercices.
*She **already did** her exercises.*

Tu **es rarement allé** en montagne.       *You **rarely went** to the mountains.*
Ils **ont longtemps parlé**.                 *They **spoke for a long time**.*
Tu **as vite fini** tes devoirs.             *You **have quickly finished** your homework.*

In the last example, note that when the verb in the passé composé (**as fini**) is translated into English as *have finished*, the word order is the same in French and English.

The placement of the long adverb modifying a verb in a simple tense or a verb in a compound tense is not significantly different. When the verb is in a compound tense, long adverbs are consistently found at the beginning, at the end, or *between* the auxiliary verb and the past participle in a French sentence.

**adverb + subject + auxiliary verb + past participle**

or

**subject + auxiliary verb + past participle + adverb**

or

**subject + auxiliary verb + adverb + past participle**
**Soudainement** le cheval **s'est cabré**.   ***Suddenly** the horse **reared**.*
Le cheval **s'est cabré soudainement**.       *The horse **reared suddenly**.*
Le cheval **s'est soudainement** cabré.       *The horse **suddenly reared**.*

### EXERCICE
### 14·9

*Rewrite each sentence changing the verb from the present tense to the passé composé and placing the adverb correctly in the sentence. There are two possible positions for the adverbs in sentences 5 and 6.*

1. J'aime bien ce gâteau. _____

2. Lise apprend vite son vocabulaire. _____

   _____

3. Gigi finit déjà son dîner. _____

4. Nous allons souvent au cinéma. _____

_____

5. Il récite passionnément le poème. _____

_____

_____

6. Elle explique longuement la leçon. _____

_____

_____

## Adverbs in negative expressions

The adverb **ne** always precedes the conjugated verb it modifies while the auxiliary adverb that completes it follows the verb in simple tenses such as present, future, or imparfait.

**subject + ne/n' + verb + auxiliary adverb + complement**
Nous + n' + irons + **pas** + au parc.
*We will **not** go to the park.*

| | |
|---|---|
| Vous **n'**avez **jamais** de monnaie. | *You **never** have any change.* |
| Je **n'**aime **plus** cette chanson. | *I do **not** like this song **anymore**.* |
| Je **ne** cherchais **rien**. | *I was **not** looking for **anything**.* |

| | |
|---|---|
| —Elle a le droit de faire cela? —**Non**. | *—Does she have the right to do that? —**No**.* |
| Je **n'**approuve **ni** tes paroles **ni** tes actions. | *I do **not** approve of your words **nor** your deeds.* |
| Cette loi **ne** change **nullement** la situation. | *This law **in no way** changes the situation.* |

The adverb **ne** and the auxiliary adverb that completes it frame the conjugated auxiliary verb **être** or **avoir** in compound tenses such as passé composé.

**subject + ne/n' + auxiliary verb + auxiliary adverb + past participle + complement**
Nous + **ne** + sommes + **pas** + allés + au parc.
*We **did not** go to the park.*

| | |
|---|---|
| Nous **n'**avons **plus** voulu jouer. | *We **did not** want to play **anymore**.* |
| Elle **n'**avait **pas** répondu. | *She **had not** answered.* |
| Je **n'**ai **jamais** volé. | *I **never** stole.* |
| Il **n'**est **nullement** mort. | *He **did not** die **at all**.* |

The adverb **ne** and the auxiliary adverb that completes it *both precede* the infinitive verb they modify in a sentence.

| | |
|---|---|
| J'ai peur de **ne plus pouvoir** le faire. | *I am afraid **I will no longer be able** to do it.* |
| Elle regrette de **ne pas l'avoir** fait. | *She is sorry **she did not do it**.* |

The adverb **ne** is sometimes found alone (its auxiliary complement **pas** being omitted) after the verbs **oser** (*to dare*), **cesser** (*to cease*), **savoir** (*to know*), and **pouvoir** (*to be able*), as well as after **voici/voilà...que**, **cela fait...que**, **il y a...que** (for a length of time).

| | |
|---|---|
| Elle **n'**ose partir sans demander permission. | *She does **not** dare leave without permission.* |
| Il **ne** cesse de neiger. | *It does **not** cease snowing.* |
| Je **ne** sais que dire. | *I do **not** know what to say.* |

| Il **ne** peut savoir cela. | He cannot know that. |
| Voici deux jours que je **n'**ai de réponse. | I have **not** had an answer for two days. |
| Cela fait un an que je **ne** le vois. | I have **not** seen him for a year. |

EXERCICE
**14·10**

*Rewrite each sentence changing the verb from the affirmative to the negative form. Use the negative adverbial expressions in parentheses, and be sure to place them correctly in the sentence.*

1. Joëlle sait toujours quoi dire. (ne...jamais)

_____

2. Elle ose dire la vérité. (ne...pas)

_____

3. Elle est timide. (ne...nullement)

_____

4. Mais elle a peur de *plaire* aux gens. (*Put* plaire *into the negative form using* ne...pas.)

_____

5. Elle a toujours été sûre d'elle-même. (ne...jamais)

_____

6. Elle s'est souvent opposée aux opinions de ses amis. (ne...pas)

_____

## Adverbs as modifiers of adjectives and other adverbs

In both English and French, adverbs sometimes serve to modify the meaning of adjectives and other adverbs. They are placed before the words they modify.

| **adverb + adjective** | **adverb + adverb** |
| assez + grand | très + patiemment |
| *pretty tall* | *very patiently* |

In the following sentences, note how the adverbs **assez, terriblement, très,** and **plutôt** modify the meaning of the adjectives:

| Il est **assez** grand pour son âge. | He is **pretty** tall for his age. |
| Je me suis sentie **terriblement** confuse. | I felt **terribly** embarrassed. |

In the the next sentences, the adverbs modify the meaning of another adverb:

| Il se comporte **très** gentiment. | He behaves **very** nicely. |
| Elle conduisait **plutôt** mal. | She was driving **rather** badly. |

The following is a list of some adverbs that often perform as modifiers of adjectives or other adverbs:

| assez | *pretty* | plus | *more* |
| aussi | *as* | plutôt | *rather* |

| | | | | |
|---|---|---|---|
| bien | *quite* | si | *so* |
| fort (*formal*) | *very* | très | *very* |
| moins | *less* | | |

| | |
|---|---|
| Il a neigé **si** longtemps que nous n'avons pas pu sortir. | *It snowed for **so** long that we have not been able to go out.* |
| Ce manteau est **aussi** chaud que l'autre. | *This coat is **as** warm as the other one.* |
| Il est **plus** grand qu'elle. | *He is tall**er** than her.* |
| Elle est **moins** exubérante aujourd'hui. | *She is **less** exuberant today.* |

EXERCICE
14·11

*Translate the following sentences into French.*

1. Isi is very strong. _____

2. Isa is quite pretty. _____

3. Isi is taller than Isa. _____

4. Isa is slimmer than Isi. _____

5. Isi is quite intelligent. _____

6. Isa is as intelligent as Isi. _____

# Adverbial phrases

In French and in English alike, adverbial phrases can have various positions in a sentence: at the beginning, at the end, or right after the verb. Therefore, use the same word order in French and in English when dealing with an adverbial phrase. Here are a few structural variations of adverbial phrases:

**adverbial phrase + subject + verb**

or

**subject + verb + adverbial phrase**

| | |
|---|---|
| Nous sommes sortis **tous les soirs**. | We went out **every night**. |
| Nous avons fait cela **à la main**. | We did that **by hand**. |
| Il est sorti **tout de même**. | He went out **anyway**. |
| Comporte-toi **comme il faut**! | Behave **properly**! |

Adverbial phrases always modify the meaning of a verb. They come in a great variety of composite structures. Following are a few common adverbial structures:

## Preposition + noun

An adverbial phrase can consist of a preposition and a noun or noun phrase.

| | | | |
|---|---|---|---|
| à bon marché | *cheaply* | d'une voix douce | *in a soft voice* |
| à bras ouverts | *with open arms* | d'une voix tranchante | *in a cutting voice* |
| à contrecœur | *reluctantly* | de jour | *during the day* |
| à la main | *by hand* | de nuit | *at night* |

| | | | |
|---|---|---|---|
| à plat ventre | *flat on the belly* | de préférence | *preferably* |
| à reculons | *backward* | en avance | *early* |
| à voix basse | *in a low voice* | en retard | *late* |
| à voix haute | *aloud* | sans cesse | *incessantly* |
| avec plaisir | *with pleasure* | | |

| | |
|---|---|
| L'invitation est écrite **à la main**. | *The invitation is **hand written**.* |
| Nous avons été accueillis **à bras ouverts**. | *We were **welcomed with open arms**.* |
| Elle est tombée **à plat ventre**. | *She fell **flat on the ground**.* |
| Ils parlent **sans cesse**. | *They speak **incessantly**.* |
| Je lirai **à voix haute**. | *I will read **aloud**.* |
| Ma montre est **en avance**. | *My watch is **fast**.* |
| Le petit garçon marche **à reculons**. | *The little boy walks **backward**.* |
| L'homme d'affaires a signé **à contrecœur**. | *The businessman signed **reluctantly**.* |
| Elle pense à lui **de jour** et **de nuit**. | *She thinks about him **day** and **night**.* |

**EXERCICE**
**14·12**

*Write L (**Logique**) or PL (**Pas logique**) on the lines according to whether the following statements are logical or not.*

1. _____ Elle est timide. Elle parle à voix haute.

2. _____ Il a beaucoup à dire. Il parle sans cesse.

3. _____ Elle voulait vendre sa maison. Elle a signé le contrat de vente à contrecœur.

4. _____ Il était heureux de nous revoir. Il nous a accueillis à bras ouverts.

5. _____ Il est dix heures dix mais sur ma montre il est dix heures. Elle est en avance.

6. _____ Mon lave-vaisselle ne marche pas. Je lave mes assiettes à la main.

## Avec + noun

This structure is often used to add emphasis to the manner in which something is done and replaces a simple adverb, for example, **avec franchise** (*with frankness*) is used instead of **franchement** (*frankly*).

| | | | |
|---|---|---|---|
| avec courtoisie | *with courtesy* | avec joie | *with joy* |
| avec élégance | *with elegance* | avec précision | *with precision* |
| avec franchise | *with frankness* | avec soin | *with attention/care* |

| | |
|---|---|
| Ecoute! Je te parle **avec franchise**. | *Listen! I am speaking to you **in all frankness**.* |
| Ce travail se fait **avec précision**. | *This work is done **with precision**.* |
| On parle aux gens **avec courtoisie**. | *One **uses courtesy** when speaking to people.* |
| Elle marche **avec élégance**. | *She walks **with elegance**.* |
| J'écris **avec soin**. | *I write **with care**.* |

*Use an adverbial phrase that includes* **avec** *to complete each sentence.*

1. Une personne honnête parle _____ .

2. Une personne polie agit _____ .

3. Une personne minutieuse fait les choses _____ .

4. Une personne élégante s'habille _____ .

5. Une personne diligente fait tout _____ .

6. Une personne patiente vous traite _____ .

## D'un air/ton or d'une façon/manière + adjective

This structure is often used to clarify whether it is the demeanor, look, appearance, or tone that is being described. Sometimes this structure replaces a simple adverb, for example, **d'un air familier** (*with a familiar look*) is used instead of **familièrement** (*in a familiar manner*).

| | | | |
|---|---|---|---|
| d'un air doux | *in a sweet way* | → | doucement |
| d'un air familier | *in a familiar manner* | → | familièrement |
| d'un air insouciant | *with a carefree look* | → | insouciamment |
| d'un air naïf | *in a naïve way* | → | naïvement |
| d'un air triste | *with a sad look* | → | tristement |
| d'un ton coléreux | *in an angry tone* | → | coléreusement |
| d'un ton méchant | *in a mean tone* | → | méchamment |

Other times, these phrases cannot be replaced by a simple adverb:

| | |
|---|---|
| d'un air blagueur | *in a joking way* |
| d'un air conciliatoire | *in a conciliatory manner* |
| d'un air songeur | *in a pensive manner* |
| d'une façon déroutante | *in a confusing way* |
| d'une façon rusée | *in a cunning way* |
| d'une manière accueillante | *in a welcoming manner* |

| | |
|---|---|
| Il la regarde **d'un air familier**. | *He looks at her **in a familiar way**.* |
| Elle le salue **d'un air triste**. | *She greets him **with a sad look**.* |
| Il m'a parlé **d'un ton coléreux**. | *He spoke to me **in an angry tone**.* |
| Ils m'ont accueilli **d'une manière accueillante**. | *They received me **in a welcoming manner**./ They **welcomed** me.* |
| Il a donné l'explication **d'une façon déroutante**. | *He gave the explanation **in a confusing way**./ He gave a **confusing** explanation.* |

*When appropriate, replace the italicized phrases with simple adverbs. If there is no such adverb, write X on the line.*

Il était une fois une petite fille qui se dirigeait (1) _____ (*d'un air insouciant*) vers la maison de sa grand-mère. En chemin, elle rencontra le loup qui la regarda (2) _____ (*d'un air familier*) et lui parla (3) _____ (*d'un ton doux*). La petite fille l'écouta (4) _____ (*d'un air naïf*). Il lui demanda (5) _____ (*d'un air blagueur*) s'il pouvait l'accompagner. Elle lui répondit que oui (6) _____ (*d'un air très conciliatoire*). Mais la petite rusée l'emmena tout droit à la maison du garde forestier qui lui dit (7) _____ (*d'un ton coléreux*) de retourner au plus vite dans la forêt.

*Replace the following adverbs with adverbial phrases that are synonymous. Use expressions such as **d'un air....***

1. tristement _____

2. élégamment _____

3. furieusement _____

4. joyeusement _____

5. soigneusement _____

6. franchement _____

Note the following adverbial phrases that consist of a preposition and an adjective:

| à présent | *presently* | en particulier | *particularly* |
|---|---|---|---|
| en général | *generally* | en premier | *first* |

**À présent**, j'habite en France.      ***Presently**, I live in France.*
**En général**, je fais très attention.      ***Generally**, I pay attention.*
J'aime les fruits, les fraises **en particulier**.      *I like fruit, strawberries **in particular**.*
Je voudrais présenter **en premier**.      *I would like to present **first**.*

And now note how the following examples of prepositional phrases can serve the function of adverbs:

| à jamais | *forever* | en bas | *downstairs/below* |
|---|---|---|---|
| au-dessous | *below* | en haut | *upstairs/above* |
| au-dessus | *above* | par contre | *on the other hand* |
| de plus | *in addition* | pour toujours | *forever* |

| | | | |
|---|---|---|---|
| Voilà ton cadeau. **De plus**, je t'invite à dîner. | *There is your gift!* ***In addition**, I am inviting you to dinner.* | | |

Le lecteur de DVD est **au-dessous**.      *The DVD player is **down below**.*
Je garderai ce souvenir **pour toujours**.      *I will keep this souvenir **forever**.*
**Par contre**, je préfère oublier cet incident.      ***On the other hand**, I prefer to forget this incident.*

The following are examples of noun phrases serving the function of adverbs:

| | | | |
|---|---|---|---|
| certains jours | *some (certain) days* | nulle part | *nowhere* |
| maintes fois | *numerous times* | tous les soirs | *every night* |

Tu regardes les nouvelles **tous les soirs**.      *You watch the news **every night**.*
**Certains jours** je travaille.      ***On certain days** I work.*
Je ne trouve mon portable **nulle part**.      *I cannot find my cell phone **anywhere**.*
Je t'ai dit **maintes fois** de le ranger.      *I told you **numerous times** to put it away.*

And here are a few more noun phrases that serve as adverbs:

| | | | |
|---|---|---|---|
| tout à coup | *suddenly* | tout d'abord | *first of all* |
| tout à fait | *entirely* | tout de même | *anyway* |
| tout à l'heure | *in a little while* | tout de suite | *right away* |

**Tout à coup**, je me sens mieux.      ***Suddenly** I feel better.*
**Tout d'abord**, faisons nos devoirs!      ***First of all**, let's do our homework!*
Je vais venir **tout de suite**.      *I am going to come **right away**.*
Il pleut mais je sors **tout de même**.      *It is raining, but I am going out **anyway**.*
Il avait **tout à fait** raison.      *He was **entirely** right.*
Téléphone-moi **tout à l'heure**!      *Call me **in a little while**!*

**EXERCICE**
**14·16**

*Fill in each blank with an adverbial phrase from the list.*

de plus / par contre / ensemble / longtemps / avec courtoisie / en particulier / là-bas / en général / ensuite / en force / d'abord / à bon marché

1. Les Robert ont décidé de faire un voyage en Corse tous _____ .

2. _____ ils vont écrire au syndicat d'initiative.

3. _____ ils écriront à l'oncle Julius qui habite _____ .

4. L'oncle Julius habite la Corse depuis _____ .

5. Il sera content de voir arriver sa famille _____

6. Cela permettra aux Robert de passer des vacances _____ car il n'y aura pas de note d'hôtel.

7. _____ c'est toujours mieux de visiter un endroit avec les gens des environs.

8. _____ les habitants d'une région connaissent tous les coins et les recoins de l'endroit, _____ les restaurants et les cafés sympa.

9. _____ , comme il a un âge avancé, est-ce qu'il connaîtra les boîtes de nuit?

10. Ils lui demanderont cela _____ .

**EXERCICE**
**14·17**

*Write this postcard text in French. Use the suggested vocabulary and beware of the placement of adverbs.*

Dear friend, I am having so much fun here in France (**s'amuser**). You have no idea (**ne pas avoir idée**) how much (**combien de**) culture and history I am learning. I will be much more knowledgeable (**avoir des connaissances**) when I finish this trip. I am so happy to be here (**heureux d'être ici**) and have no regrets at all (**regret**) that I am spending so much money. French people are very polite and welcoming (**polis et accueillants**). You cannot imagine (**imaginer**) how enriching this trip is (**enrichissant**)! See you soon!

_____

_____

_____

_____

_____

_____

# ·15· Using prepositions and prepositional phrases

## Prepositions

Prepositions help link words and establish relationships between them. They can be single words such as **à** (*at, to, in*), **de** (*from, of*), and **pour** (*to, in order to*); these are called simple prepositions. They can also be compound phrases such as **afin de** (*in order to*) and **grâce à** (*thanks to*); these are called complex prepositions. Here are some examples of simple and complex prepositions:

| SIMPLE PREPOSITIONS | | COMPLEX PREPOSITIONS | |
|---|---|---|---|
| à | *at, in, to* | à cause de | *because of* |
| après | *after* | à côté de | *next to* |
| avant (de) | *before* | à propos de | *regarding* |
| chez | *at/to someone's place* | au centre de | *in the center of* |
| contre | *against* | au-delà de | *beyond* |
| dans | *in* | au-dessous de | *underneath* |
| de | *of, from* | au-dessus de | *above, over* |
| en | *in, of, on* | au lieu de | *instead of* |
| entre | *between* | au milieu de | *in the middle of* |
| jusque | *until* | au sujet de | *concerning* |
| malgré | *in spite of* | de la part de | *from* |
| pendant | *during* | de peur de | *for fear of* |
| pour | *for* | en face de | *across from* |
| sans | *without* | grâce à | *thanks to* |
| sous | *under* | loin de | *far from* |
| sur | *on* | près de | *near* |
| vers | *toward* | quant à | *as for* |

Consider the following sentences that include prepositional phrases:

| | |
|---|---|
| Je n'ai rien **contre toi**. | *I have nothing **against you**.* |
| Il est **à l'école**. | *He is **at school**.* |
| J'habite **à Miami**. | *I live **in Miami**.* |
| **Grâce à mes parents** j'ai fini mes études. | ***Thanks to my parents**, I finished my studies.* |
| Il s'est arrêté **au milieu de la rue**. | *He stopped **in the middle of the street**.* |
| Je dois te parler **au sujet de la réunion**. | *I have to talk to you **about the meeting**.* |

Remember that the preposition **à** as well as any complex preposition that has **à** as its second component must contract with the article **le** to produce **au** and with the article **les** to produce **aux**.

| | |
|---|---|
| Je vais **au marché**. | *I am going **to the market**.* |
| Ils sont **aux îles Seychelles**. | *They are **in the Seychelles Islands**.* |
| **Grâce aux dons**, ils ont atteint leur but. | ***Thanks to the gifts**, they reached their goal.* |
| Je serai là. **Quant aux autres**, je ne sais pas. | *I will be there. **As for the others**, I do not know.* |

Similarly, the preposition **de** as well as any complex preposition that has **de** as its second component must contract with the article **le** to produce **du** and with the article **les** to produce **des**.

| | |
|---|---|
| L'agent est **au milieu du carrefour**. | *The policeman is **in the middle of the intersection**.* |
| Ton sac à dos est **au-dessous du mien**. | *Your backpack is **below mine**.* |
| Ce train circule **au-delà des banlieues**. | *This train runs **beyond the suburbs**.* |
| Cette conférence est **au sujet de la poésie**. | *This conference is **about poetry**.* |

# Prepositional phrases

Many sentences include one or more prepositional phrases. A prepositional phrase consists of a preposition followed by a noun (sometimes accompanied by an adjective), a pronoun, or an adverb. Prepositional phrases are powerful tools in building sentences as they provide supporting details.

**preposition + noun**
en + banlieue
Elle aime vivre **en banlieue**.  *She likes living **in the suburbs**.*

**preposition + pronoun**
chez + moi
Dînons **chez moi**!  *Let's have dinner **at my house**!*

**preposition + adverb**
près d' + ici
Je connais un bon café **près d'ici**.  *I know a good café **near here**.*

When a prepositional phrase includes a verb as in the following example, it is an infinitive clause. You may review Unit 10 for more on infinitive clauses introduced by prepositions.

**preposition + verb → prepositional clause**
Téléphone **au lieu d'écrire**!  *Call **instead of writing**!*

**EXERCICE**

**15·1**

*Identify the prepositional phrase(s) in each sentence by underlining it/them.*

1. J'allais faire un séjour chez ma tante Irène en France.

2. À la dernière minute tante Irène a décidé de m'emmener en Italie.

3. J'ai donc pris l'avion pour Rome au lieu de celui pour Paris.

4. À côté de moi, il y avait un jeune homme très sympa.

5. Nous avons beaucoup bavardé en cours de route.

6. Pendant le voyage, nous avons appris à nous connaître.

7. À la fin du voyage, nous étions amis.

8. C'est grâce à ma tante Irène que je l'ai rencontré.

___

EXERCICE

15·2

*Reconstruct each sentence by placing the fragments in the appropriate order.*

1. au marché / est allé / Luc / pour / acheter / des légumes

___

2. sa copine Mireille / a rencontré / il / des salades / devant / le stand

___

3. ils / leurs achats / ont fait / beaucoup discuter / sans

___

4. puis / ils / du coin / sont allés / au café

___

5. au sujet / les deux amis / ont eu / de vacances / une discussion / d'un projet

___

6. chez eux / puis / ils / sont rentrés

___

# Using the prepositions à, chez, de, and en

These prepositions are among the most frequently used prepositions in the French language. They are often used to express possession or to indicate locations.

## Using à and de to express possession

The prepositional phrase **à** + noun/stress pronoun following the verb **être** helps build sentences in which something belongs to someone. See Unit 12 to review stress pronouns.

**subject + être + à + noun or stress pronoun**
Ce chien + est + à + mon voisin.
Ce chien est **à mon voisin**.                This dog belongs **to my neighbor**.
Cette voiture est **à ma mère**.              This car belongs **to my mother**.
Ce livre est **à moi**.                       This book belongs **to me**.
Il n'est pas **à toi**.                       It does not belong **to you**.
Cette montre est **à lui**.                   This watch belongs **to him**.

The prepositional phrase **de** + noun helps build phrases that express possession.

**noun + de + noun**
la maison + de + Ginette
la maison **de Ginette**            *Ginette's* house
le sac **d'Ariane**                 *Ariane's* purse
le pull **de sa sœur**              *her sister's* sweater
les clefs **de la maison**          *the keys of the house*

## EXERCICE 15·3

*Using the English as a guide, complete each sentence in French.*

1. This is Luc's house.

   C'est la maison _____.

2. It belonged to his father.

   Elle était _____.

3. But now it belongs to him.

   Mais maintenant elle est _____.

4. The roof of the house is very old.

   _____ est très vieux.

5. He will repair it when he gets the deed of the house.

   Il le fera réparer quand il recevra l'acte notarié _____.

6. The town's only construction company belongs to his cousin.

   La seule entreprise de construction _____.

## EXERCICE 15·4

*Using the verb **être** followed by the preposition **à**, build sentences in which you say that an object belongs to the person(s) in parentheses.*

1. la poupée (Suzette) _____

2. le sac à dos (l'alpiniste) _____

3. le couteau (le boucher) _____

4. les valises (les passagers) _____

5. le sac à main (la dame) _____

6. la Peugeot (M. Lemaire) _____

# Using à and de to express purpose or quality

Some prepositional phrases including **à** serve to express the purpose for which something is intended.

**noun + à + noun**

le sac + à + dos

| | |
|---|---|
| Où est ma brosse **à dents**? | *Where is my **tooth**brush?* |
| Il nous faut une boîte **aux lettres**. | *We need a **mail**box.* |
| Donne-moi une cuillère **à soupe**. | *Give me a **soup** spoon.* |
| Cherche la planche **à repasser**! | *Look for the **ironing** board!* |
| Voilà la canne **à pêche**! | *There is the **fishing** line!* |

Some prepositional phrases including **de** are used to indicate the material out of which something is made.

**noun + de/d' + noun**

les gants + de + laine

| | |
|---|---|
| J'aime les gants **de laine**. | *I like **woolen** gloves.* |
| Elle préfère les tasses **de porcelaine**. | *She prefers **china** cups.* |
| Regarde ce joli vase **de cristal**! | *Look at this pretty **crystal** vase!* |
| C'est une clôture **de fer**. | *It is an **iron** gate.* |

Note that the preposition **en** is often used in the same way as **de** for materials.

les gants **de laine** = les gants **en laine**
les tasses **de porcelaine** = les tasses **en porcelaine**
le vase **de cristal** = le vase **en cristal**
la clôture **de fer** = la clôture **en fer**

---

**EXERCICE**
## 15·5

*On the lines provided, write the letter of the correct translation for each item on the left.*

1. _____ a teaspoon
2. _____ a coffee cup
3. _____ a washing machine
4. _____ a coffee grinder
5. _____ a laundry pin
6. _____ a steamboat

a. une épingle à linge
b. une machine à laver
c. un bateau à vapeur
d. une tasse à café
e. une cuillère à thé
f. un moulin à café

---

**EXERCICE**
## 15·6

*Use the appropriate preposition and a word from the list to complete each sentence.*

cristal / or / soie / caoutchouc / laine / bois

1. J'ai une jolie robe _____.

2. Tu as un beau pull _____.

---

3. Ces pneus _____ sont pour la bicyclette.

4. Ces vases _____ sont très chers.

5. Ces bijoux _____ sont magnifiques.

6. Cette cuillère _____ sert à mélanger la salade.

## Using à and de to tell time

In formal settings, the French use the twenty-four-hour clock to indicate the time of day, but in familiar conversation they use twelve hours as we do. See how the following prepositional phrases correspond to the English terminology of A.M. or P.M.

Il s'est réveillé à une heure **du matin.**   *He woke up at one o'clock **in the morning.***
Le goûter est à trois heures **de l'après-midi.**   *The snack is at three o'clock **in the afternoon.***
Je rentre à six heures **du soir.**   *I get home at six **in the evening.***

The prepositions **à** and **de** are used to express **at** and **from** a specific time.

Le cours commence **à huit heures.**   *The class starts **at eight o'clock.***
Il se termine **à 10 h 30.**   *It ends **at 10:30.***
Elle travaille **de midi à minuit.**   *She works **from noon till midnight.***

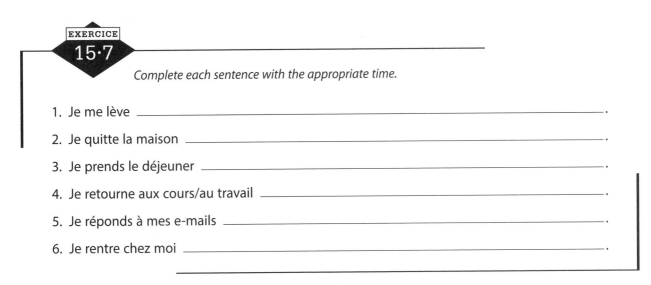

EXERCICE
15·7

*Complete each sentence with the appropriate time.*

1. Je me lève _____.

2. Je quitte la maison _____.

3. Je prends le déjeuner _____.

4. Je retourne aux cours/au travail _____.

5. Je réponds à mes e-mails _____.

6. Je rentre chez moi _____.

## Using à, en, chez, and de to indicate location

The prepositional phrase **à** + place helps indicate *where*. Remember to contract the preposition **à** with the article **le** (→ **au**) and with the article **les** (→ **aux**).

à l'école          *in/to school*
au coin           *on/to the corner*
au bureau         *at/to the office*
aux champs        *in/to the fields*
à la plage        *at/to the beach*

| à la gare | at/to the train station |
| à la maison | at home/home |

Prepositional phrases including **à/au/aux** and **de/du/des** as well as **en** are used to indicate geographical areas, destinations, and origination points.

| Elle habite **à New York**. | *She lives **in New York**.* |
| Je vais **au Canada**. | *I am going **to Canada**.* |
| Ils sont **au Québec**. | *They are **in Québec**.* |
| Nous allons **en France**. | *We are going **to France**.* |
| Je pars **en Alsace**. | *I am leaving **for Alsace**.* |
| Ils habitent **en Australie**. | *They live **in Australia**.* |
| Elle vit **en Algérie**. | *She lives **in Algeria**.* |
| Il est **de Bordeaux**. | *He is **from Bordeaux**.* |
| Elle revient **de Bruxelles**. | *She is coming back **from Brussels**.* |
| Nous revenons **d'Asie**. | *We are back **from Asia**.* |
| Elle vient **du Québec**. | *She comes **from Québec**. (province)* |
| Elles sont **des États-Unis**. | *They are **from the United States**.* |

The prepositional phrase **chez** + noun/stress pronoun serves to express *at* or *to* someone's residence or place of business.

| J'ai rendez-vous **chez le médecin**. | *I have an appointment **at the doctor's**.* |
| Rejoins-moi **chez Denise**! | *Meet me **at Denise's**!* |
| C'est très joli **chez elle**. | *It is very pretty **at her house**.* |
| Ce café s'appelle **Chez Philippe**. | *This café's name is **At Philip's**.* |
| Je vais **chez mes grands-parents**. | *I am going **to my grandparents' house**.* |
| Téléphone-moi **chez eux**. | *Call me **at their house**.* |
| Demain je resterai **chez nous**. | *Tomorrow I will stay at **our house**.* |

**EXERCICE**

## 15·8

*Complete each sentence appropriately, using translations of the words in parentheses.*

1. On trouve du pâté de foie gras _____. (*in Alsace*)

2. On fait du champagne _____. (*in Champagne*)

3. On trouve la Tour Eiffel _____. (*in Paris*)

4. Le Conseil de l'Europe se trouve _____. (*in Strasbourg*)

5. Le Festival du Film a lieu _____. (*in Cannes*)

6. La ville de Marseilles est _____. (*in Provence*)

7. On mange un couscous excellent _____. (*in Algeria*)

8. Il y a un beau festival de neige _____. (*in Montreal*)

*Complete each sentence by telling where the people just came from.*

1. Il est New Yorkais. Il vient d'arriver _____ .

2. Elle est allemande. Elle vient d'arriver _____ .

3. Il est mexicain. Il vient d'arriver _____ .

4. Elle est australienne. Elle vient d'arriver _____ .

5. Ils sont parisiens. Ils viennent d'arriver _____ .

6. Elle est suisse. Elle vient d'arriver _____ .

# Using à and en for transportation

Prepositional phrases **à** and **en** + noun are often used with means of transportation.

| | |
|---|---|
| Jean va au gym **à pied**. | *Jean goes to the gym **on foot**.* |
| Mireille part en vacances **en train**. | *Mireille leaves on vacation **by train**.* |
| Je vais au Louvre **en métro**. | *I am going to the Louvre **by subway**.* |
| Il va en Tunisie **en avion**. | *He goes to Tunisia **by plane**.* |
| Marie va au travail **en bus**. | *Marie goes to work **by bus**.* |
| Quelquefois elle y va **à vélo/en vélo**. | *Sometimes she goes there **by bike**.* |

*Tell where each location is and how you get there from where you live.*

EXAMPLE:     Québec est <u>au Canada</u>. J'y vais <u>en avion</u>.

1. Paris est _____ . J'y vais _____ .

2. Washington, D.C. est _____ . J'y vais _____ .

3. Mexico City est _____ . J'y vais _____ .

4. La statue de la Liberté est _____ . J'y vais _____ .

5. L'Alamo est _____ . J'y vais _____ .

6. Mon café préféré est _____ . J'y vais _____ .

# Varying structures and word order in prepositional phrases

Complete sentences often include a variety of prepositional phrases such as preposition + noun, e.g., **en soie** (*out of silk*); preposition + pronoun, e.g., **chez moi** (*at my house*); preposition + verb, e.g., **pour aimer** (*in order to love*); preposition + adverb, e.g., **près d'ici** (*near here*).

## Prepositional phrases including nouns

There are numerous prepositional noun phrases. Generally these will occupy the same position in French and in English. Consider the following sentence:

| | |
|---|---|
| Il est parti **à l'école en voiture avec son copain Marc avant huit heures**. | *He left **for school by car with his friend Marc before eight o'clock**.* |

There are four prepositional phrases in this sentence. They serve to establish where, how, around what time, and with whom someone left. The prepositions used in this sentence link the compound verb **est parti** to various *nouns*:

- **À** introduces a place: **l'école**
- **En** introduces a means of transportation: **voiture**
- **Avec** introduces a companion: **son copain**
- **Avant** introduces a time: **huit heures**

| | |
|---|---|
| Nous allons **au cours du soir à la Sorbonne**. | *We attend **night classes at the Sorbonne**.* |
| **Pour tes amis**, tu ferais tout. | ***For your friends**, you would do everything.* |
| **Après le concert**, on ira boire un pot. | ***After the concert**, we'll go for a drink.* |
| On se tutoie **entre copains**. | *We use the **tu** form **between friends**.* |
| Il adore se promener **en moped avec sa copine**. | *He loves to go for a ride **on his moped with his girlfriend**.* |
| **Pendant les vacances**, on s'amuse **du matin au soir**. | ***During vacation**, we have fun **day and night**.* |

Be aware that a French prepositional phrase does not necessarily translate as a prepositional phrase in English. In French there are verbs that are always followed by a preposition (thereby introducing a prepositional phrase), whereas their English counterparts are not followed by a preposition (these are often followed by a direct object—not a prepositional phrase).

| **verb + prepositional phrase** | **verb + direct object** |
|---|---|
| Tu joues + **du violon**. | *You play + **the violin**.* |

The phrase *to play the violin* includes *no* preposition in English, but the phrase **jouer du violon** includes the preposition **de**, which contracts with the article **le** to produce **du** (or with the article **les** to produce **des**). Many **faire** idioms include the preposition **de** in French, whereas the English translation does not.

| | |
|---|---|
| Elles font **de la musique**. | *They are playing **music**.* |
| Ils font **du camping**. | *They are **camping**.* |
| Nous faisons **des mathématiques**. | *We are studying **mathematics**.* |
| On fait **du yoga**. | *We are doing **yoga**.* |
| Je fais **de l'exercice**. | *I am **exercising**.* |

Similarly, some French verbs are followed by the preposition **à**, which contracts with the article **le** to produce **au** and with the article **les** to produce **aux**.

| | |
|---|---|
| Nous jouons **aux cartes**. | *We play **cards**.* |
| Elle roule **à vélo**. | *She rides **the bike**.* |

| | |
|---|---|
| Tu as réussi **à l'examen**. | *You passed **the exam**.* |
| Vous assisterez **à la conférence**. | *You will attend **the conference**.* |
| Je ne peux pas renoncer **à ce voyage**. | *I cannot give up **this trip**.* |

On the other hand, there are verbs that are followed by a preposition in English (thereby introducing a prepositional phrase), whereas their French counterparts are not followed by a preposition (these are followed by a direct object—not a prepositional phrase).

| **verb + direct object** | **verb + prepositional phrase** |
|---|---|
| Je cherche + **un restaurant**. | *I am looking + **for a restaurant**.* |
| Nous regardons **le mannequin**. | *We are looking **at the model**.* |
| Ils écoutent **la radio**. | *They listen **to the radio**.* |

In addition, be aware of phrases such as **le cours du soir** (*the night class*). These prepositional phrases (which include two nouns) follow reverse word order in the English translation from French. When you encounter them, remember that the French phrase will position the main idea (the fact that it is a class) in first place followed by the detail (it is offered at night):

| FRENCH WORD ORDER | ENGLISH WORD ORDER |
|---|---|
| **main idea + detail/description** | **detail/description + main idea** |
| **le cours** + du soir | *the night + **class*** |

Note how *class* (**cours**) comes before *night* (**soir**) in the French phrase whereas it is the opposite in the English phrase. Here are some other examples of such prepositional phrases:

| | |
|---|---|
| la salle de bains | *the bathroom* |
| le livre de français | *the French book* |
| la classe de mathématiques | *the mathematics class* |
| la machine à laver | *the washing machine* |
| la cuillère à café | *the coffee spoon* |
| la glace à la vanille | *vanilla ice cream* |

**EXERCICE**

**15·11**

*Complete each sentence with a preposition only when necessary. Place an X on the line when no preposition is needed.*

1. Marc a perdu son équipement de tennis. Il cherche ses chaussures _____ tennis depuis ce matin.

2. Il doit _____ écouter sa mère. Elle lui dit toujours de les ranger.

3. Il va téléphoner _____ son copain Nicolas pour voir s'il les a vus.

4. Nicolas est en train de regarder _____ un match de foot au stade.

5. Marc ne peut donc pas jouer _____ tennis aujourd'hui. Zut!

6. Par contre, il peut jouer _____ piano. Il a un récital le mois prochain.

*Express the following ideas in French. Beware of word order.*

1. *the French class*: français/classe _____

2. *the living room*: séjour/salle _____

3. *the fruit salad*: fruits/salade _____

4. *the book index*: matières/table _____

5. *the essay topic*: essai/sujet _____

6. *the math problem*: maths/problème _____

## Prepositional phrases that include pronouns

Prepositional phrases may include stress pronouns such as **moi**, demonstrative pronouns such as **celui-ci**, possessive pronouns such as **le mien**, and interrogative pronouns such as **quoi**.

| | |
|---|---|
| Il est juste **en face de moi**. | *He is just **across from me**.* |
| Assieds-toi **entre nous**! | *Sit **between us**!* |
| **Pour eux**, tout va très bien. | ***For them**, all is very well.* |
| **Chez vous**, on discute beaucoup. | ***At your house**, there is a lot of discussion.* |
| Elle ne peut pas vivre **sans lui**. | *She cannot live **without him**.* |
| **Entre ceux-ci**, je préfère celui-ci. | ***Among those**, I prefer this one.* |
| Mets ta main **dans la mienne**! | *Put your hand **into mine**!* |
| **De quoi** parles-tu? | ***What** are you talking **about**?* |
| **Avec qui** sors-tu? | ***With whom** are you going out?* |

Once again, beware of making appropriate contractions whenever the prepositions **à** and **de** or complex prepositions including **à** or **de** are followed by the articles **le** and **les**.

| | |
|---|---|
| **Par rapport aux nôtres**, ces dessins sont beaux. | ***Compared with ours**, these drawings are beautiful.* |
| Il est toujours gentil **à l'égard des siens**. | *He is always nice **toward his own** (people).* |

## Prepositional phrases that include adverbs

A preposition may also introduce other function words such as adverbs. This type of prepositional phrase is often idiomatic.

| | |
|---|---|
| Tu habites **près d'ici**. | *You live **near here**.* |
| La poste n'est pas **loin de là**. | *The post office is not **far from there**.* |
| Je m'en vais. **À bientôt**! | *I am leaving. **See you soon**!* |
| Bon! **À demain**! | *Good! **See you tomorrow**!* |
| **En/De plus**, tu ne réponds jamais. | ***In addition**, you never answer.* |

**EXERCICE**

**15·13**

*Complete each sentence appropriately, using translations of the words in parentheses. Use the familiar **tu** form for* you *when necessary.*

1. J'ai garé ma voiture _____ la tienne. (*next to*)

2. Je suis _____. (*at your house*)

3. Où es-tu? Je t'attends. Je ne veux pas aller au concert _____. (*without you*)

4. J'ai deux billets et j'ai payé très cher _____. (*for these tickets*)

5. _____ j'adore ce groupe. (*In addition*)

6. Ah bon! Tu es _____. (*at your neighbor's*)

7. Heureusement que tu n'es pas _____. (*far from here*)

8. _____ parlez-vous? (*Of what*)

9. Rentre vite! Il peut venir _____ s'il veut. (*with us*)

10. Non? Alors dis-lui _____! (*See you soon*)


**EXERCICE**

**15·14**

*Read the following paragraph, then answer the questions in complete sentences. Be sure to include prepositional phrases such as **à la maison** (at home).*

Paul habite à Québec, au Canada. Il vit encore chez ses parents. Il arrive au bureau à 9 h moins 10. Il travaille chaque jour de 9 h du matin à 5 h du soir. Le lundi il va à l'université où il suit des cours de programmeur. Les autres jours il rentre chez lui. Quelquefois il voyage aux États-Unis pour rencontrer des clients.

1. Dans quelle ville habite Paul?

_____

2. Dans quel pays est la ville de Québec?

_____

3. Où est-ce qu'il vit encore?

_____

4. Où est-ce qu'il va chaque matin?

_____

5. À quelle heure est-ce qu'il commence à travailler?

_____

6. Où est-ce qu'il va le lundi après le travail?

_____

7. Où est-ce qu'il va les autres jours après le travail?

   _____

8. Où est-ce qu'il voyage quelquefois?

   _____

*Write a short description of where you live and what your daily routine is like. Follow the suggested guidelines in the vocabulary provided.*

La ville où j'habite / le pays où est la ville / là où je vis maintenant / où je vais chaque matin / à quelle heure je quitte la maison / où je vais après le travail ou les cours

1. _____

2. _____

3. _____

4. _____

5. _____

6. _____

# Using present and past participles

·16·

## Participial clauses

Clauses are called participial when they include either a present participle (also called a gerund) or a past participle. These structures are rather formal and more frequently used in writing than in speaking. Consider the following examples of participial clauses:

>**gerund + direct object**
>**ayant** + cours
>*having* class

>**past participle + prepositional phrase**
>**arrivé** + à l'aéroport
>*arrived* at the airport

| | |
|---|---|
| **Ayant cours** à huit heures, elle s'est levée tôt. | ***Having class*** *at eight o'clock, she got up early.* |
| **Arrivée** à l'heure au cours, elle était soulagée. | ***Having arrived*** *on time to class, she was relieved.* |

## Using a gerund

Gerunds such as **faisant** (*doing*) are used in French and in English whenever the action of the participial clause takes place at the same time as the action in the main clause—both actions might take place in the present, past, or future. The gerund is formed by dropping the **-ons** ending from the first-person plural (**nous**) form of the verb in the present tense and replacing it with **-ant** (excepting the irregular verbs **avoir, être,** and **savoir**):

>aller → nous all**ons** → all → all**ant**
>choisir → nous choisiss**ons** → choisiss → choisiss**ant**
>attendre → nous attend**ons** → attend → attend**ant**

Examples of simple gerunds are as follows:

| | | | |
|---|---|---|---|
| allant | *going* | descendant | *going down* |
| ayant | *having* | étant | *being* |
| cherchant | *looking for* | faisant | *doing* |
| choisissant | *choosing* | perdant | *losing* |
| comprenant | *understanding* | sachant | *knowing* |

Gerunds are more frequently used in writing than in speaking. They are used to emphasize cause-and-effect relationships or simultaneity of actions when the subject is the same in both the main and dependent clauses.

**Faisant trop de fautes**, il s'est arrêté.     *Making too many mistakes, he stopped.*
**Passant devant ta maison**, j'ai décidé de     *Passing in front of your house, I decided to*
    te rendre visite.     *pay you a visit.*

Note that a less formal approach would consist in using a subordinate clause instead of a participial clause.

**Faisant** trop de fautes     *making too many mistakes*
= **parce qu'il faisait** trop de fautes     *because he was making too many mistakes*

**Passant** devant ta maison     *passing in front of your house*
= **au moment où je passais** devant ta maison     *at the time I was passing in front of your house*

EXERCICE
16·1

*Complete each sentence with the gerund of the verb in parentheses.*

1. Anne veut s'arrêter à la pharmacie en _____ en ville. (aller)

2. Elle s'est écorchée le genou en _____ dans l'escalier. (tomber)

3. C'est en _____ qu'elle a raté une marche. (se dépêcher)

4. Pauvre Anne! Elle aurait dû faire attention en _____. (descendre)

5. Elle aurait pu éviter cet accident en _____ la rampe. (saisir)

6. Enfin! En _____ bien, cela peut arriver à n'importe qui. (réfléchir)

EXERCICE
16·2

*Replace each subordinate clause with a gerund.*

1. parce que je sais = _____

2. parce que nous préparons = _____

3. parce que je passe = _____

4. parce que nous avons = _____

5. parce que tu es = _____

6. parce que nous ne pouvons pas = _____

*Complete each sentence with one of the answers you provided in exercise 16-2.*

1. _____ dans ta rue en chemin pour la bibliothèque, je m'arrête chez toi.

2. _____ mon meilleur ami, tu es toujours prêt à m'aider.

3. _____ un examen d'anglais lundi, nous devons réviser nos notes.

4. _____ le bac littérature, c'est une matière importante pour nous.

5. _____ rater le bac, il faut travailler comme des fous.

6. _____ qu'il ne reste que quelques mois avant le bac, j'ai encore un peu de courage.

## Using a past gerund

Gerunds in their compound form such as **ayant fait** (*having done*) are used in French and in English whenever the action of the participial clause clearly precedes the action in the main clause. A past gerund compound form consists in the auxiliary verb **ayant** or **étant** followed by a *past participle*. Consider the following list of past gerund forms using **ayant**:

| | | | |
|---|---|---|---|
| ayant cherché | *having looked for* | ayant fait | *having done* |
| ayant choisi | *having chosen* | ayant perdu | *having lost* |
| ayant été | *having been* | ayant pris | *having taken* |
| ayant eu | *having had* | | |

In the following sentences, note that the action expressed in the gerund precedes the action in the main clause:

| | |
|---|---|
| **Ayant réfléchi à la situation**, elle est prête à prendre une décision. | *Having reflected upon the situation, she is ready to make a decision.* |
| **Ayant pris la mauvaise route**, elle s'est perdue. | *Having taken the wrong road, she got lost.* |
| **Ayant vainement cherché l'autoroute**, elle s'est arrêtée à un hôtel. | *Having looked for the highway in vain, she stopped at a hotel.* |

In the following examples, note the various spellings of the past participle that follow the auxiliary **étant**. The past participles used after **être** must reflect the gender and number of the person or thing being referred to.

| | |
|---|---|
| étant monté/montée/montés/montées | *having gone up* |
| étant allé/allée/allés/allées | *having gone* |
| étant né/née/nés/nées | *having been born* |
| étant sorti/sortie/sortis/sorties | *having gone out* |

| | |
|---|---|
| **Etant allée au marché la veille**, elle avait tous les ingrédients. | *Having gone to the market the day before, she had all the ingredients.* |
| **Ayant été élue présidente**, elle convoqua l'assemblée. | *Having been elected president, she called the assembly.* |
| **Etant morts en 1937**, ils n'ont pas vécu la deuxième guerre. | *Having died in 1937, they did not live to see the second war.* |

Note that, in French, a past infinitive clause can replace a participial clause that includes a compound gerund. In English the structure remains the same in both cases.

| | |
|---|---|
| Ayant réfléchi... | *Having reflected . . .* |
| = Après avoir réfléchi... | *After having reflected . . .* |
| | |
| Ayant été élue... | *Having been elected . . .* |
| = Après avoir été élue... | *After having been elected . . .* |

**EXERCICE**
**16·4**

*Complete each sentence with a past participle, using the verbs in parentheses.*

1. Ayant _____ son voyage d'affaires, Arthur se préparait à rentrer chez lui. (terminer)

2. Étant _____ par la Bourgogne, il s'est arrêté dans quelques vignobles. (passer)

3. Ayant _____ à sa femme de lui acheter un bon rouge, il lui a acheté quelques bouteilles de bon vin de Bourgogne. (promettre)

4. Ayant _____ beaucoup de temps, il a dû s'arrêter dans un hôtel pour la nuit. (perdre)

5. Le lendemain, ayant bien _____, il a repris la route. (dormir)

**EXERCICE**
**16·5**

*Rewrite each underlined clause as a past gerund clause.*

1. Parce que nous sommes partis trop tôt, nous avons raté l'annonce.

   _____

2. Après avoir annoncé les fiançailles, ils se sont embrassés.

   _____

3. Après avoir dansé toute la soirée, ils se sont retirés.

   _____

4. Après avoir entendu la nouvelle, nous avons regretté de ne pas être restés.

_____

5. Parce que nous étions déjà rentrés à la maison, c'était trop tard.

_____

## Using gerunds to express cause and effect

Sometimes a gerund clause expresses a cause while the main clause expresses the effect. In that case, in French and English alike, the participial clause precedes the main clause. Note the comma after the participial clause. Consider the following participial clauses, which include the simple gerunds: **étant** (*being*), **chantant** (*singing*), and **voyant** (*seeing*):

**participial clause + main clause → cause and effect**

| | |
|---|---|
| **Le bus étant en retard**, nous avons pris le taxi. | ***The bus being late,*** *we took the cab.* |
| **Le serveur chantant à tue-tête**, la salle s'est mise à rire. | ***The waiter singing at the top of his lungs,*** *the room broke out laughing.* |
| **Se voyant perdre**, elle s'est énervée. | ***Seeing herself losing,*** *she got agitated.* |

Note that subordinate adverbial clauses (more frequently used in speaking) can replace the participial clauses in the previous example sentences:

| | |
|---|---|
| Le bus étant en retard... | *The bus being late . . .* |
| = Parce que/Puisque le bus était en retard... | *Because/Since the bus was late . . .* |
| | |
| Se voyant perdre,... | *Seeing herself losing . . .* |
| = Comme elle se voyait perdre,... | *As she saw herself losing . . .* |

Some participial clauses include the compound gerund form to express that the action of the dependent participial clause precedes the action of the main clause. In the following examples, the actions of **ayant travaillé** (*having worked*), **étant né** (*having been born*), and **ayant été témoin** (*having witnessed*) precede the actions in the main clauses:

| | |
|---|---|
| **Ayant travaillé tout l'été**, il est épuisé. | ***Having worked all summer,*** *he is exhausted.* |
| **Étant né en France**, il est français. | ***Being born in France,*** *he is French.* |
| **Ayant été témoin de l'accident**, il a fait une déclaration. | ***Having witnessed the accident,*** *he made a report.* |

## Using gerunds to focus on a specific moment

Sometimes a gerund describes the action performed by the object of the verb in the main clause. In that case, in French and English alike, the participial clause follows and completes this object. Note that the actions in both the main and participial clauses occur simultaneously.

**subject + verb + object + present participle + prepositional phrase**
J'ai + aperçu + l'oiseau + **s'envolant** + **de sa cage**.
*I saw the bird **flying out of his cage**.*

| | |
|---|---|
| Nous observons l'enfant **jouant dans le sable**. | *We are observing the child **playing in the sand**.* |
| Nous étions fascinés par la comète **tombant du ciel**. | *We were fascinated by the comet **falling out of the sky**.* |

A participial clause including a gerund can be replaced by a relative clause as in the following examples:

J'ai aperçu l'oiseau **s'envolant** de sa cage. = J'ai aperçu l'oiseau **qui s'envolait** de sa cage.
Nous observons l'enfant **jouant** dans le sable. = Nous observons l'enfant **qui joue** dans le sable.

## Using the gerund after the preposition **en**

These participial clauses usually underscore the simultaneity of the actions in the main and dependent clauses. The preposition **en** (*while*), which introduces the clause, is often accompanied by the adverb **tout** to further stress the simultaneity of the actions.

**main clause + (tout) en + gerund + direct object**
Il est tombé + en + descendant + l'escalier.
*He fell **while** coming down the stairs.*

| | |
|---|---|
| Elle criait de joie **en entendant les nouvelles**. | *She was screaming with joy **upon hearing the news**.* |
| Il faisait ses devoirs **tout en écoutant son iPod**. | *He was doing his homework **while listening to his iPod**.* |
| Elle pleurait **tout en décrivant l'incident**. | *She was crying **while describing the incident**.* |

Note the cause-and-effect relationship (added to simultaneity of actions) between the two clauses in the following sentences:

| | |
|---|---|
| Il a fait des progrès **en travaillant dur**. | *He made progress **by working hard**.* |
| Elle est devenue célèbre **en composant des chansons**. | *She became famous **by composing songs**.* |

In the following examples, note how a participial clause can be placed before the main clause in French and in English to stress the action of that participial clause. In this case, the adverb **tout** is often added in a French sentence. A comma ends the participial clause in both English and French. Also note that the subject in the main and participial clauses is the same.

**(tout) en + gerund + main clause**
**Tout en** + mangeant + elle faisait des texto.
***All the while*** *she was eating, she was text-messaging.*

**Tout en répondant,** je fouillais dans mon sac.   ***All the while I was answering***, *I was looking through my purse.*

Note that, in this sentence, the person was doing both actions of answering *and* looking, simultaneously.

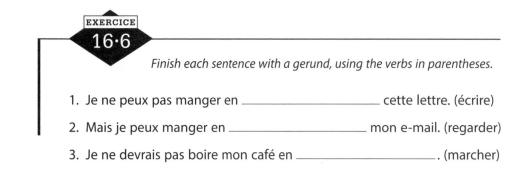

**EXERCICE**
**16·6**

*Finish each sentence with a gerund, using the verbs in parentheses.*

1. Je ne peux pas manger en _____ cette lettre. (écrire)

2. Mais je peux manger en _____ mon e-mail. (regarder)

3. Je ne devrais pas boire mon café en _____. (marcher)

4. Par contre je peux boire mon eau tout en me _____. (promenant)

5. Je peux lire le journal tout en _____ la télé. (regarder)

6. Mais je ne peux pas lire le journal en _____ de la bicyclette. (faire)

*Complete each sentence appropriately, using the verbs in parentheses.*

1. Elle parlait au téléphone tout en _____. (conduire)

2. C'est en _____ deux choses à la fois qu'on prend des risques. (faire)

3. En se _____ dans une zone interdite, elle a eu une contravention! (garer)

4. Elle n'a fait qu'aggraver la situation en _____ d'expliquer ses raisons à l'agent. (essayer)

5. Tout en l'_____, l'agent a écrit sa contravention. (écouter)

6. On apprend beaucoup en _____ des erreurs, n'est-ce pas? (faire)

## Using a past participle

Some participial clauses include a past participle such as **terminé** (*finished*), **choisi** (*chosen*), **vendu** (*sold*). These clauses are shortcuts; they are used instead of adverbial clauses.

| | |
|---|---|
| **Son devoir terminé**, il s'est couché. | *His work done, he went to bed.* |

The participial clause **Son devoir terminé** could be replaced by an adverbial clause: **Quand il a terminé son devoir** (*When he finished his assignment*) or by a past infinitive clause: **Après avoir terminé son devoir** (*After finishing his assignment*).

Consider the following participial clauses and note that the English translations often require the addition of a conjugated verb (*is/was*). Also note that the past participle agrees in gender and number with the noun it refers to.

| | |
|---|---|
| **Une fois le dîner servi**, je m'assiérai. | *Once dinner is served, I will sit down.* |
| **La vieille auto vendue**, il fallait bien en acheter une autre. | *The old car having been sold, it was necessary to buy another one.* |
| **Le modèle de voiture choisie**, il fut facile de conclure l'affaire. | *Once the car model was chosen, it was easy to conclude the deal.* |
| **Minutieusement examinés**, les patients auront un rapport complet. | *Thoroughly examined, the patients will get a complete report.* |

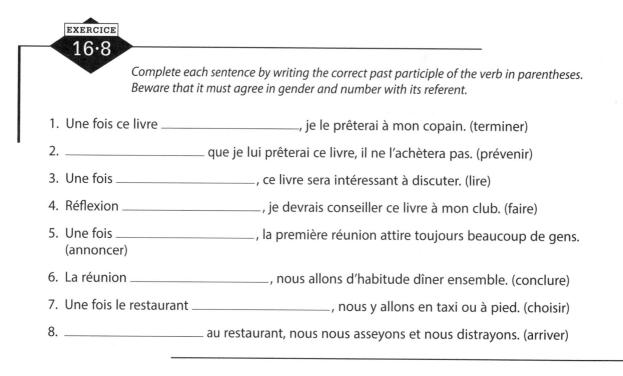

*Complete each sentence by writing the correct past participle of the verb in parentheses. Beware that it must agree in gender and number with its referent.*

1. Une fois ce livre _____, je le prêterai à mon copain. (terminer)

2. _____ que je lui prêterai ce livre, il ne l'achètera pas. (prévenir)

3. Une fois _____, ce livre sera intéressant à discuter. (lire)

4. Réflexion _____, je devrais conseiller ce livre à mon club. (faire)

5. Une fois _____, la première réunion attire toujours beaucoup de gens. (annoncer)

6. La réunion _____, nous allons d'habitude dîner ensemble. (conclure)

7. Une fois le restaurant _____, nous y allons en taxi ou à pied. (choisir)

8. _____ au restaurant, nous nous asseyons et nous distrayons. (arriver)

*Using the fragments, make logical French sentences. Add appropriate punctuation.*

1. avec mon cousin français / ayant décidé / correspondre / de / regulièrement / réviser mon français / j'ai dû

_____

2. faire / quelques exercices / je peux / chaque jour / que mon dîner soit prêt / en attendant

_____

3. en étudiant / tout / écouter / je peux / ma musique favorite

_____

4. faite / réflexion / d'avoir acheté / je suis content(e) / ce livre

_____

5. terminés / une fois / tous les exercices / bien mieux / j'écrirai

_____

## Using past participles in the passive voice

In the passive voice, the subject of the verb, rather than performing the action, is now being *subjected to* the action. In the following example, *the room* is the subject of the verb *to clean*, but it is not doing the action of cleaning:

La chambre **sera nettoyée**.                    *The room **will be cleaned**.*

Note that the French past participle **nettoyée** agrees in gender and number (feminine singular) with the subject **la chambre**.

The verb in the passive voice may be in the present, past, or future tense, and the word order is always the same.

**subject + être + past participle**
La chambre + **a été** + nettoyée.
*The room has been cleaned.*

L'argent **est dépensé** sans scrupules.        *Money **is spent** without scruples.*
La vieille poste **sera rasée**.                 *The old post office **will be torn down**.*
Le voleur **a été arrêté**.                      *The thief **was arrested**.*
La voiture **est inspectée** en ce moment.       *The car **is being inspected** at this moment.*
Les gens **étaient séparés**.                    *The people **were separated**.*

The passive voice is not used as frequently in French as it is in English. In French there are other alternatives. The most frequently encountered alternative is the use of the impersonal pronoun **on**. Consider how the previous sentences could be stated using **on**:

**On dépense** l'argent sans scrupules.          *People spend money without scruples.*
**On rasera** la vieille poste.                  *They will tear down the old post office.*
**On a arrêté** le voleur.                       *They arrested the thief.*
**On inspecte** la voiture en ce moment.         *Someone is inspecting the car right at this moment.*
**On avait séparé** les gens.                    *They had separated the people.*

---

**EXERCICE**

**16·10**

*Complete each French sentence by putting the verb in parentheses in the appropriate form.*

1. Picasso _____ quelquefois _____ comme un peintre français. (décrire)

2. En fait, il est né en Espagne où son talent d'artiste _____ _____ alors qu'il est très jeune. (reconnaître)

3. Il _____ _____ par la France. (fasciner)

4. En Provence où il _____ _____, il poursuit sa carrière d'artiste. (établir)

5. _____ _____ partout sans argent, ses notes de café _____ _____ avec des dessins. (se promener/payer)

6. Mais c'est à Paris qu'il _____ _____ le plus. (louer)

7. Ses tableaux et ses poteries _____ _____ au plus haut prix. (estimer)

*Translate each sentence into French using the vocabulary provided.*

1. The house is sold. (la maison/vendre)

   _____

2. The windows are washed. (les fenêtres/laver)

   _____

3. The lawn has been mowed. (le gazon/tondre)

   _____

4. The yard has been cleaned. (la cour/nettoyer)

   _____

5. The sign has been removed. (le panneau/enlever)

   _____

6. The bushes have been trimmed. (les buissons/tailler)

   _____

# Making transitions

Transitional words or phrases serve to link parts of a sentence or to connect one sentence to another as well as one paragraph to another. They help build organized paragraphs that can be read smoothly, and help to ultimately construct extended pieces of writing such as letters.

## Linking thoughts within a sentence

Smooth transitions from one thought to another within a sentence are clearly important to communicate effectively. This can be achieved by the use of adverbs and conjunctions.

## Using coordinating and subordinating conjunctions

Using conjunctions will help sentences flow in a logical manner, making your message clear to the reader. These conjunctions may serve in a variety of ways such as adding an idea, e.g., **et** (*and*); explaining an idea, e.g., **car** (*for*); or opposing an idea, e.g., **bien que** (*even though*). You may review Unit 6 for coordinating conjunctions and Units 7 and 8 for subordinating conjunctions.

### Coordinating conjunctions

Coordinating conjunctions such as **et** (*and*), **car** (*for*), **ou** (*or*), **mais** (*but*), **donc** (*so*), and **ni...ni** (*neither . . . nor*) are commonly used to link two or more verbs, nouns, adverbs, adjectives, or clauses.

| | |
|---|---|
| Elle a fait le lavage **et** la vaisselle. | *She did the wash **and** the dishes.* |
| Il est allé manger **car** il avait faim. | *He went to eat **for** he was hungry.* |
| Elle veut aller au cinéma **ou** au restaurant. | *She wants to go to the movies **or** to the restaurant.* |
| Il avait fini **donc** il est parti. | *He had finished, **so** he left.* |
| Il ne veut **ni** nager **ni** marcher. | *He does not want to swim **nor** walk.* |
| Elle est fatiguée **mais** elle veut finir son travail. | *She is tired but wants to finish her work.* |

## Subordinating conjunctions

Subordinating conjunctions link two clauses. Some conjunctions govern the subjunctive mood. The following are some commonly used subordinating conjunctions:

| | | | |
|---|---|---|---|
| alors que | *while* | pendant que | *while* |
| bien que | *although* | pourvu que | *provided that* |
| parce que | *because* | tandis que | *while* |

Il est parti tôt **parce qu'**il était pressé.　　*He left early **because** he was in a hurry.*
Elle dansait **alors que/tandis que** je chantais.　　*She was dancing **while** I was singing.*

In the following sentences, note that the conjunctions **bien que** and **pourvu que** are followed by a verb in the subjunctive mood:

Elle a planté des fleurs **bien qu'**elle n'y
　connaisse pas grand-chose.
Je te pardonne **pourvu que** tu ne le
　fasses plus.

*She planted flowers **even though** she does not
　know anything about gardening.*
*I forgive you **provided** you do not do this
　again.*

---

### EXERCICE 17·1

*Complete each sentence with one of the following coordinating conjunctions.*

ni / et / donc / mais / car / ou

1. Comme sports, je fais de la marche _____ de la natation.

2. Je n'aime ni courir _____ escalader les montagnes.

3. Pour nager, je vais à la piscine _____ à la plage.

4. J'adore la mer _____ quelquefois les vagues sont trop hautes pour nager.

5. Je vais quand même souvent à la plage _____ je peux toujours y faire de la marche.

6. Je fais beaucoup d'exercice physique, _____ je suis en assez bonne forme.

---

### EXERCICE 17·2

*Complete each sentence with one of the following subordinating conjunctions.*

alors que / tandis que / parce que / pourvu que / bien que / pendant que

1. Comme sports, Mimi monte et descend l'escalier une ou deux fois par jour _____ moi, je vais au gym, au parc et à la plage.

2. Mimi croit qu'elle est en forme _____ elle ne soit pas malade.

3. Je ne suis pas contente _____ je sais que Mimi ne fait pas assez d'exercice.

4. _____ je sois plus âgée et plus raisonnable, Mimi ne m'écoute pas.

5. La plupart du temps Mimi écoute des CD, couchée sur son lit, _____ moi, j'écoute mon iPod tout en marchant.

6. Je m'inquiète pour Mimi _____ c'est ma petite sœur.

## Using adverbs and adverbial conjunctions

Just like coordinating and subordinating conjunctions, adverbs and adverbial conjunctions can be classified in categories such as adding, contrasting, illustrating, and sequencing ideas.

### Addition

It is sometimes good style to use an adverb or adverbial clause such as the following to illustrate or provide an additional detail in a sentence:

| | | | |
|---|---|---|---|
| ainsi que | *as well as* | également | *also/too* |
| aussi | *also/too* | encore | *still* |
| d'ailleurs | *besides* | | |

| | |
|---|---|
| L'eau était trop froide pour y nager; il y avait **aussi** de grandes vagues. | *The water was too cold to swim in it; **also** there were big waves.* |
| J'ai apporté les boissons; j'ai **également** fait un dessert. | *I brought the drinks; I **also** made a dessert.* |
| Il a nettoyé l'évier mais il y avait **encore** des débris de verre. | *He cleaned the sink, but **still** there was some broken glass in it.* |

Note: Unlike the adverb *also*, which is often used at the head of a sentence or clause in English, **aussi**, **également**, and **encore** should never appear at the head of a French sentence but rather after the verb.

**subject + verb + aussi/encore**
Il + avait + encore...
*He still had . . .*

| | |
|---|---|
| Elle enseigne le violon **ainsi que** le piano. | *She teaches the violin **as well as** the piano.* |
| Il a rendu le livre; **d'ailleurs** il ne l'avait pas lu. | *He returned the book; **besides** he had not read it.* |

Note: It is not unusual to use a coordinating conjunction such as **et** or **mais** as well as an adverb to make a transition from one thought to another. Remember that a great majority of adverbs follow the verb in a French sentence. Consider the following examples:

| | |
|---|---|
| Il a pris la retraite **mais** il travaille **encore** un peu. | *He retired **but** he **still** works a little.* |
| Il répond au téléphone **et** donne **aussi** les rendez-vous. | *He answers the phone **and also** gives appointments.* |

### Contrast

In some instances, adverbs or adverbial phrases such as the following help transition from one idea to another by establishing a contrast:

| | | | |
|---|---|---|---|
| au lieu de cela | *instead of that* | pourtant | *yet* |
| cependant | *however* | malgré tout | *in spite of everything/ all the same* |
| sinon | *otherwise* | | |

Tu devais surveiller les enfants; **au lieu de cela**, tu dormais.

Prends ton petit déjeuner; **sinon** tu auras faim.

*You were supposed to watch the children; **instead of that**, you were sleeping.*

*Have your breakfast; **otherwise** you will be hungry.*

## Emphasis

In other instances, adverbs or adverbial phrases such as the following help transition from one idea to another by adding emphasis to what has already been stated:

| | | | |
|---|---|---|---|
| bien sûr que | *of course* | en fait | *in fact* |
| certainement | *certainly* | naturellement | *naturally* |
| en effet | *indeed* | sûrement | *surely* |

Quand on m'a demandé de venir, **bien sûr que** je suis venue.

Je croyais que c'était l'adresse correcte; **en fait** elle était fausse.

Quand on l'a insulté, **naturellement** il s'est révolté.

*When they asked me to come, **of course** I came.*

*I thought that it was the correct address; **in fact** it was wrong.*

*When they insulted him, **naturally** he rebelled.*

## Illustration

Adverbs or adverbial phrases such as the following help transition from one idea to another by giving an example or an illustration:

| | | | |
|---|---|---|---|
| autrement dit | *in other words* | par exemple | *for example/for instance* |
| en particulier | *specifically* | surtout | *especially* |

J'adore les pierres précieuses, **par exemple** les rubis.

Il dessine beaucoup d'animaux, **en particulier** les chats.

J'aime bien le Colorado **surtout** en été.

*I adore precious stones, **for example** rubies.*

*He draws many animals, **specifically** cats.*

*I like Colorado **especially** in the summer.*

## Time sequence

Often, adverbs or adverbial phrases such as the following help transition from one idea to another by establishing a time sequence:

| | | | |
|---|---|---|---|
| actuellement | *at the moment* | enfin | *finally* |
| alors | *then/so* | ensuite | *then* |
| après | *afterward* | finalement | *finally* |
| autrefois | *formerly* | maintenant | *now* |
| avant | *before* | par la suite | *afterward* |
| bientôt | *soon* | puis | *then* |
| d'abord | *first (of all)* | | |

Il est inscrit à l'Université de Paris **mais actuellement** il est en vacances.

**Avant** il ne faisait pas de gym **mais maintenant** il en fait tous les jours.

Il a pris une douche, **puis** il s'est habillé **et enfin**, il a pu partir.

*He is enrolled at the University of Paris, **but currently** he is on vacation.*

***Before** he did not do any exercise, **but now** he does some every day.*

*He took a shower, **then** he got dressed, **and finally** he was able to leave.*

*Complete each sentence with an appropriate transition word or phrase from the list provided.*

tandis que / mais / car / et / bien que / ou / puisque / donc / ainsi que

1. J'ai toujours rêvé d'aller à Monaco _____ je n'en ai jamais eu l'occasion.

2. _____ nous serons sur la Côte d'Azur cet été, je veux vraiment y aller.

3. Je veux jouir de la vue le long de la mer _____ nous passerons par de petits ports de pêche.

4. À Monaco, nous pourrons voir la Changée des Gardes _____ le célèbre casino.

5. Il paraît qu'il y a de nombreux cafés et restaurants; _____ nous déjeunerons là-bas.

6. Il faudra aussi acheter un souvenir _____ nous n'aimions pas trop dépenser pour ce genre de choses.

*Choose the appropriate transitional word or phrase to complete each sentence in the following paragraph.*

pourtant / et / ainsi que / mais actuellement / bientôt / en effet / bien que

Le jeune Sarkozy se distinguait déjà au lycée par son talent de négociateur (1) _____ son charme. Il savait énoncer clairement ses arguments (2) _____ affirmer ses points de vue. (3) _____ il n'était pas arrogant, simplement sûr de lui. Il n'avait que vingt ans quand il s'est affilié à la campagne électorale de Jacques Chirac. (4) _____ les deux hommes avaient des convictions communes, (5) _____ Sarkozy ait changé de direction par la suite. (6) _____ Sarkozy a réussi à faire une belle carrière politique. Élu président de la république française, il est devenu leader d'une importante nation européenne et a su (7) _____ s'affirmer sur la scène internationale. (8) _____ le président Sarkozy fait face à un nombre de problèmes, mais «Qui vivra verra!»

*Reconstitute each sentence of this paragraph by placing the sentence fragments in the correct order and adding punctuation. Pay particular attention to transitional words such as* **sinon** *or* **aussi** *that provide important clues.*

1. encore beaucoup à apprendre / mais il me reste / j'ai beaucoup appris

_____

2. ainsi que de la grammaire / j'étudie du vocabulaire / il faut que

_____

3. aussi / la culture française / comprendre mieux / je voudrais

_____

4. c'est frustrant / être patient / sinon / il faut / quand on apprend une langue

_____

5. de faire des progrès / en particulier / je vais continuer / bien sûr qu'avec un peu de diligence / dans l'art d'écrire

_____

6. quelques phrases / je sais écrire / actuellement

_____

7. un paragraphe entier / je pourrai écrire / mais bientôt

_____

# Linking sentences and paragraphs

Smooth, orderly, and logical transitions from one sentence to the next, and from one paragraph to another, are key to creating clear meaning and flow in any document. This can be achieved by using prepositional and adverbial phrases, impersonal expressions, verbs, and conjunctions. These structures are here organized according to their meaning rather than their grammatical definition.

## Expressing personal viewpoints

You may begin a sentence with a phrase such as **Selon moi** or with a verb phrase such as **Je crois** to make it clear that you are giving your own point of view. Here are some examples followed by a paragraph in which you will notice how transitional words allow the smooth development of ideas:

| | |
|---|---|
| Selon moi | _In my opinion_ |
| À mon avis | _In my opinion_ |
| D'après moi | _In my opinion_ |
| Je crois que | _I believe that_ |
| Je ne crois pas que | _I do not believe that_ |
| Je pense que | _I think that_ |
| Je ne pense pas que | _I do not think that_ |
| Je suis convaincu(e) que | _I am convinced that_ |

**Je ne pense pas que** ce problème soit grave. **Selon moi**, ce voyage est bien organisé. **Je crois que** nous reviendrons. **D'après moi**, on devrait remercier le guide. **Je suis convaincue qu**'il est honnête.

_**I do not think that** this problem is serious. **In my opinion**, this trip is well organized. **I believe that** we will come back. **In my opinion**, we should thank the guide. **I am convinced that** he is honest._

# Expressing certainty or uncertainty

You may begin a sentence with one of many impersonal expressions that help convey varying degrees of certainty or uncertainty. Remember that expressions that convey uncertainty must be followed by a verb in the subjunctive mood. (See Unit 8.) The following expressions are frequently used in French. Note the use of transitional words in the short paragraph following these expressions:

| FOLLOWED BY INDICATIVE MOOD | | FOLLOWED BY SUBJUNCTIVE MOOD | |
|---|---|---|---|
| Il est certain que | *It is certain that* | Il n'est pas certain que | *It is not certain that* |
| Il est évident que | *It is evident that* | Il est possible que | *It is possible that* |
| Il est probable que | *It is probable that* | Il est peu probable que | *It is improbable that* |
| Il va de soi que | *It is self-evident that* | Il est contestable que | *It is questionable/ debatable that* |

Ce n'est pas clair. **Il est contestable qu'il** ait gagné. Quelle surprise! **Il est certain qu'**on ne peut pas tout prévoir. Mais quel mensonge! **Il est évident que** la vérité est rare. Il est si têtu. **Il n'est pas certain qu'**on puisse raisonner avec lui. Il n'écoute pas. **Il est peu probable qu'**il fasse ce qu'on lui demande.

*It is not clear. **It is questionable that** he won. What a surprise! **It is certain that** we cannot predict everything. But what a lie! **It is evident that** truth is rare. He is so stubborn. **It is not certain that** we can reason with him. He does not listen. **He is not likely to** do what they ask.*

# Illustrating a point

You may begin a sentence with one of the following terms when you are ready to give evidence for the point you are making. Note the use of transitional words in the short paragraph following these expressions:

| | |
|---|---|
| Notamment | *Notably/In particular* |
| Par exemple | *For example* |
| On peut préciser que | *Let us point out that/One should point out that* |
| On peut souligner que | *Let us stress that* |

Il avait des raisons très claires pour commettre le délit. **On peut préciser qu'**il y avait beaucoup réfléchi. Mais il a fait plusieurs erreurs. **Par exemple**, le mois dernier, il a oublié de payer une facture. Et il avait un dossier: il avait été emprisonné plusieurs fois, **notamment** l'an dernier.

*He had very clear reasons to commit the felony. **One should point out that** he had thought about it a lot. But he made several mistakes. **For example**, last month he forgot to pay a bill. And he had a record: he had been incarcerated several times, **in particular** last year.*

# Giving a reason

Except for **comme**, which must begin a sentence in order to mean *as/since*, you may use the following terms *to begin* or *develop* a sentence when you want to explain why. Note the use of transitional words in the short paragraph following these expressions:

| | |
|---|---|
| À cause de | *Because of* |
| Comme | *As/Since* |
| Étant donné que | *Given that* |
| Parce que | *Because* |
| Puisque | *Since* |

À **cause de** l'examen ce matin, Mireille était pressée. **Étant donné qu'**elle était en retard, elle a décidé de prendre la voiture de sa sœur. **Comme** elle en avait besoin tout de suite, elle l'a prise sans demander. Ce n'était pas sympa **parce que** la sœur de Mireille a eu très peur quand elle n'a pas vu sa voiture.

*Because of the exam this morning, Mireille was in a hurry. Given that she was late, she decided to take her sister's car. Since she needed it immediately, she took it without asking. It was not nice, because Mireille's sister got very scared when she did not see her car.*

## Stating a consequence

You may use the following terms when you want to show consequences. Note the use of transitional words in the short paragraph following these expressions:

| | |
|---|---|
| Ainsi | *Thus* |
| C'est pour cette raison que | *It is for this reason that* |
| C'est pourquoi | *That is why* |
| Donc | *So/Thus* |
| Par conséquent | *Consequently* |
| Voilà pourquoi | *That is why* |

L'économie n'est pas très bonne. **Ainsi** Jacques a perdu son travail. **Voilà pourquoi** il en cherche un autre. **C'est aussi pour cette raison qu'**il regarde les petites annonces chaque jour. Il a rendez-vous chez un employeur demain. **Donc** il faut qu'il prépare son CV.

*The economy is not very good. **Thus** Jacques lost his job. **That's why** he is looking for another. **It is also for this reason** that that he looks at ads every day. He has an appointment with an employer tomorrow. **So** he has to prepare his résumé.*

## Stating a contrast

There are many expressions that help compare and contrast. Here are a few common ones. Note the use of transitional words in the short paragraph following these expressions:

| | | | |
|---|---|---|---|
| Au contraire | *On the contrary* | Malgré | *Despite* |
| Cependant | *However* | Même si | *Even though/Even if* |
| D'autre part | *On the other hand* | Par contre | *On the other hand* |
| En dépit de | *In spite of* | Pourtant | *Yet* |
| Mais | *But* | | |

Le jeune homme était vendeur dans un grand magasin. **Malgré** le fait qu'il gagnait bien sa vie, il désirait faire des études de kinésithérapeute. Il était très bon en anatomie **même s'**il n'avait pas poursuivi ses études. **D'autre part**, comment allait-il payer ses factures? **Même si** ses études allaient durer quelques années, il serait patient.

*The young man was a salesman in a department store. **Despite** the fact that he earned a good living, he wanted to become a physical therapist. He was good in anatomy **even if** he had not pursued his studies. **On the other hand**, how was he to pay his bills? **Even if** his studies were going to last a few years, he would be patient.*

## Establishing a sequence

To show a sequence of events in a sentence or paragraph, you may use any of the previously seen adverbs or adverbial conjunctions, which are used to begin and develop sentences, as well as the following expressions, which may be useful when developing an argument. Note the use of transitional words in the short paragraph following these expressions:

| | |
|---|---|
| En premier lieu | *In the first place* |
| Premièrement | *First/Firstly* |
| En deuxième lieu | *In the second place* |
| Deuxièmement | *Secondly* |
| En troisième lieu | *In the third place* |
| Troisièmement | *Thirdly* |
| En dernier lieu | *Lastly* |

| | |
|---|---|
| Non, je ne suis pas allé en Corse. **En premier lieu**, je ne connaissais personne là-bas. **En deuxième lieu**, je n'avais plus que deux jours de vacances et **en troisième lieu**, on m'a invité à rester à Eze. | *No, I did not go to Corsica. **In the first place**, I did not know anybody there. **In the second place**, I only had two days vacation left, and in **the third place**, I was invited to stay in Eze.* |

## Concluding

You may use one of the following terms when you finish an argument, an illustration, or an explanation. In the paragraph following these expressions, note how transitional terms make the entire paragraph easy to read and understand:

| | |
|---|---|
| En conclusion | *To conclude* |
| En résumé | *To summarize* |
| En somme | *In short* |
| Somme toute | *All in all* |

| | |
|---|---|
| Je n'étais pas du tout satisfait du service à votre hôtel. **Premièrement**, le personnel n'était pas attentif: **par exemple**, on a oublié de me réveiller le premier matin. **Deuxièmement**, ma chambre n'a pas été nettoyée pendant deux jours. **Troisièmement,** on m'a facturé pour un film que je n'ai pas vu. **En conclusion**, le service était lamentable. | *I was not at all satisfied with the service at your hotel. **First**, the personnel were not attentive: **for example**, they forgot to wake me up on the first morning. **Secondly**, my room was not cleaned for two days. **Thirdly**, I was charged for a movie I did not see. **To conclude**, the service was deplorable.* |

**EXERCICE**
## 17·6

*Circle the appropriate transition from the choices in parentheses to complete each sentence.*

Je suis désolée de ne pas pouvoir accepter votre invitation. (1) (Probablement, Malheureusement) mon mari et moi serons en plein déménagement. Mon mari vient d'apprendre qu'il va travailler dans une succursale de sa banque dans une ville voisine et (2) (c'est pourquoi, parce que) nous devons emballer tous nos effets aussitôt que possible. (3) (Tandis que, Cependant) je dois vous dire que nous apprécions beaucoup votre amitié et (4) (pourtant, même si) nous habitons à une certaine distance, nous voulons continuer de vous voir. (5) (Puisque, Certainement) nos enfants ont le même âge et s'entendent bien, il est important que nous fassions des efforts pour nous voir souvent. (6) (Ainsi que, Donc) le fait que nous ne soyons plus voisins ne devrait pas nous empêcher de rester amis.

*Translate the phrases in parentheses to complete each sentence.*

1. _____ qu'il fasse mauvais temps aujourd'hui. (*It is not at all sure*)

2. _____ que nous aurons de la pluie. (*It is probable*)

3. _____ que nos amis viennent. (*It is not certain*)

4. _____ que la meilleure équipe gagne ce match. (*It is not evident*)

5. _____ que tous les gens soient honnêtes. (*It is debatable*)

*Circle the most appropriate choice to complete each sentence.*

1. (Par conséquent, À mon avis), beaucoup de gens ne font pas confiance aux promesses des politiciens.

2. (Je doute, Je crois) que beaucoup d'entre eux ont été déçus ces dernières années.

3. (D'après moi, Je suis convaincue) que les choses peuvent changer.

4. Nous aurons bientôt une nouvelle vague de politiciens, (je crois, je ne pense pas).

5. Il suffit que nous votions raisonnablement, (je pense, j'espère).

6. (Malgré, Selon moi), tout est possible!

7. (C'est pourquoi, En dépit) je vais voter dans ces élections.

8. (Au contraire, Ainsi) je ferai mon devoir de citoyen.

*Outline the five steps you take to prepare and write an essay for class, using expressions such as **en premier lieu** with the following ideas.*

1. _____

(réfléchir et organiser les idées)

2. _____

(réviser et finir le plan)

3. _____

(commencer à écrire et développer l'essai)

4. _____

(relire et faire des corrections à l'essai)

5. _____

(rendre l'essai au prof et quitter la salle de classe)

*Reconstitute each sentence of this paragraph by placing the sentence fragments in the correct order and adding punctuation. Let the transitional word clues such as **C'est pourquoi** guide you.*

1. est toujours complexe / selon moi / la politique

_____

2. qu'il est difficile / de dire toute la vérité / je suis convaincu / pour un politicien / et rien que la vérité

_____

3. à admettre / la vérité est quelquefois difficile / il est certain que

_____

4. que les gens / il va de soi / notamment / n'aiment pas entendre la vérité / quand elle est désagréable

_____

5. peu de politiciens ont le courage / de toujours dire la vérité / étant donné que / il faut observer leurs actions de très près

_____

6. c'est pourquoi / et les interviews / je suis les débats

_____

*Translate the following paragraph using the imparfait and passé composé tenses. Remember that the words* **aussi** *and* **également** *cannot head a sentence in French.*

*Formerly I was very shy. I used to worry (s'inquiéter) a lot when I had to talk, in particular before a group of people. Also, I always blushed (rougir) in front of people. But soon I learned to calm down (se calmer). Now I can even make presentations (faire des interventions) in front of an audience. Naturally this did not happen (se passer) in one day.*

# Letter writing and messaging

French and English formats of letter writing are quite similar in the way letters are addressed but often differ in the way they are closed. In both languages there is a formal style used for legal matters, business, and trade, and there is a familiar style used with friends and relatives.

## Addressing an envelope

When writing a person's address on an envelope, the order of lines is the same in English and in French but the order in which information is given on those lines varies slightly.

The number of the house or building should be separated from the name of the street by a comma. However, that rule is frequently disregarded.

| | |
|---|---|
| 19, rue Roethig | *or* 19 rue Roethig |
| 40, boulevard des Alouettes | *or* 40 boulevard des Alouettes |

Beware that in French-speaking countries, a street (**rue**) may be called **allée** (*alley*), **chemin** (*path*), **quai** (*riverside*), **promenade** (*promenade*) or other such creative names. These substitutes for **rue** are sometimes capitalized because they have become an inherent part of the location.

| | |
|---|---|
| 136, Allée des Aubépines | *or* 136 Allée des Aubépines |
| 22, Promenade des Anglais | *or* 22 Promenade des Anglais |

The zip code (**le code postal**) consists of five digits and appears before the name of the town or city in a French address. In France the first two digits of the zip code identify the county (**le département**) in which the person resides.

| | |
|---|---|
| **13**004 Marseille | **69**002 Lyon |
| France | France |

In France's overseas departments and territories, the first three digits identify the town or city.

**971**00 Basse-Terre
Guadeloupe

When writing to Québec, Canada, remember that the first language of the province is French; try to follow the rule of the comma after the street number. Also be sure to indicate **Québec** in parentheses after the town/city *and then* the zip code.

99, avenue Jacques Cartier
Montréal (Québec) H1X 1X1

In addition, a person's title is usually omitted in English, but not in French. Titles may be abbreviated on an envelope as follows. But do not use abbreviations in the body of the letter itself.

Docteur/Dr                         Doctor/Dr.
Maître/Me                          Esquire/Esq.
Madame/Mme                         Madam/Mrs.
Mesdames/Mmes
Mademoiselle/Mlle                  Miss/Miss
Mesdemoiselles/Mlles
Monsieur/M.                        Mister/Mr.
Messieurs/MM.
Professeur/Pr                      Professor/Prof.

Compare the following formats:

| ENGLISH | FRENCH | FRENCH |
| --- | --- | --- |
| Paul Smith | Monsieur Jules Lemand | M. Jules Lemand |
| 215 Riverside Road | 19, rue Roethig | 19, rue Roethig |
| Colorado Springs, CO 80918 | 67 000 Strasbourg | 67 000 Strasbourg |

When writing to a person who lives with a relative or rents a room in another person's home, add a line after the person's name to whom you are writing. This will be followed by the name and address of the home's owner.

Mlle Michelle Verban
Chez Mme Aubin
12, rue du Maréchal Foch
5660 Liège
Belgique

When writing to a company rather than a specific person, write the company's name on the first line, then the specific department and/or the name of the person (if applicable) on the second line, the street address on the third line, the zip code followed by the city on the fourth line, and the country on the fifth line. See the following example:

Société Générale
Section Assurances (*Insurance Department*)/Mlle Butin
29, boulevard Haussmann
75009 Paris
France

**EXERCICE**
**18·1**

*Using the information provided, write each address as if on an envelope.*

1. avenue Leclerc / 12 / Monique Meru / Lille / Madame / 59000 / France

_____

_____

_____

_____

2. 75009 / MM. / Royen et Sanson / Société Productrice d'Electricité / Paris / boulevard Haussmann / 10

_____

_____

_____

_____

3. Fort de France / Martinique / 5 / rue de la Liberté / Hôtel Le Lafayette / 97200

_____

_____

_____

_____

# Writing a letter

In both an informal and formal French letter, there usually does not appear any address at the top: A business letter is written on letterhead that provides the sender's information, and a personal letter is often written on personalized stationery that also provides the sender's information.

## Place and date

Regardless of whether or not letterhead is used, the sender's location (usually a city) appears at the top right of a letter and is separated from the date by a comma as follows:

> Avignon, le 11. 3. 2008

## Salutations

In French and in English, the main difference between informal and formal salutations is the use of a title used in formal letters.

### Informal salutations

In an informal letter to a friend or relative, use the word **cher** (_dear_) in the form that is appropriate (masculine, feminine, plural) before the person's name. You may also add the corresponding possessive article **mon**, **ma**, **mes** (_my_) before the adjective **cher**.

| | |
|---|---|
| **Cher** François | _Dear_ François |
| **Mon cher** François | _My dear_ François |
| **Chère** Michelle | _Dear_ Michelle |
| **Ma chère** Michelle | _My dear_ Michelle |
| **Chers** François et Michelle | _Dear_ François and Michelle |
| **Chers** amis | _Dear_ friends (males or mixed group) |
| **Chères** amies | _Dear_ friends (females) |
| **Mes chères** amies | _My dear_ friends (female group) |

## Formal salutations

In a formal letter, you may use a salutation with or without a name. If you know the person to whom you are writing, use the appropriate form of the word **cher**. If you do not know the person, use only the title.

**Writing to a known person:**

| | |
|---|---|
| **Chère** madame, | *Dear Madam,* |
| **Chère** madame Flaubert, | *Dear Mrs. Flaubert,* |

**Writing to an unknown person:**

| | |
|---|---|
| Monsieur, Madame, | *To whom it may concern,* |
| Monsieur, | *Sir,* |
| Messieurs, | *Dear Sirs,* |

With individuals who bear a professional title, use **monsieur** or **madame** followed by the professional title. Remember that according to the dictionary of the French Academy, some professions such as **écrivain** (*writer*), **juge** (*judge*), and **docteur** (*doctor*) do not have a feminine form. However, in Québec and parts of Switzerland, it has become standard practice to use a feminine form for these professions: e.g. **la professeure** (*female teacher*) and **l'écrivaine** (*female writer*).

| | |
|---|---|
| Monsieur le Directeur/Madame la Directrice, | *Dear Director,* |
| Monsieur le Professeur/Madame le Professeur, | *Dear Professor,* |
| Monsieur le Docteur/Madame le Docteur, | *Dear Doctor,* |

# Closings

There are numerous closing formulas for both informal and formal letters. Many of them differ greatly from closings you would use in English.

## Informal closings

In English and in French the closing of a letter will depend on the degree of intimacy one shares with the intended reader. Sometimes the closing is an entire sentence (which ends with a period); sometimes it is just a phrase or a word (which usually ends with a comma or an exclamation mark). As these expressions cannot be translated literally, note that many include the notion of friendship (**amitié**), and others reflect the fact that the French *kiss* (**baisers/bises**) rather than *hug*.

| | |
|---|---|
| Je vous envoie mes amitiés./Amitiés. | *Regards,* |
| Je vous envoie mon très amical souvenir. | *Best regards,* |
| Je vous envoie mes pensées bien amicales. | *Best wishes,* |
| Amicalement,/Cordialement, | *Yours sincerely,* |
| Chaleureusement, | *Warm regards,* |
| Bien à toi/Ton ami(e) dévoué(e), | *Yours truly,* |
| Je t'embrasse. | *Love,/With love,* |
| Bons baisers! | *Lots of love,* |
| Bises! | *Hugs and kisses!* |
| Grosses bises! | *Lots of hugs and kisses!* |

## Formal closings

Formal French closing formulas tend to be long and flowery. They cannot be translated literally into English, because in English a formal closing is quite simply the word *Sincerely*. Here are a few examples of some frequently used French formulas. Note that the title embedded in the closing (sir, madam, miss) must refer to the title used in the opening salutation.

Je vous prie d'agréer, madame/monsieur/mademoiselle, l'expression de mes sentiments distingués.

Veuillez agréer, madame/monsieur/mademoiselle, mes cordiales salutations.

Je vous prie d'accepter, madame/monsieur/mademoiselle, mes sincères salutations.

The final closing of a letter will be your signature. Sometimes it will be followed by a post-script (P.S.), which will yield some additional information that was not included in the letter.

### EXERCICE 18·2

*Using the information provided, write three lines that give the date, the salutation, and the closing of each letter.*

1. Paris / July 4, 2008 / Doctor Mason (your physician)

_____

_____

_____

2. Metz / May 23, 2009 / Jeanine Rosier (your girlfriend)

_____

_____

_____

### EXERCICE 18·3

*Using the information in the following paragraph, compose a note that Tina is writing to a French friend named Marie-Josée who is presently in Cannes with her aunt. Include proper opening and closing expressions.*

Depuis que Marie-Josée est partie à Cannes, Tina s'ennuie beaucoup. Elle n'a personne pour l'accompagner au cinéma. Marie-Josée manque terriblement à Tina. Elle ne peut pas attendre qu'elle revienne de France. Mais elle espère que Marie-Josée s'amuse quand même en France. Elle demande comment ça lui plaît là-bas et lui dit de donner le bonjour à sa tante.

_____

_____

_____

_____

_____

_____

_____

_____

*Write a note to a woman who is renting an apartment in Nice. Tell her you saw her ad online, and you very much like the description of the apartment and the monthly rental fee. Add that you hope the apartment is still for rent and that you would like to see it when you are in Nice on June 15. Ask if that is convenient and say that you are waiting for a reply. Use proper opening and closing expressions.*

_____

_____

_____

_____

_____

_____

_____

_____

_____

*Write a letter to Mr. Fauchon, the manager of a hotel on the Left Bank (**Rive Gauche**) in Paris where you have stayed before. Tell him you and your spouse have stayed at his hotel on several occasions and would like to reserve a room for two weeks in July. You would like your usual room with a view of the Eiffel Tower. You also want breakfast included in the room rate. Ask if you could have a discounted rate since you are a regular customer. Thank him courteously. Use proper opening and closing expressions.*

_____

_____

_____

_____

_____

_____

_____

_____

_____

_____

_____

_____

# E-mails

Using e-mails for formal and informal communication has become a way of life all over the world. In French, e-mail is most commonly called by its English name, **le e-mail**, but it is also called **le courriel** (especially in Canada) or **le courier électronique** (*electronic mail*). The format of e-mails is the same in French as it is in English.

EXERCICE
18·6

*Follow the directions for each exercise.*

1. Write an e-mail to Mme Sorot, a friend of the family who hosted you in France and just forwarded your mail to you. Tell her you just received the package containing the mail she had the kindness to send you. Add that you will always remember the days you spent as her guest. Thank her for having sent your mail to you and close appropriately.

_____

_____

_____

_____

_____

_____

_____

2. Write an e-mail to your friend Jonathan. Tell him to please send you his new phone number in France. Tell him that if he is available this afternoon, you would like to talk to him. Tell him to answer quickly.

_____

_____

_____

_____

_____

# Text messaging

Text messaging is called **le texto** in French. The essential idea of text messaging is to express oneself with the least number of characters, making use of pure reliance on sounds, abbreviations, and acronyms to convey a message. Beware that it is customary not to use accents in text messages. Consider the following examples of French abbreviations and acronyms used in text messaging:

| | | | | | |
|---|---|---|---|---|---|
| A2m1 | À demain. | *See you tomorrow.* | FDS | fin de semaine | *weekend* |
| ALP | À la prochaine. | *See you soon.* | G | j'ai | *I have* |
| auj | aujourd'hui | *today* | Je t'M | Je t'aime. | *I love you.* |
| BAL | boîte aux lettres | *mailbox* | KDO | cadeau | *gift* |
| BCP | beaucoup | *a lot* | Koi29 | Quoi de neuf? | *What's new?* |
| Bjr | Bonjour. | *Hello.* | Mr6 | Merci. | *Thanks.* |
| C | c'est | *it is* | Pkoi | Pourquoi? | *Why?* |
| CPG | C'est pas grave. | *It does not matter.* | rdv | rendez-vous | *date/appointment* |
| DSL | Désolé(e). | *Sorry.* | STP | S'il te plait. | *Please.* |
| DQP | Dès que possible. | *As soon as possible.* | | | |

# Common abbreviations used in informal communication

Along with the previously mentioned shortcuts in written communication, there are many other words in French that are commonly abbreviated in written *and* spoken communication. Here are a few examples:

| | | |
|---|---|---|
| un apart | un appartement | *an apartment* |
| cet aprem | cet après-midi | *this afternoon* |
| le cine | le cinéma | *the movie theater* |
| un/une coloc | un/une colocataire | *a cotenant* |
| dac | d'accord | *OK* |
| la fac | la faculté | *the school* (university) |
| le foot | le football | *soccer* |
| le frigo | le réfrigérateur | *the fridge* |
| impec | impeccable | *terrific* |
| le petit dej | le petit déjeuner | *breakfast* |
| une promo | une promotion | *a promotion* |
| un/une proprio | un/une propriétaire | *an owner* |
| un resto | un restaurant | *a restaurant* |

**EXERCICE**

**18·7**

*Write a text message to a friend. Thank her/him for a birthday gift that you like a lot. Also ask if she/he wants to go to the movies. Set the time for the date at eight o'clock.*

_____

_____

_____

_____

# Using colloquial expressions and structures

In Unit 18, you learned to build sentences for formal and informal communication. You will now see some expressions called colloquialisms; these are only used in very informal communication. Although there are colloquialisms that are strictly limited to a certain area, this unit will introduce colloquialisms commonly used in all French-speaking regions.

## Exclamatory expressions

Some exclamations beginning with **qu'est-ce que** and **ce que** (*how*) are used only in colloquial language. The speaker uses exclamations typical of informal conversational communication to emphasize admiration, praise, or just the opposite: contempt, disdain, scorn, dislike, and so on. Note the following constructions and how they are used:

> **Qu'est-ce que/Ce que + declarative sentence + !**
> **Qu'est-ce que** + tu es bête + !
> *You are so silly! (**How** silly you are!)*

> **Qu'est-ce qu'**elle m'énerve!      *Boy, does she bother me!*
> **Ce que** nous riions!      *We were laughing so much!*
> **Ce qu'**ils plaisantaient!      *(You can't imagine) How they used to joke!*

> **Qu'est-ce que + subject + verb + comme + noun + !**
> **Qu'est-ce que** + tu + fais + **comme** + fautes + !
> *How many mistakes you make!*

In these idiomatic colloquial expressions, the expression **ce que** is used to introduce the action that is remarkable in its magnitude or frequency while the preposition **comme** is used to introduce the category in which magnitude or frequency occurs.

> **Ce que** tu manges **comme** sucreries!      *How many sweets you eat!*
> **Ce qu'**elles ont fait **comme** progrès!      *How much progress they made!*

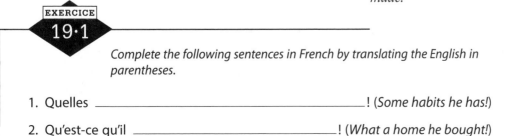

**EXERCICE**
**19·1**

Complete the following sentences in French by translating the English in parentheses.

1. Quelles _____! (*Some habits he has!*)

2. Qu'est-ce qu'il _____! (*What a home he bought!*)

3. Qu'est-ce que tu _____! (*What crazy things you did!*)

4. Ce qu'ils _____! (*They are so nice!*)

5. Ce que _____! (*This is so easy!*)

6. Qu'est-ce qu'elle _____! (*How beautiful she is!*)

*For each situation on the left, write the letter from the column on the right of your most likely reaction.*

1. _____ Jean-Jacques fait son propre lavage.

2. _____ Ses parents lui offrent une voiture.

3. _____ Il gagne un million à la loterie.

4. _____ Il va au gymnase tous les jours.

5. _____ Il marque deux buts à chaque match.

a. Qu'est-ce qu'il joue bien!

b. Qu'est-ce qu'il est discipliné!

c. Ce qu'il a comme chance!

d. Ce qu'ils sont généreux!

e. Ce qu'il est en forme!

## Short replies

The following expressions are short answers to *yes* or *no* questions or examples of simple replies to comments:

| | | | |
|---|---|---|---|
| Absolument. | *Absolutely.* | Je parie que non. | *I bet not. (I bet you that it is not so.)* |
| Bien sûr que non. | *Of course not.* | | |
| Bien sûr que oui. | *Of course.* | Je parie que oui. | *I bet so. (I bet you that it is so.)* |
| C'est bidon. | *It's worthless.* | | |
| C'est ça. | *That's right.* | Laisse tomber! | *Forget it!* |
| C'est nul. | *It sucks.* | Mais enfin! | *Come on!* (disbelief/ disapproval) |
| C'est pas vrai. | *It's not true.* | | |
| Ça marche. | *That's fine.* | (Mais) Évidemment. | *(But) of course.* |
| Ça se voit. | *That's obvious.* | (Mais) Quand même! | *Come on!* (disbelief/ disapproval) |
| Ça va. | *OK.* | | |
| Ça va de soi. | *That's obvious.* | Naturellement. | *Naturally.* |
| Ça y est. | *That's it.* | Pardi! | *Of course!* |
| Du tout. | *Not at all.* | Pas grave. | *Not to worry.* |
| Enfin! | *Finally!* | Peu importe. | *No matter.* |
| Exactement. | *Exactly.* | Tout à fait. | *That's it.* |
| Fais gaffe! | *Watch out!* | Tu penses bien. | *Of course.* |
| | | Vrai de vrai. | *It's true.* |

Circle one of the words or expressions from the choices in parentheses to complete Suzanne's answer appropriately.

1. Tu aimes les examens?

   *Suzanne*: (Pas grave / Du tout), Rémy!

2. Tu vas étudier pour l'examen de demain?

   *Suzanne*: (Tu penses bien / Enfin)! Je veux réussir.

3. Moi, je crois que je vais échouer.

   *Suzanne*: (Enfin / Mais enfin), Rémy!

4. Tu crois qu'il va être difficile, cet examen?

   *Suzanne*: (C'est nul / Je parie que oui).

5. J'ai vraiment peur, Suzanne.

   *Suzanne*: (Ça se voit. / Ça y est!), Rémy. Calme-toi!

6. Tu veux qu'on étudie ensemble?

   *Suzanne*: (Mais évidemment / Vrai de vrai) !

Complete each sentence by filling in the blanks with the correct translations of the expressions in parentheses.

1. —Zut! J'ai brûlé le rôti! —_____, on peut commander une pizza! (*Not to worry*)

2. —Je suis vraiment désolé! —_____! (*Forget it*)

3. —Tu veux sérieusement une pizza? —_____! (*It's true*)

4. —On va en commander une à la nouvelle pizzeria? —_____! (*That's fine*)

5. —Bon. Je téléphone tout de suite. —_____! (*OK*)

6. —Tu es vraiment gentil, tu sais! —_____! (*Of course*)

# Short questions

The following expressions have an interrogative structure but are used to express surprise rather than to ask a real question:

| | |
|---|---|
| C'est à dire? | *Meaning?* |
| Comment ça? | *What do you mean?* |
| Et alors? | *So what?* |
| Et après? | *So what?* |
| Qu'est-ce que tu racontes? | *What are you talking about?* |
| Quoi? | *What?* |
| Sans blague? | *No kidding?* |
| Tu dis? | *What?* |
| Tu te paies ma tête? | *Are you taking me for a fool?* |

**EXERCICE**
**19·5**

*Choose one of the words or expressions from the choices in parentheses to complete each of Joëlle's answers to Eric appropriately.*

1. Dis donc, Joëlle, j'ai vu Mireille tomber de son vélo.

   *Joëlle*: (Quoi / Tu te paies ma tête)? Elle s'est fait mal?

2. Je crois qu'elle jouait à la malade.

   *Joëlle*: (Comment ça / Sans blague)? Je ne comprends pas.

3. Tu sais, elle voulait probablement attirer notre attention.

   *Joëlle*: (Et après / Qu'est-ce que tu racontes)?Mireille n'est pas comme ça, voyons!

4. Tu ne vois pas qu'elle est jalouse de sa sœur?

   *Joëlle*: (Et alors / Tu dis)? Je ne vois pas ça du tout, Eric!

5. Ce matin, elle a mis le pull de Josie.

   *Joëlle*: (Et après / Tu dis)? Ça se fait entre sœurs.

6. Tu es une vraie mère poule.

   *Joëlle*: (C'est à dire / Tu te paies ma tête)? Explique un peu.

## Using reflexive pronouns for emphasis

Reflexive pronouns are sometimes used even though they are not necessary to add emphasis to an action. This is a familiar form of speech. Consider the following examples:

| | |
|---|---|
| Je vais l'acheter. | *I am going to buy it.* |
| Je vais **me** l'acheter. | |
| | |
| Tu les choisis toi-même. | *You choose them yourself.* |
| Tu **te** les choisis toi-même. | |
| | |
| Il cherche une femme intelligente. | *He is looking for an intelligent woman.* |
| Il **se** cherche une femme intelligente. | |

In the following examples, note the use of **être** as an auxiliary verb when the reflexive pronoun is added. Also note that the past participles (**mangé/trouvé**) do not agree with the reflexive pronouns because the pronouns do not serve as direct object pronouns: *We did not eat ourselves./ You did not find yourselves.*

Nous avons mangé une grosse tarte.        *We ate a big tart!*
Nous **nous** sommes mangé une grosse tarte!

Vous avez trouvé des parfums délicieux.        *You found delicious perfumes.*
Vous **vous** êtes trouvé des parfums délicieux.

### EXERCICE
### 19·6

*Rewrite the following sentences replacing the italicized verbs with the reflexive pronoun structure used in familiar speech.*

1. Les Dupuis *ont acheté* une ferme à la campagne.

_____

2. M. Dupuis *a choisi* une vieille ferme pas très chère près de Paris.

_____

3. Mme Dupuis *a trouvé* tout de suite de beaux géraniums.

_____

4. Elle *a* déjà *décoré* toutes les fenêtres de sa ferme.

_____

# Using the impersonal pronoun **on**

Although the pronoun **on** is sometimes used in formal contexts where it is the English equivalent of *one*, it is most frequently used in informal French as a replacement for *we, you, they, someone, everyone,* or *people*.

**On** ne parle pas la bouche pleine.        *One does not speak with a full mouth.*
**On** écoute ses parents!        *You should listen to your parents!*
**On** m'a assuré que ce produit est bon.        *People assured me that this product is good.*
Qu'est-ce qu'**on** fait ce weekend?        *What should/can we do this weekend?*
Allez, **on** y va!        *Come on, let's go!*
**On** s'entend bien, toi et moi.        *We get along well, you and I.*

### EXERCICE
### 19·7

*Rewrite the following sentences in a more formal manner by replacing **on** with **nous**.*

1. On va arroser les géraniums aujourd'hui.

_____

2. On ira au village acheter des provisions.

_____

3. Après le déjeuner, on va tailler les rosiers.

_____

4. En fin d'après-midi, on fera une promenade à cheval.

_____

5. On brossera les chevaux demain.

_____

## Adding a pronoun after a subject-noun

In familiar conversations, a subject-noun may be followed by a pronoun that is ordinarily unnecessary. Consider the following examples:

Ton père est sympa.                  *Your father is nice.*
Ton père, **il** est sympa.

Sa maison est grande.                *His/Her house is big.*
Sa maison, **elle** est grande.

José et moi allons partir.           *José and I are going to leave.*
José et moi, **nous** allons partir.

Louise et Jules vont venir.          *Louise and Jules are going to come.*
Louise et Jules, **ils** vont venir.

EXERCICE
19·8

*Rewrite the following sentences in a more formal manner by omitting unnecessary pronouns.*

1. Les Dupuis, ils adorent l'équitation.

_____

2. M. Dupuis, il monte vraiment bien à cheval.

_____

3. Mme Dupuis, elle est encore débutante.

_____

4. Leurs chevaux, ils sont doux.

_____

## Dropping parts of speech

Another colloquialism consists in dropping parts of speech such as **ne** in negative structures or **il** in impersonal expressions.

# Dropping **ne/n'** in negative structures

Since the adverbial part of the structure (**pas, plus, jamais, rien, personne**) is sufficient to convey a negative meaning, the **ne** part of the negative structure is frequently dropped in familiar communication.

| | |
|---|---|
| Il **ne** faut pas que tu arrives en retard.<br>Il faut pas que tu arrives en retard. | *You must not arrive late.* |
| **Ne** fais pas ça!<br>Fais pas ça! | *Don't do that!* |
| Je **n'**ai jamais volé.<br>J'ai jamais volé. | *I never stole.* |
| Elle **n'**a plus rien.<br>Elle a plus rien. | *She has nothing left.* |
| Il **n'**est pas jaloux.<br>Il est pas jaloux. | *He is not jealous.* |

# Dropping the pronoun **il** in impersonal expressions

In impersonal expressions such as **il y a** (*there is*) and **il faut** (*it is necessary*), the subject cannot be anything other than **il**; this subject is therefore omitted in familiar communication.

| | |
|---|---|
| **Il** y a trop de sel dans cette soupe.<br>Y a trop de sel dans cette soupe. | *There is too much salt in this soup.* |
| **Il** y aura beaucoup de monde.<br>Y aura beaucoup de monde. | *There will be a lot of people.* |
| **Il** y avait une tâche sur la chemise.<br>Y avait une tâche sur la chemise. | *There was a stain on the shirt.* |
| **Il** faut bien manger, mon petit.<br>Faut bien manger, mon petit. | *You must eat well, my little one.* |

EXERCICE
## 19·9

*Add the missing elements of speech to make the following familiar paragraph more formal.*

M. Rateau (1) _____ va pas au bureau aujourd'hui. (2) _____
y a une manifestation qui cause de gros bouchons au centre-ville. (3) _____
faudra attendre que ce soit terminé pour pouvoir circuler librement. (4) _____
suffit d'être patient et de suivre les nouvelles. Il (5) _____ a qu'à travailler un
peu à la maison, c'est tout!

# Writing

·20·

After accomplishing the tasks in the previous units of this book, you can now put your new skills into practice. It is indeed time for you to realize just how much you have learned and to apply this new knowledge in a more flexible and personal fashion. You may not remember how to perform every structure presented to you but that may not be necessary for you to communicate effectively. Feel free to use familiar structures but do not be afraid to try out less familiar ones. Finally, take the opportunity to create your own piece of extended writing.

## Let's practice!

In this section, you will combine series of given words to produce sentences and paragraphs; you will make changes to given sentences to create new ones; finally you will produce your own writing.

**EXERCICE 20·1**

*Use the adverbs, adjectives, interrogative phrases, and pronouns provided in the list to complete the sentences in the following paragraph.*

alors / demain / est-ce que / chouette / qui / moi / en / vous / l'

(1) _____ il fera beau. (2) _____, profitons-en et allons à la plage! (3) _____ vous voulez pique-niquer sur la plage? Ce serait (4) _____, non? (5) _____, j'apporterai à manger. (6) _____ apportera les boissons? Toi, Mireille? Merci. Et Francine propose d'apporter une salade niçoise. Qu'est-ce que vous (7) _____ pensez? (8) _____ êtes d'accord! Eh bien, (9) _____ aussi. J'adore la salade niçoise. Bon. La musique, c'est moi qui (10) _____ apporterai! À demain, les amis!

**EXERCICE 20·2**

*Use the sentence fragments to write original sentences. Add any necessary words such as transitions and conjunctions, use appropriate punctuation, and conform to the grammar cues in parentheses.*

1. plus facile / apprendre le français / utiliser un livre bien écrit (*adjective + infinitive / present participle clause or subordinate clause with* quand)

   _____

   _____

2. faire tous les exercices de ce livre / pour élargir ma base de français / il faut (*subordinate clause with subjunctive*)

   _____

   _____

3. de temps en temps / il faut réviser / tout / on a appris (*relative clause—no antecedent*)

   _____

   _____

4. ajouter / en même temps / de nouvelles notions grammaticales / des mots de vocabulaire / il faut (*infinitive clause*)

   _____

   _____

5. utiliser ces connaissances de français / voyager / communiquer / amis / collègues / lire journaux / quel plaisir (*exclamatory sentence / infinitive clause / present participle clause*)

   _____

   _____

6. formidable / comprendre / une autre langue / une autre culture / vraiment / ne pensez-vous pas (*interrogative sentence / infinitive clause*)

   _____

   _____

7. ce chapitre / plus amusant / m'exprimer / plus personnelle / d'une façon / plus créative / il permet (*comparative form of adjectives / adverbial structure / subordinate clause with* parce que)

   _____

   _____

8. après / finir ce livre / voudrais pratiquer / amis français (*past infinitive clause*)

   _____

   _____

9. l'année prochaine / suivre un autre cours de français / avoir le temps / si (*conditional clause with* si *and present tense*)

   _____

   _____

10. surpris(e) / comprendre et apprendre / tant / français / content (*exclamatory sentence / adjective followed by past infinitive clause*)

_____

_____

_____

EXERCICE
20·3

*In the following sentences, change the boldface words and expressions to words that will restore the basic ideas in the fairy tale* Sleeping Beauty (La Belle au Bois Dormant).

Il était une fois un roi et une reine **qui ne voulaient absolument pas d'enfants** (1) _____. **Mais** (2) _____ la reine est tombée enceinte et a accouché d'une petite fille **vraiment horrible** (3) _____. Le roi et la reine **la détestaient** (4) _____. Ils ont invité sept **vieilles** (5) _____ fées au palais pour offrir des cadeaux à leur **horrible** (6) _____ fillette. **Heureusement** (7) _____ ils ont oublié d'inviter la plus **jeune** (8) _____ des fées du royaume. La **jeune** (9) _____ fée **n'a pas jeté de mauvais sort** (10) _____ à la princesse. L'une des sept **vilaines** (11) _____ fées a promis que la fillette serait **tuée** (12) _____ par un prince.

EXERCICE
20·4

*Write a personal narrative describing the best moment in your life. You must use the imperfect and passé composé tenses. Use descriptive adjectives to describe this special moment, transitional words and adverbs to enrich and give details of what happened, and exclamatory words to show how you felt. Try to use at least one present or past participle clause, one relative clause, and one past infinitive clause.*

*The questions provided for each prompt aim at guiding your writing. The models you will find in the Answer Key are based on them. However, feel free to make any changes you deem necessary.*

A. **Ma première voiture.** Était-ce le plus beau jour de votre vie? Vous et votre père/mère, vous êtes-vous levé(e)s tôt ce matin-là? Vous êtes-vous rendu(e)s à la salle de vente des voitures d'occasion? Comment s'appelait le représentant qui vous a accueillis et vous a demandé si vous étiez prêt(e)s à acheter une voiture? A quelle heure êtes-vous reparti(e)s? Comment vous sentiez-vous dans votre voiture? Quelle sorte de cadeau était-ce? Inoubliable? Fantastique?

_____

_____

_____

_____

_____

B. **La lettre de l'université.** Qu'attendiez-vous de savoir au mois de mars ou d'avril? Alliez-vous ouvrir la boîte à lettres tous les jours? Pourquoi? Comment se passaient les longues journées sans nouvelles? Et puis, qu'est-ce qui s'est passé un jour? Était-ce la lettre que vous attendiez? Comment avez-vous ouvert la lettre (tout doucement, avec crainte, impatiemment)? Est-ce que c'était une invitation à vous rendre à une session d'orientation? Votre rêve se réalisait-il?

_____

_____

_____

_____

_____

_____

_____

_____

# Let's write dialogues!

In this section, you will create your own dialogues. This will allow you to practice asking and answering questions.

EXERCICE
20·5

*Write a dialogue in which you are trying to get your money back (**se faire rembourser**) for an electric razor purchased in a department store. Give at least two reasons to the salesperson why you want to return the item. Be sure to use appropriate forms of address (**vous** and a title such as **monsieur** or **madame**); use courteous expressions such as "**Pardonnez-moi**." The salesperson should ask questions such as "Why are you returning this item?"/"Did you bring your receipt?"/"May I have your credit card?"*

Moi: _____

_____

Vendeur: _____

_____

Moi: _____

_____

Vendeur: _____

_____

Moi: _____

_____

Vendeur: _____

_____

Moi: _____

_____

Vendeur: _____

_____

EXERCICE
20·6

*Write a dialogue between yourself and a man or a woman you are meeting for the first time at a friend's house. Ask at least three questions to get to know that person, but offer some information about yourself as well. Remember to be formal since you are meeting the person for the first time. The following are some suggested questions and answers:*

—*Is it the first time you've come to André's place? —Yes, how about you?*
—*Oh! We are very good friends. Where did you meet him? —At the university's coffee shop. We were waiting in line. So we chatted.*
—*Oh! So you, too, are studying business? —Yes, that's it! And you, are you a student?*
—*Yes, I am studying . . .*

Moi: _____

_____

Une connaissance: _____

_____

Moi: _____

_____

Une connaissance: _____

_____

Moi: _____

_____

Une connaissance: _____

_____

Moi: _____

_____

*Write a dialogue between yourself and a good friend. Remember to use familiar terms. (You may use a few colloquialisms such as "**j'aime pas**" or "**Y a**.") Suggested questions and answers are as follows:*

—Hey, feel like going to the movies tonight? —I don't mind. What's playing?

—There is a new adventure movie downtown with Gérard Depardieu. —I don't like that too much! I prefer comedies. Anything funny at the movies?

—I am going to see on the Internet. I'll send you a text message in a moment. OK? —OK. Hear from you in a little while.

Moi: _____

_____

Gigi: _____

_____

Moi: _____

_____

Gigi: _____

_____

Moi: _____

_____

Gigi: _____

_____

*In this section, you will practice formal writing by composing a complete letter (opening, body, and closing). Write a letter to M. Ramoneau, the manager of a hotel where you stayed recently and where you enjoyed wonderful service. Be sure to open and close the letter appropriately. You may use the following questions to guide your writing:*

Pour quelle raison écrivez-vous (pour remercier ou féliciter quelqu'un)? Quand étiez-vous à cet hôtel? / Pendant combien de temps? / Avec qui? / Était-ce la première fois? / Est-ce le syndicat d'initiative de Poitiers qui vous a recommandé cet hôtel?

Quels employés vous ont le mieux servi (le directeur ou le chef du restaurant, un serveur ou une serveuse au café, le concierge)? / Quels services très spéciaux vous ont-ils rendus (des soins très attentifs, un plat spécial, des réservations dans un restaurant ou pour un spectacle, une bouteille de vin)?

Comptez-vous revenir bientôt? / Allez-vous recommander cet hôtel à vos amis?

_____

_____

_____

_____

# Review and extension

This chapter combines topics and provides opportunities to review the essentials presented in the main body of the book in a more global and more contextual form. Summary charts and summary outlines are presented for at-a-glance review; the learner can go back into the referenced chapters for more details when deemed necessary.

    **I.** Declarative sentences with adverbs and noun-objects [chapters 1 and 14]

    **II.** Declarative sentences with object pronouns [chapters 1, 12–14]

    **III.** Interrogative sentences [chapters 2 and 3]

    **IV.** Independent clauses including declarative, interrogative, imperative, and exclamatory structures [chapters 1–6]

    **V.** Dependent clauses [chapters 7–10, 16]

    **VI.** Nouns and noun phrases as complements of prepositions [chapters 11 and 15]

## I. Declarative sentences with adverbs and noun-objects

[*See chapters 1 and 14.*]

### Affirmative declarative sentences

Affirmative declarative sentences include at the very least a subject and a verb. They may include direct and/or indirect objects (direct objects are placed before indirect objects).

| Subject + verb | Subject + verb + adverb | Subject + verb + objects + adverb of time OR adverb of time + Subject + verb + objects | Subject + verb + short adverb + objects |
|---|---|---|---|
| **Nous partons.** *We are leaving.* | **Nous partons** vite. *We leave quickly.* | **Vous offrez** des cadeaux aux enfants aujourd'hui. *You give some gifts to the children today.* OR Aujourd'hui, **vous offrez** des cadeaux aux enfants aujourd'hui. *Today, you give some gifts to the children.* | **Les étudiants donnent** souvent de bonnes réponses au professeur. *The students often give good answers to their teacher.* |

**213**

**EXERCICE**

**21·1**

*Reconstruct each sentence by placing the fragments in the appropriate order.*

1. regarde / des films / souvent / d'horreur / Nadine

   _____

2. collectionne / elle / d'Halloween / des masques

   _____

3. Ses amis / le soir d'Halloween / toujours / aux enfants / des bonbons / donnent

   _____

4. achète / chaque année / Nadine / un costume différent

   _____

5. Elle / son costume / parfois / à ses petits frères / montre / et à ses petites sœurs

   _____

6. admire / et les masques de Nadine / tout le monde / les costumes

   _____


**EXERCICE**

**21·2**

*Reconstruct each sentence by placing the fragments in the appropriate order.*

1. admirons / les stars / nous / passionnément

   _____

2. attribuons / nous / à nos stars / toutes sortes de qualités

   _____

3. les stars / de nos jours / des marques publicitaires / représentent

   _____

4. toujours / de la star / les grandes marques / disséminent / une image flatteuse

   _____

5. relance / la collaboration de la star avec une marque / parfois / la carrière de la star

   _____

6. la nécessité d'une telle collaboration / on / bien / comprend

   _____

# Negative declarative sentences

The word order in negative declarative sentences is the same as in affirmative sentences but includes the negative adverbs ne/pas, ne/jamais, ne/rien, ne/plus, ne/personne, ne/que.

- ◆ **Ne** always precedes the verb.
- ◆ **Pas, jamais, rien,** and **plus** are placed right after the conjugated form of the verb in the present tense, after the conjugated form of **aller** in the near future, or in a two-verb structure, before the past participle of the verb in the passé composé.

| | |
|---|---|
| Les étudiants **ne donnent pas** de bonnes réponses [au professeur]. | *The students do not give good answers [to their teacher].* |
| Les étudiants **ne vont pas donner** de bonnes réponses [au professeur]. | *The students are not going to give good answers [to their teacher].* |
| Les étudiants **n'ont pas donné** de bonnes réponses [au professeur]. | *The students did not give good answers [to their teacher].* |

- ◆ **Personne** and **que** follow the same pattern in the present tense but appear after the infinitive verb in the near future or in two-verb structures, and after the past participle in the passé composé.

| | |
|---|---|
| Je **ne vois personne**. *I do not see anyone.* | Il **n'a qu'**un enfant. *He has only one child.* |
| Je **ne vais voir personne**. *I am not going to see anyone.* | Il **ne va avoir qu'**un enfant. *He is going to have only one child.* |
| Je **n'ai vu personne**. *I saw no one.* | Il **n'a eu qu'**un enfant. *He had only one child.* |

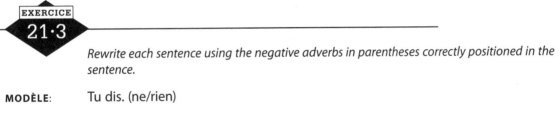

EXERCICE
21·3

*Rewrite each sentence using the negative adverbs in parentheses correctly positioned in the sentence.*

**MODÈLE:** Tu dis. (ne/rien)

**RÉPONSE:** Tu ne dis rien.

1. Nous mangeons les escargots. (ne/jamais)

   _____

2. Vous écoutez. (ne/personne)

   _____

3. Vous faites tout le dimanche. (ne/rien)

   _____

4. Les enfants jouent. (ne/plus)

   _____

5. Elle a invité. (ne/personne)

   _____

6. Ils ont vu un spectacle. (ne/que)

_____

7. Tu vas au concert? (ne/pas)

_____

8. Vous allez chanter. (ne/plus)

_____

**EXERCICE**
**21·4**

*Rewrite each sentence using the negative adverbs in parentheses correctly positioned in the sentence. Beware of the varying tenses.*

**MODÈLE:**     Nous nous sommes bien amusés. (ne/pas)

**RÉPONSE:**     Nous ne nous sommes pas bien amusés.

1. Aujourd'hui, je veux des fruits et de la tarte. (ne/ni...ni)

_____

2. Demain, je vais inviter. (ne/personne)

_____

3. Hier, j'ai lu. (ne/rien)

_____

4. Maintenant, je voudrais jouer à ce jeu. (ne/plus)

_____

5. L'an dernier, j'allais au marché. (ne/jamais)

_____

6. Plus tard ce soir, je vais aller. (ne/nulle part)

_____

7. Généralement, je réussis à mes examens de Français. (ne/que)

_____

8. Hier j'ai nagé et bronzé. (ne/ni...ni)

_____

# II. Declarative sentences with object pronouns

[*See chapters 1, 12, 13, and 14.*]

## Direct object pronouns in affirmative declarative sentences

The pronouns **le, la, l'**, and **les** are direct object pronouns; they replace previously mentioned people or things, they receive the action of the verb, and they precede the verb when it is in its simple one-word form.

| **le** | **la** | **l'** | **les** |
|---|---|---|---|
| Nous le voulons. | Tu la prends. | Je l'aime. | Tu les as? |
| *We want it/him.* | *You take it/her.* | *I love it/him/her.* | *Do you have them?* |

In the following question, the noun phrase **tes amis** receives the action of the verb **chercher** directly (it is not preceded by a preposition) and is therefore its direct object. In the answer to the question, the noun phrase **tes amis** is replaced by the direct object pronoun **les**. Note the position of the pronoun **les:** right before the verb **cherche** in the present tense.

_____Tu cherches tes amis?　　　　　*Are you looking for your friends?*
_____Oui, je les cherche.　　　　　*Yes, I'm looking for them.*

The responder to the initial question is then asking his/her own follow-up question in which the verb is now in the passé composé.

_____Tu cherches tes amis?　　　　　*Are you looking for your friends?*
_____Oui, je les cherche. **Tu les a vus?**　　*Yes, I'm looking for them.* ***Have you seen them?***

Note the direct object pronoun is now before the helping verb **avoir**—not before the past participle **vus**. Also note that since French past participles agree in gender and number with a preceding direct object, the past participle **vu** (of the verb voir) is now ending in -*s*.

_____Tu **les** a vus?　　　　　*Have you seen them?*

---

**EXERCICE**
**21·5**

*Answer each question with a direct object pronoun appropriately positioned in the sentence. All questions and answers are in the present tense.*

**MODÈLE:**　　Il prend le bus? _____ Oui, _____

RÉPONSE:　　Il le prend.

1. Tu aimes les fruits? _____ Oui, _____

2. Tu écoutes la radio? _____ Oui, _____

3. Tu écris le texto? _____ Oui, _____

4. Tu as la clé de la maison? _____ Oui, _____

5. Tes parents font la cuisine? ____ Oui, _____

6. On fait les courses? ____ Oui, _____

7. Tes parents cherchent ta petite sœur? ____ Oui, _____

8. Tes parents trouvent ta sœur? ____ Oui, _____

EXERCICE
21·6

*Answer each question with a direct object pronoun appropriately positioned in the affirmative answer. All questions and answers are in the passé composé or the near future.*

**MODÈLE:**   Les enfants ont fait les lits? ____ Oui, _____

RÉPONSE :   Ils les ont faits.

1. Les enfants ont écrit leurs essais? ____ Oui, _____

2. Marie a préparé son dîner? ____ Oui, _____

3. Jérémy a passé l'aspirateur? ____ Oui, _____

4. Tu as lavé ta voiture? ____ Oui, _____

5. Tes parents ont sorti la poubelle? ____ Oui, _____

6. Tu vas bientôt couper le gazon? ____ Oui, _____

7. Tes amis vont nettoyer le salon? ____ Oui, _____

8. Ta mère va finir son gâteau? ____ Oui, _____

# Indirect object pronouns in affirmative declarative sentences

The pronouns **lui** and **leur** are indirect object pronouns; they replace previously mentioned people, receive the action of the verb indirectly because the people were part of a noun phrase that includes the preposition **à**, and are placed before the verb in its simple one-word form.

| **lui** | **lui** | **leur** |
|---|---|---|
| Tu parles **à Thomas**? | Tu parles **à Chloé**? | Tu téléphones **à tes amis**? |
| —Oui, Je **lui** parle souvent. | —Oui, Je **lui** parle souvent. | —Oui, je leur téléphone. |
| *Do you talk to Thomas?* | *Do you talk to Chloé?* | *Do you call your friends?* |
| —*Yes, I talk **to him** often.* | —*Yes, I talk **to her** often.* | —*Yes, I call **them** often.* |

Note that the noun phrase [à + person(s)] can appear with the contracted form of [à + le] or [à + les] as in the following sentences:

| **lui** | **lui** | **leur** |
|---|---|---|
| Tu réponds **au prof**? | Tu offres quelque chose **au client**? | Qu'est-ce que tu donnes **aux enfants**? |
| ____Oui, Je **lui** réponds. | ____Oui, Je **lui** offre un bon. | ____Je **leur** donne des bonbons. |
| *Do you answer the teacher?* | *Do you give the client something?* | *What do you give to the children?* |
| ____*Yes, I answer him.* | ____*Yes, I give him a voucher.* | ____*I give them candy.* |

**Indirect object pronouns are required with special verbs like plaire, falloir, and manquer.**

[*See chapter 13.*]

| Cet article ne **lui** plaît pas. | *She does not like this article.* |
|---|---|
| Leurs parents **leur** ont manqué. | *They missed their parents.* |
| Qu'est-ce qu'il **te** faut? | *What do you need?* |

**EXERCICE**
**21·7**

*Answer each question with an indirect object pronoun appropriately positioned in the sentence. Start each answer with the subject pronoun nous.*

MODÈLE: Tu écris à tes copains? ____ Oui, _____

RÉPONSE: Nous leur ecrivons.

1. Vous obéissez à vos parents? ____ Oui, _____

2. Vous allez répondre à votre professeur? ____ Oui, _____

3. Vous avez écrit à votre grand-mère? ____ Oui, _____

4. Vous donnez des cadeaux d'anniversaire à vos amis? ____ Oui, _____

5. Vous avez envoyé les courriels aux clients? ____ Oui, _____

6. Vous promettez des choses à vos amis? ____ Oui, _____

7. Vous allez désobéir à votre patron? ____ Non, _____

8. Vous allez poser une question au serveur? ____ Oui, _____

*Answer each question with an indirect object pronoun appropriately positioned in the sentence.*

MODÈLE:    Le dentiste t'a fait mal? _____ Oui, _____

RÉPONSE :   Il m'a fait mal.

1. La mauvaise nouvelle t'a fait de la peine? _____ Oui, _____

2. Il va te rester de l'argent après vos vacances? _____ Oui, _____

3. Une carte de crédit te suffit? _____ Oui, _____

4. Il nous faut une chambre d'hôtel? _____ Oui, _____

5. Cet hôtel te parait cher? _____ Oui, _____

6. La vue sur la plage va nous manquer? _____ Oui, _____

7. Le décor de la chambre du premier étage t'a plu? _____ Oui, _____

8. Et la musique de l'ascenseur, elle plaît aux clients? _____ Oui, _____

## Object pronouns in negative declarative sentences

French object pronouns include direct and indirect object pronouns, and adverbial pronouns **y** and **en**.

| Direct object pronouns [replace noun phrases other than prepositional] | Indirect object pronouns [replace à + person(s)] | Direct or indirect object pronouns [replace person(s)] | Adverbial pronouns y and en [y replaces à + thing and en replaces de + thing(s) / 0person(s)] |
|---|---|---|---|
| le, la, l', les | lui, leur | me, te, se, nous, vous | y, en |

◆ Object pronouns precede the simple one-word form of a verb and follow the negative adverb **ne**:

Il **ne lui envoie rien**.                    *He does not send him/her anything.*
Des chocolats? Je **n'en veux pas**.          *Chocolates? I do not want any.*

◆ Object pronouns precede the infinitive verb and follow the negative adverb **pas/jamais/plus** in the near future or in two-verb structures:

Je **ne** veux **pas t'inviter**.             *I do not want to invite you.*
La plage? Nous **n'allons plus** y aller.     *The beach? We are not going to go there anymore.*

◆ Object pronouns precede the helping verb and follow the negative adverb **ne** in the passé composé:

Je **ne leur ai jamais** parlé.                          *I never spoke to them.*
Vous **ne vous** êtes **pas** levés à l'heure.           *You did not get up on time.*

*Answer each question with the appropriate object pronoun that replaces the bold part of the question. Position the pronoun correctly in the sentence and start each answer with the subject pronoun je.*

MODÈLE:      Tu as parlé **à ton professeur?** _____ Non, _____

RÉPONSE:     Je ne lui ai pas parlé.

1. Tu as fini **tes examens?** _____ Non, _____

2. Tu as eu **de bonnes notes** en cours de Français? _____ Non, malheureusement, _____

3. Tu as aidé **tes amis** à étudier? _____ Oui, naturellement, _____

4. Tu vas encore **aux cours?** _____ Non, _____ .
   C'est terminé.

5. Tu vas **m'**accompagner **au café?** _____ Non, _____ ; je n'ai pas le temps.

6. Tu vas expliquer **aux copains** pourquoi tu ne viens pas? _____ Oui, bien sûr, _____

7. Tu n'as pas besoin **d'une tasse de café?** _____ Non, pas du tout, _____

8. Bon, tu prends **le bus** pour rentrer? _____ Oui, _____ tout de suite.

*Following the prompts, answer each question using one or two object pronoun(s) that appropriately respond to the bold parts of the question.*

MODÈLE:      Thomas **t'**a montré **son projet?** _____ Non/pas _____

RÉPONSE:     Non, il ne me l'a pas montré.

1. Thomas a répondu **au texto de Cécile?** _____ Non/pas encore

_____

2. Cécile a bien envoyé **ce texto?** _____ Non/peut-être pas

_____

3. Elle **t'**a montré **le texto**? _____ Non/que le début

_____

4. Et toi, tu envoies **des invitations** aussi? _____ Non/jamais

_____

5. Ah bon. Tu n'offres jamais **ton aide à Cécile**? _____ Non/jamais/à personne

_____

6. Arrête! Tu dis **des bêtises**. _____ Oui/bien sûr/tout le temps

_____

7. Bon. Tu racontes toujours **les vieilles blagues de notre enfance** ? _____ Ah non/plus

_____

8. Tu **m'**offres **un verre de vin**? _____ Non, désolé/rien/je dois partir

_____

## Reflexive pronouns in declarative sentences

Reflexive verbs are accompanied by the pronouns **me/te/se/nous/vous/se**; these can have a direct or indirect object function either for reflexive or reciprocal actions.

| Reflexive usage | Function of the pronoun | Reciprocal usage | Function of the pronoun |
| --- | --- | --- | --- |
| Je **me** lave. *I wash myself.* | **me** is a direct object (laver quelqu'un) | / | |
| Tu **te** promènes. *You are walking (yourself).* | **te** is a direct object (promener quelqu'un) | / | |
| Elle **se** demande. *She asks herself/wonders.* | **se** is an indirect object (demander à quelqu'un) | / | |
| Nous **nous** habillons. *We dress ourselves* | **nous** is a direct object (habiller quelqu'un) | Nous **nous** regardons. *We look at each other.* | **nous** is a direct object (regarder quelqu'un) |
| Vous **vous** lavez les mains. *You are washing your hands (to yourselves).* | **vous** is an indirect object (laver les mains à quelqu'un) | Vous **vous** embrassez. *You kiss each other.* | **vous** is a direct object (embrasser quelqu'un) |
| Elles **se** rasent les jambes. *They shave their legs (to themselves).* | **se** is an indirect object (raser les jambes à quelqu'un) | Ils **s'**écrivent. *They write to each other.* | **s'** is an indirect object (écrire à quelqu'un) |

Remember that, in an affirmative or negative declarative sentence, the reflexive pronoun matching the subject pronoun precedes the infinitive verb in the near future (or in a two-verb structure):

Je vais **me** promener. — *I am going to take a walk.*
Elle ne peut pas **se** raser. — *She cannot shave.*

♦ In an affirmative or negative declarative sentence, the reflexive pronoun precedes the helping verb **être** in the passé composé:

Nous **nous** sommes levés tôt.  
Les filles ne **se** sont pas maquillées.

*We got up early.*  
*The girls did not put on their make-up.*

**EXERCICE**
**21·11**

*Using all the phrase fragments, reconstruct each sentence. The first three sentences require the present tense, the fourth requires the near future, and the last four sentences require passé composé. Be sure to place the correct reflexive pronoun appropriately in the sentence.*

**MODÈLE:**    ce matin / se laver / elle

RÉPONSE:    Ce matin, elle s'est lavée.

1. Généralement / Monique / se promener / dans le quartier / tôt le matin

   _____

2. Généralement / nous / se laver et s'habiller / pendant ce temps

   _____

3. Généralement / vous / s'arrêter / au café / en route

   _____

4. Aujourd'hui / vous / aller / se préparer / dans la chambre

   _____

5. Ce matin, tu / se coiffer/bien

   _____

6. Ce matin / je / se brosser les dents / avant toi

   _____

7. Ce matin, papa / se raser

   _____

8. Ce matin / nous / se dépêcher

   _____

*Using all the parts of each sentence, reconstruct each sentence, using the passé composé for all the reflexive verbs. Be sure to place the correct reflexive pronoun appropriately in the sentence.*

**MODÈLE:**    Mireille / se laver

RÉPONSE:    Mireille s'est lavée.

1. Mireille / se lever avant le reste de la famille

_____

2. Moi, son frère, je / se cacher

_____

3. Mireille / se dépêcher de sortir

_____

4. Alec, le copain de Mireille, / se rendre chez nous

_____

5. Alec et Mireille / se rencontrer devant notre maison

_____

6. Alec et Mireille / s'embrasser

_____

7. Alec et Mireille / se promener un peu ensemble

_____

8. Alec et Mireille / se séparer

_____

9. A neuf heures, Alec et Mireille / se rendre à l'université séparément

_____

10. Ils / se revoir au cours de physique

_____

# III. Interrogative sentences

[*See chapters 2 and 3.*]

## Yes/No questions

This type of question includes at the very least a subject and a verb. There are several ways to ask these questions.

- ◆ Intonation questions have the same word order as a declarative sentence; the higher pitch at the end of the sentence denotes an interrogation. These questions have a familiar tone.
- ◆ *Est-ce que* questions have the same word order as a declarative sentence once the phrase *est-ce que* has appeared. This type of question can be found in both familiar and formal settings.
- ◆ The oui/non, n'est-ce pas style of question conveys a familiar tone whereas adding *n'est-ce pas* is a little more formal.
- ◆ The inversion style of question requires that the places the subject pronoun and verb occupied in a declarative sentence be reversed. This type of question is often more formal.

| Intonation | Est-ce que | Oui/non/n'est-ce pas | Inversion |
|---|---|---|---|
| Tu pars? | Est-ce que tu pars? | Tu pars, oui? | Pars-tu? |
| | | Tu pars, non? | |
| | | Tu pars, n'est-ce pas? | |
| *Are you leaving?* | *Are you leaving?* | You are leaving, right? | *Are you leaving?* |

Remember to insert -**t**- in the singular third person (with the pronouns il/elle/on) that does not end in a consonant for liaison purposes. Also remember that an inversion is usually not appropriate (there are a few exceptions) when the subject pronoun is **je**.

| Declarative sentence with subject-pronoun | Interrogative sentence with inversion |
|---|---|
| Vous chantez. *You sing.* | Chantez-vous? *Do you sing?* |
| Il chante. *He sings.* | Chante-t-il? *Does he sing?* |
| Elle va chanter. *She is going to sing.* | Va-t-elle chanter? *Is she going to sing?* |

The inversion style of questioning exists when the subject is a noun rather than a pronoun but the type of inversion does not require making an inversion between the subject and the verb; instead the personal subject pronoun that would replace the subject noun is added to the verb (il/elle/ils/elles).

| Declarative sentence with subject-noun | Inversion question |
|---|---|
| Pauline chante. *Pauline sings.* | Pauline chante-t-elle? *Does Pauline sing?* |
| Le professeur parle. *The teacher is speaking.* | Le professeur parle-t-il? *Is the teacher speaking?* |
| Les filles aiment danser. *The girls like to dance.* | Les filles aiment-elles danser? *Do the girls like to dance?* |

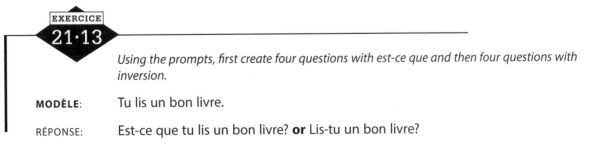

**EXERCICE**

**21·13**

*Using the prompts, first create four questions with est-ce que and then four questions with inversion.*

**MODÈLE:**  Tu lis un bon livre.

**RÉPONSE:**  Est-ce que tu lis un bon livre? **or** Lis-tu un bon livre?

1. Antoine travaille au restaurant.

2. Il n'a pas de vacances.

_____

3. Tu vas en voyage.

_____

4. Vous partez aujourd'hui ou demain.

_____

5. Nathalie reste à la maison.

_____

6. Les chiens restent chez les voisins.

_____

7. Tu vas t'amuser tout seul.

_____

8. Tu peux nous envoyer des texto.

_____

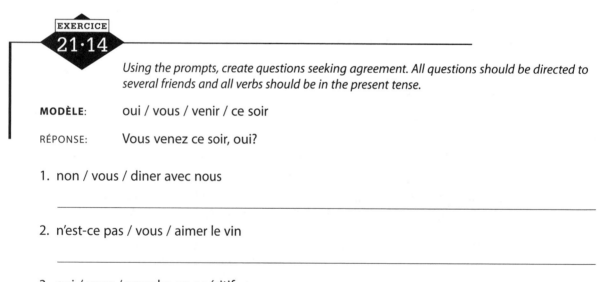

EXERCICE
21·14

*Using the prompts, create questions seeking agreement. All questions should be directed to several friends and all verbs should be in the present tense.*

**MODÈLE:**     oui / vous / venir / ce soir

RÉPONSE:     Vous venez ce soir, oui?

1. non / vous / diner avec nous

_____

2. n'est-ce pas / vous / aimer le vin

_____

3. oui / vous / prendre un apéritif

_____

4. non / vous / rester chez nous / ce soir

_____

5. n'est-ce pas / on / attendre les amis

_____

6. oui / on/ pouvoir parler de politique

_____

7. non / vous / être d'accord

_____

8. n'est-ce pas / vous / avoir la nationalité française

_____


## Interrogative sentences with precise interrogative words

◆ A **who** question can only use this format: [qui or qui est-ce qui] + [verb].
◆ A **what** question can use two different formats depending on whether the **what** is the subject or object; **what** can occasionally be the subject of the verb as in: **Qu'est-ce qui se passe?** or **Qu'est-ce qui arrive?** (What is happening?). Usually, though, **what** is the object of the verb and can be used with an *est-ce que*–type format or an *inversion* format.

| Qui/qui est-ce qui + verb | Que/object + [verb + hyphen + subject pronoun] | qu'est-ce que / object + subject + verb |
|---|---|---|
| Qui écoute? *Who listens?* | Que veux-tu? *What do you want?* | Qu'est-ce que nous mangeons? *What are we eating?* |
| Qui est-ce qui vient? *Who is coming?* | Que regardent-ils? *What are they watching?* | Qu'est-ce que Mario cherche? *What is Mario looking for?* |

◆ Questions about when, how, why, and how many can be posed using various formats.

| Intonation | Est-ce que | Inversion |
|---|---|---|
| Quand tu arrives? *When will you arrive?* | Quand est-ce que tu arrives? *When will you arrive?* | Quand arrives-tu? *When will you arrive?* |
| Comment tu vas? *How are you doing?* | Comment est-ce que tu vas? *How are you doing?* | Comment vas-tu? *How are you doing?* |
| Pourquoi tu ris? *Why are you laughing?* | Pourquoi est-ce que tu ris? *Why are you laughing?* | Pourquoi ris-tu? *Why are you laughing?* |
| Combien de jours on a? *How many days do we have?* | Combien de jours est-ce qu'on a? *How many days do we have?* | Combien de jours a-t-on? *How many days do we have?* |

**EXERCICE**
**21·15**

*Use the proper question word required for the structure and the meaning of the question. Select from the list to complete each question.*
qui / qu'est-ce qui / quand / pourquoi / où / comment / combien de temps / qu'est-ce que

**MODÈLE:**     part avec toi?

**RÉPONSE:**     Qui part avec toi?

1. _____ tu pars, ce soir ou demain?

2. _____ tu vas, à New York ou à Boston?

3. _____ tu vas à l'aéroport, en taxi ou en train?

4. _____ va t'attendre là-bas, Thomas ou Raymond?

5. _____ est-ce que Thomas va t'attendre?

6. _____ vous allez faire demain ensemble?

7. _____ Thomas ne travaille-t-il pas? Est-il en vacances?

8. _____ va se passer si Thomas n'est pas là quand tu arrives?

**EXERCICE**
## 21·16

*Use the various fragments to construct a coherent question that refers to the near future. Whenever **est-ce que** is not part of the elements provided, use an inversion-type interrogative structure.*

**MODÈLE:** envoyer / nous / quand / cette lettre

RÉPONSE: Quand allons-nous envoyer cette lettre?

1. inviter / tu /qui

_____

2. est-ce que / ne pas inviter / tu / Kevin / pourquoi

_____

3. décorer la salle / tu / comment

_____

4. est-ce que / danser / on / où

_____

5. qu'est-ce que / manger / nous

_____

6. être DJ / qui

_____

7. qu'est-ce qui / se passer / si on boit trop

_____

8. est-ce que / les invités / rester / combien de temps

_____

# IV. Independent clauses including declarative, interrogative, imperative, and exclamatory structures

[*See chapters 1–6.*]

An independent clause:

- ◆ includes at least a subject and a verb (it may or may include adverbs; it may or may not be followed by a complement)
- ◆ may be affirmative or negative
- ◆ expresses a complete thought

This type of clause can be declarative, interrogative, imperative, or exclamatory.

| Declarative | Interrogative | Imperative | Exclamatory |
|---|---|---|---|
| Le soleil se lève (à six heures). *The sun rises (at 6 a.m.).* | Où vas-tu (maintenant)? *Where are you going (now)?* | Ne te dépêche pas! *Do not hurry!* | Qu'elle est intelligente! *How smart she is!* |

**EXERCICE**
**21·17**

*Identify the part of each sentence that is an independent clause. Note that it may be the entire sentence.*

**MODÈLE:**   Ne nous arrêtons pas dans ce café qui est si loin de la route!

**RÉPONSE:**   Ne nous arrêtons pas dans ce café

1. J'aime beaucoup ce spectacle.

   _____

2. Qu'est-ce que tu penses de la performance?

   _____

3. L'actrice principale est géniale.

   _____

4. Tu es bien silencieuse après avoir exprimé ton opinion.

   _____

5. J'aimerais bien que tu m'écoutes un peu mieux.

   _____

6. Comment sais-tu que c'est la dernière performance?

   _____

7. Ne garde pas le silence!

   _____

8. Allons-y avant que tout le monde se lève!

   _____

*Use the various fragments of a sentence provided to construct a coherent independent clause. Take note of the interrogative or exclamatory/imperative punctuation marks when they are provided; if none is provided, make it a declarative sentence.*

MODÈLE: est-ce que / boire un verre de vin / voudrais/tu?

RÉPONSE: Est-ce que tu voudrais boire un verre de vin?

1. nous promener / allons!

_____

2. fait beau / il / aujourd'hui

_____

3. veux / tu / aller / où?

_____

4. un match de football / il y a / intéressant

_____

5. près du zoo / pouvons / plus tard / nous / nous reposer?

_____

6. d'une glace / j'ai envie

_____

7. deux dollars / donne-moi!

_____

8. cette glace / que / est bonne!

_____

# V. Dependent clauses

[*See chapters 7–10, 16.*]

## Dependent clauses with verbs in the indicative mood

This type of clause does not exist independently from a main clause which contains the essential idea. The main clause is followed by the conjunction **que** and a dependent clause which elaborates on or completes the essential idea. If the essential idea communicates a fact or a certainty, then the verb in the dependent clause is in the indicative mood, which includes tenses such as the present, near future, and passé composé.

**[Main verb or adjectival phrase = fact or certainty] + que + subject + verb in the indicative mood**

Je sais qu'il va pleuvoir.            *I know (that) it is going to rain.*
Il est sûr que nous allons réussir.     *It is sure (that) we are going to succeed.*
Elle dit que tu es égoïste.           *She says (that) you are selfish.*

## Dependent clauses with verbs in the subjunctive mood

If the essential idea communicates a doubt, an uncertainty, a wish, or a feeling, then the verb in the dependent clause is in the subjunctive mood, which for all practical purposes includes a present and a past tense.

**[Main verb or adjectival phrase = non-fact / uncertainty / wish / feeling] + que + subject + verb in the subjunctive mood]**

Je doute qu'il fasse beau demain.       *I doubt (that) it will be nice tomorrow.*
Il n'est pas certain que nous puissions réussir.   *It is not certain (that) we can succeed.*
Elle voudrait que je sois plus patient.     *She would like me to be more patient.*
Tu es contente que nous t'aidions?       *Are you happy (that) we help you?*

**EXERCICE**
**21·19**

*Combine the two sentences provided into one well-structured sentence that includes an independent and a dependent clause.*

**MODÈLE:**    A. Je pense. Il va pleuvoir.       B. Je voudrais. Il va pleuvoir.

**RÉPONSE:**    A. Je pense qu'il va pleuvoir.     B. Je voudrais qu'il pleuve.

1. A. Je sais. Tu vas arriver à l'heure.

   _____

   B. Je suis content. Tu vas arriver à l'heure.

   _____

2. A. Elle pense. C'est élégant.

   _____

   B. Elle veut. C'est élégant.

   _____

3. A. Vous dites. Il aime ça.

   _____

   B. Vous voudriez. Il aime ça.

   _____

4. A. Le professeur dit. Vous allez rendre vos devoirs.

   _____

   B. Le professeur veut. Vous allez rendre vos devoirs.

   _____

5. A. Je suis certain. La voiture va bien marcher.

_____

B. Je ne suis pas certain. La voiture va bien marcher.

_____

EXERCICE
21·20

*Reconstruct each sentence by placing the fragments in the appropriate order.*

MODÈLE:     demande / il / nous / finissions / que

RÉPONSE:     Il demande que nous finissions.

1. je / que / suis content / tu viennes

_____

2. voudrait / que / tu / il / sois heureux

_____

3. elle / que / dit / c'est l'heure de partir

_____

4. nous / que / savons /le temps / va changer

_____

5. vous / que / êtes sûr / le bus / à l'heure /est

_____

6. ils / que / nous soyons là / commandent

_____

7. je / que / pense / sont sympa / ces gens

_____

8. que / tu / nous / pouvons venir / réponds

_____

## Dependent clauses introduced by the relative pronouns qui, que, où, and dont

**Relative clauses allow adding detail about something or someone mentioned in the main clause.** Review the following examples. The verb in the relative clause is generally in the indicative mood (unless the verb in the main clause is a verb such as *chercher* or *demander*).

| qui (= subject) + verb | que (= direct object) + subject + verb | où + subject + verb | dont + subject + verb |
|---|---|---|---|
| | | | (the verb is used with the preposition **de**: parler de/avoir besoin de, etc.) |
| Je te montre <u>la maison</u> **qui** est à vendre. *I am showing you the house which is for sale.* | C'est <u>la maison</u> **que** tu veux vendre? *Is this the house you want to sell?* | C'est la ville où il est né. *This is the town where he was born.* | Tu as vu <u>le monument</u> **dont** j'ai parlé? *Did you see the monument which I talked about?* |
| C'est <u>la fille</u> **qui** est si gentille. *This is the girl who is so nice.* | C'est <u>la fille</u> **qu'**on a invitée. *This is the girl we invited.* | C'est l'appartement où j'habite. *This is the apartment where I live.* | Voilà le <u>stylo</u> **dont** tu as besoin. *There is the pen you need.* |

EXERCICE
21·21

*Combine two sentences into one, using a relative pronoun to link them.*

MODÈLE:   Nous aimons ce plat. Tu l'as fait?

RÉPONSE:   Nous aimons ce plat que tu as fait.

1. C'est une touriste. Elle a perdu son sac.

   _____

2. Voilà l'avion. Elle va le prendre.

   _____

3. C'est le café. On peut prendre le petit déjeuner.

   _____

4. Où est le billet? Je l'ai acheté il y a quelques minutes.

   _____

5. Elle cherche la personne. La personne a trouvé son sac.

   _____

6. C'est la porte. Il y a beaucoup de gens.

   _____

7. Tu vois la personne? Je parlais d'elle.

   _____

8. C'est un sujet important. Nous avons parlé de ce sujet hier.

   _____

*Reconstruct each sentence by placing the fragments in the appropriate order.*

**MODÈLE**: qui fait / tu sais / le cours?

RÉPONSE: Tu sais qui fait le cours?

1. où est / je me demande / notre serveuse?

_____

2. le plat / tu peux commander / que j'aime?

_____

3. dont j'ai parlé / au café / Je t'invite

_____

4. que nous voulions / quelqu'un est assis / à la table

_____

5. la serveuse / voilà / que nous avons d'habitude

_____

6. nous apporte / les boissons / elle / dont nous avons envie

_____

7. qu'il nous faut / c'est le menu

_____

8. qui était assis / où est le client / à notre table?

_____

## Dependent clauses introduced by prepositions

Dependent clauses introduced by the prepositions pour, avant de, après, and en require special verbal structures.

◆ **de + infinitive**

J'ai envie **de me baigner**.            *I feel like swimming.*
Zoë a peur **de se tromper**.            *Zoë is afraid to make a mistake.*

◆ **Pour/avant de + infinitive**

J'ai besoin de la voiture **pour aller** en ville.     *I need the car to go to town.*
Je prends une douche **avant de m'habiller**.     *I take a shower before getting dressed.*

- **Après + past infinitive**

  Nous nous brossons les dents **après avoir mangé**.

  *We brush our teeth after eating.*

  Nous avons mangé **après être rentrés**.

  *We ate after getting home.*

- **En + present participle**

  J'apprends beaucoup **en faisant** ce travail.

  *I learn a lot while doing this work.*

  On apprend toujours **en voyageant**.

  *We always learn while traveling.*

**EXERCICE 21·23**

*Write the letter of the clause that best completes a sentence. If there are two possible answers, write both letters.*

1. _____ Ma copine voudrait manger.       a. en chantant

2. _____ Elle prend sa raquette.           b. pour communiquer rapidement

3. _____ Elle conduit la voiture.          c. après avoir joué

4. _____ Elle fait une sieste.             d. pour avoir de bonnes notes

5. _____ Elle étudie bien.                 e. avant de regarder la télé

6. _____ Nous écrivons des texto.          f. pour jouer au tennis

**EXERCICE 21·24**

*Reconstruct each sentence by placing the fragments in the appropriate order.*

1. Thomas / apprend / chantant / le français / en

   _____

2. Son instructeur / conclure la leçon/ l'interroge / avant de

   _____

3. Ses copains / dans le salon / jouer avec lui / avoir attendu / veulent / après

   _____

4. Les garçons / racontant / en / des histoires drôles / s'amusent

   _____

5. Thomas / jouer / pour / cherche / au foot /son ballon

   _____

6. Sa sœur Béatrice / au foot / a envie /avec les garçons / de jouer

   _____

7. Thomas / jouer / la laisser / refuse de

_____

8. Ses copains / jouer / de la laisser / lui demandent

_____

# VI. Nouns and noun phrases as complements of prepositions

*[See chapters 11 and 15.]*

## Nouns as complements of nouns

Nouns that complement another noun are often introduced by the prepositions de, à, and en.

**Nouns preceded by de**
(for description or possession)
Le ski est un **sport d'hiver**.
  *Skiing is a winter sport.*
C'est le **fils d'Arthur**.
  *This is Arthur's son.*

**Nouns preceded by en**
(to indicate the substance or material)
Je porte un **pull en laine**. *I wear a
  woolen sweater.*
C'est une **montre en or**. *This is a gold
  watch.*

**Nouns preceded by à**
(to indicate purpose or characteristic)
C'est une **assiette à soupe**.
  *This is a soup plate.*
C'est une **zone à problème**.
  *It is a hazardous area.*

**Nouns preceded by de**
(same usage as **en**; less frequently used)
Je préfère les **clôtures de fer**. *I prefer iron gates.*

Les **dents d'or** ne se font presque plus. *Gold
  teeth are barely made anymore.*

EXERCICE
21·25

*On the lines provided, write the letter of the phrase that best completes each sentence.*

| | | | |
|---|---|---|---|
| 1. _____ | Les pirates avaient souvent des dents. | a. | de français |
| 2. _____ | Sophie a une belle robe. | b. | de Marie |
| 3. _____ | Tu préfères les toits. | c. | de sport |
| 4. _____ | Les rois avaient des résidences. | d. | en bois |
| 5. _____ | Il y a une belle table. | e. | d'été et d'hiver |
| 6. _____ | Voilà le professeur. | f. | en soie |
| 7. _____ | Je ne trouve pas mes chaussures. | g. | en tuiles rouges |
| 8. _____ | Nous adorons notre cours. | h. | d'or |

## EXERCICE 21·26

*Complete the following sentences according to the prompts.*

**MODÈLE:** Vous allez souvent aux _____ . (sports/hiver)

ANSWER: sports d'hiver

1. Je voudrais une _____ sur cette table basse. (lampe/verre)

2. Tu peux m'acheter un _____ . (service/assiettes/porcelaine)

3. Il nous faut un _____ dans la cheminée. (feu/bois)

4. Paul voudrait une _____ pour la ferme. (porte/fer forgé)

5. C'est notre _____ . (maison/campagne)

6. C'est l'ancienne _____ . (maison/mes grands-parents)

7. Il y a des (tapisseries/soie) aux _____ . (murs/la salle à manger)

8. Nous avons encore  au salon. (l'horloge/mon grand-père)

## EXERCICE 21·27

*Reconstruct each sentence by placing the fragments in the appropriate order.*

1. Thomas / un pull / en / cherche / laine

   _____

2. lui / trouve / en / Chloé / un / en coton

   _____

3. de / le pull / Thomas / nouveau / va bien / lui

   _____

4. une robe / essaie / Chloé / soie / de

   _____

5. Chloé / de / jolie / est /la robe

   _____

6. vêtements / de / le rayon / super / est

   _____

7. est/ce magasin / une zone / dans/à / circulation restreinte

   _____

8. boutiques / de / une chaîne / haut de gamme / c'est

   _____

# Nouns and noun phrases as complements of adjectives

Nouns or noun phrases that complement an adjective are preceded by prepositions such as **de**, à, **en**, and **par**.

**Adjective + preposition + noun/adjectival noun phrase**

La route est **encombrée de multiples débris**.
*The road is filled with lots of debris.*

Ce livre est **destiné aux adolescents**.
*This book is aimed at adolescents.*
La table est **faite en matière recyclable**.
*The table is made out of recyclable matter.*
Il était **obsédé par la publicité**.
*He was obsessed by publicity.*

**Examples of [adjective + preposition] combinations**

couvert de, rempli de, chargé de, responsable de, fan de, fier de, capable de, satisfait de
indispensable à, nécessaire à, sensible à, essentiel à, utile à
fabriqué en, bâti en, décoré en, riche en, vendu en, divisé en
choqué par, surpris par, enchanté par, autorisé par, effectué par

### EXERCICE 21·28

*Complete the following sentences according to the prompts. Be sure to insert the appropriate preposition.*

**MODÈLE:** Nous avons une _____. (maison/bâtie/terre)

ANSWER: maison bâtie en terre

1. Notre villa est _____. (construite/pierre)

2. Elle est couverte _____. (une nouvelle toiture/zinc)

3. Cette toiture n'est pas _____. (sensible/humidité)

4. Jean a été _____. (surpris/l'architecture)

5. Jean n'est pas très _____. (fan/ce style)

6. Le zinc est _____. (résistant/l'eau)

7. Le travail a été _____. (effectué/un artisan-couvreur)

8. L'artisan qui a fait le toit est _____. (fier/son travail)

### EXERCICE 21·29

*Reconstruct each sentence by placing the fragments in the appropriate order.*

**MODÈLE:** surpris / sont/ l'article / par / ils

ANSWER: Ils sont surpris par l'article.

1. rempli / mon livre / de / lectures intéressantes / est

2. destiné / il est / comme moi / à des jeunes

3. douze chapitres / en / divisé / il est

4. riche / il est / analyses culturelles / en

5. sont / par / enchantés / la diversité / les étudiants / des lectures

6. l'apprentissage / utiles / les leçons / à / sont

7. est /la grammaire / à / indispensable / à / de / l'apprentissage / la langue

8. ce livre / de / très satisfaits / sommes / nous

# Nouns in prepositional phrases that complement the verb

Many nouns or noun phrases preceded by prepositions complement a verb; these prepositional phrases often have an adverbial function—indicating where, when, and how something occurs; in some cases, the prepositional phrases may be structurally required by the verb. The following chart provides some examples.

| Preposition + noun (phrase) [where] | Preposition + noun (phrase) [when or how] | Preposition + noun (phrase) [structural or idiomatic] |
|---|---|---|
| **chez** mon ami (*to/at my friend's house*) | **à** l'heure (*on time*) <br> **en** avance (*early*) <br> **en** retard (*late*) | jouer **du** piano (*play the piano*) <br> jouer **au** foot (*play soccer*) <br> jouer **aux** cartes (*play cards*) |
| **à** la salle de sport (*to/at the gym*) | 3h **du** matin (*3 in the morning*) <br> 2h **de** l'après-midi (*2 in the afternoon*) | faire **de** la physique (*study physics*) <br> faire **du** yoga (*practice yoga*) |
| **dans** une école de danse (*in a dance school*) <br> **en** ville (*in town*) | **pendant** la journée (*during the day*) <br> **avant** mon premier cours (*before my first class*) <br> **après** le diner (*after dinner*) | entrer **dans** une maison (*enter a house*) <br> donner **sur** un jardin (*look onto a garden*) |
| **en** France (*to/in France*) <br> **au** Mexique (*to/in Mexico*) <br> **à** Paris (*to/in Paris*) <br> **sur** le bureau (*on the desk*) | **en** voiture (*by car*) <br> **en/à** vélo (*by bike*) <br> **à** pied (*on foot*) <br> **avec** un ami (*with a friend*) <br> **en** pyjama (*in pyjamas*) | assister **à** un concert (*attend a concert*) <br> plaire **à** une personne (*be liked/admired*) |

**EXERCICE**

**21·30**

*Reconstruct each sentence by placing the fragments in the appropriate order.*

1. Luc / au / en / va / vacances / Canada

_____

2. Montréal / à / séjourner / va / il / dans / d'accueil / une famille

_____

3. chez / les Richelieu / va / il / rester

_____

4. viennent / France / des Richelieu / de / les ancêtres

_____

5. voyagent / les Richelieu / parfois / France / en

_____

6. ne veut pas / Luc / rester / l'hôtel / à

_____

7. plus à l'aise / est / d'ami / dans / il / sa chambre

_____

8. les Richelieu / Luc / accompagne / au marché / des restaurants / à / et / en ville

_____

EXERCICE
21·31

1. _____ Je voulais aller                                   a. du français

2. _____ J'étais à                                          b. en avance

3. _____ J'ai traversé l'Atlantique                          c. à pied

4. _____ Je fais                                             d. au canada

5. _____ Je joue                                             e. après le diner

6. _____ Le film va commencer dans une heure. Tu es          f. Montréal

7. _____ J'aime me promener au parc                          g. en avion

8. _____ On peut regarder un film                            h. au Monopoly

*Louise sent his parents an email upon arriving at his cousin's house. Complete the message according to the prompts in parentheses.*

Je suis arrivé 1. _____ (at my cousin's) Josiane hier à neuf heures
2. _____ {in the evening}. Ma chambre a une 3. _____
(view over) la rivière. Cette chambre me plaît et elle semble plaire aussi 4. _____
(the dog) Rexi. Il est toujours 5. _____ (in my room), 6. _____
(on my bed). Demain, je vais aller 7. _____ (to town) avec Josiane et,
8. _____ (during the day) nous allons faire les magasins. Le soir, on va assister
9. _____ (a concert) 10. _____ (with some of Josiane's friends).

# Answer key

## 1   Declarative sentences and word order

**1·1**    1. Mon frère est très jeune.    2. Il a dix-huit ans.    3. Il s'appelle Marc.    4. Je l'ai appelé hier./Je lui ai téléphoné hier.    5. Il n'était pas à la maison./Il n'était pas chez lui.    6. Il me répondra bientôt.

**1·2**    1. Lili et Mélanie; jouent    2. Leur maman; fait    3. Le papa; travaille    4. Les dessins animés; sont    5. Le poulet; rôtit    6. Les petites filles; se lavent

**1·3**    1. Le contrôleur demande les billets.
          S         V         O
   2. Les passagers ont composté leurs billets.
           S        V          O
   3. Je lis mon livre.
       S V      O
   4. J'admire les illustrations.
       S V         O
   5. Mon voisin regarde le journal.
          S       V        O
   6. Il parle à sa femme.
      S V        O

**1·4**    1. N   2. N   3. P   4. P   5. N   6. P

**1·5**    1. l'anniversaire de Viviane    2. une fête    3. None    4. Viviane    5. le repas    6. la chaîne hi-fi

**1·6**    1. une voiture    2. les voitures confortables    3. un rêve    4. la performance de la voiture    5. des sièges de velours    6. son mari

**1·7**    1. un film aux étudiants/élèves    2. une note à ses étudiants/élèves    3. leur devoir    4. leur travail à leurs parents    5. un petit cadeau à leurs enfants

**1·8**    1. Jean habite la ville de Paris.    2. Lucie est la femme de Jean.    3. Les parents de Jean achètent une maison à Jean et à Lucie.    4. Lucie et Jean partent en lune de miel aujourd'hui.    5. Nous avons lu l'annonce de leur mariage dans le journal.    6. Ils vont passer une semaine à Tahiti.

**1·9**    1. Aujourd'hui mon ami/copain Jean et moi étudions le français.    2. Nous parlons déjà le français.    3. Nous finissons toujours notre travail.    4. Nous donnons notre travail au professeur/á l'enseignant.    5. Quelquefois j'aide mon ami/copain.    6. Il m'aide aussi.

**1·10**    1. Je n'achète jamais de vin ici.    2. L'employé n'est pas très aimable.    3. Je n'aime pas payer de prix élevés.    4. Le propriétaire ne dit jamais bonjour.    5. Nous ne perdons pas de temps ici.

**1·11**    1. plus    2. jamais    3. personne    4. rien    5. rien/personne

**1·12**    1. J'ai jeté mon ancien téléphone parce que je n'en voulais plus.    2. Mais je ne peux trouver mon nouveau cellulaire nulle part.    3. Ces jours-ci je ne me rappelle plus rien.    4. Bon. Je ne peux appeler personne d'autre ce soir.    5. Je n'oublierai plus jamais de le remettre dans mon sac.

## 2     Interrogative sentences and word order

**2·1**    1. Mon copain est en retard?   2. Tu as ma liste?   3. Le passager est patient?   4. Nous attendons?   5. Il y a un taxi au coin?   6. Il fait chaud ici?

**2·2**    1. Tu as compris les instructions?   2. À ton avis, elles étaient claires?   3. On va arriver à faire ce travail?   4. Tu es certain que ce ne sera pas trop difficile?   5. Tu veux commencer ce soir?   6. Tu ne crains pas d'échouer?

**2·3**    1. Oui./Pas encore./Pas ici.   2. Si./Pas encore./Pas ici.   3. Si./Pas encore./Pas ici.   4. Oui./Pas encore./ Pas ici.   5. Oui./Pas encore.   6. Si./Pas encore.

**2·4**    1. pas   2. jamais   3. plus   4. personne   5. rien

**2·5**    1. Est-ce que le soleil brille aujourd'hui?   2. Est-ce qu'on va à la plage?   3. Est-ce que tu as envie de prendre le petit déjeuner sur la terrasse?   4. Est-ce qu'on ira nager dans la mer après le petit déjeuner?   5. Est-ce que tu es encore un peu endormi?   6. Est-ce que tu as besoin d'une bonne douche?

**2·6**    1. Marie écoute-t-elle bien les conseils de sa maman?   2. Est-elle attentive?   3. Les frères jumeaux travaillent-ils ensemble?   4. Sont-ils inséparables?   5. Ne vois-tu pas le bus?   6. Faut-il se dépêcher?

**2·7**    1. Aimez-vous cette robe, mademoiselle?   2. Puis-je recommander une paire de chaussures, mademoiselle?   3. Avez-vous besoin d'un foulard, mademoiselle?   4. Etes-vous prête à payer, mademoiselle?   5. Avez-vous une carte de crédit, mademoiselle?   6. Aimeriez-vous/Voudriez-vous un sac, mademoiselle?

**2·8**    Suggested answers: 1. Pardonnez-moi/Pardon, mademoiselle, aimez-vous cette robe?   2. Pardonnez-moi/ Pardon, mademoiselle, puis-je recommander une paire de chaussures?   3. Pardonnez-moi/Pardon, mademoiselle, avez-vous besoin d'un foulard?   4. Excusez-moi de vous déranger mademoiselle, êtes-vous prête à payer ?   5. Pardonnez-moi/Pardon, mademoiselle, avez-vous une carte de crédit?   6. Pardonnez-moi/Pardon, mademoiselle, aimeriez-vous/voudriez-vous un sac?

**2·9**    1. Préfères-tu un citron pressé, un coca ou une bière?   2. Arrivez-vous cet après-midi ou demain?   3. Désirent-ils aller à la plage ou nager dans la piscine?   4. Achetons-nous le parasol, la chaise-longue ou une serviette?   5. Veulent-elles voir un film ou dîner au restaurant?   6. Dormez-vous dans le lit ou sur le canapé?

**2·10**   1. d   2. e   3. a   4. b   5. c

**2·11**   1. Tu aimes ce livre, pas vrai?   2. Tu sais qui l'a écrit, n'est-ce pas?   3. Cet auteur est bon, tu ne penses pas?   4. C'est un maître du suspense, non?   5. Tu as lu son livre précédent, pas vrai?

## 3     Precise questions

**3·1**    1. Qui est-ce que   2. Qui est-ce que   3. Qui est-ce qui   4. Qui est-ce qui   5. Qui est-ce qui   6. Qui est-ce qui

**3·2**    1. Whom did you meet last night? —An old friend.   2. Whom did you invite? —The family.   3. Whom is Raymond going to congratulate? —His new employee.   4. Whom are you looking for? —The saleslady.   5. Whom do your parents prefer? —Me, of course.   6. Whom does Suzanne kiss? —Her boyfriend.

**3·3**    1. appelez-vous   2. invitez-vous   3. avez-vous vu   4. préférez-vous   5. allez-vous chercher   6. allez-vous renvoyer

**3·4**    1. c   2. e   3. a   4. b   5. d

**3·5**    1. aimez-vous recevoir comme cadeaux   2. vous offrent vos parents   3. dites-vous quand on vous donne un cadeau   4. faites-vous pour vous amuser   5. n'aimez-vous pas faire le jour de votre annniversaire

**3·6**    1. Que   2. Qu'   3. Qu'est-ce que   4. Qu'est-ce que   5. Qu'est-ce qui   6. Que

**3·7**    1. Tu vas où maintenant?/Où tu vas maintenant?   2. Tu vas au travail comment?/Comment tu vas au travail?   3. Tu rentres quand aujourd'hui?/Quand tu rentres aujourd'hui?   4. Pourquoi tu ne manges pas?   5. Tu veux combien de café?/Combien de café tu veux?   6. Ça va comment?/Comment ça va?

**3·8**    1. Où est-ce que tu vas maintenant?   2. Comment est-ce que tu vas au travail?   3. Quand est-ce que tu rentres aujourd'hui?   4. Pourquoi est-ce que tu ne manges pas?   5. Combien de café est-ce que tu veux?   6. Comment est-ce que ça va?

**3·9**    1. Quelle heure est-il?    2. Quelle est sa date de naissance?    3. Quel est son numéro de téléphone?    4. Quel temps fait-il aujourd'hui?    5. Quelles sont ses couleurs favorites?    6. Quel choix est-ce que j'ai?

**3·10**    1. Comment    2. Où    3. Quelle    4. Que    5. Où/Comment    6. Où/Comment    7. Où/Qui/Comment    8. Où/Comment    9. Où/Comment    10. Qui

**3·11**    1. Où    2. Qu'    3. Qu'est-ce qu'    4. Qu'est-ce qui    5. où    6. Qu'

**3·12**    1. D'où es-tu?    2. Où vas-tu?    3. Depuis quand étudies-tu le français?    4. Quand vas-tu finir cet exercice?    5. Jusqu'à quand vas-tu attendre?    6. À qui écris-tu la plupart de tes e-mails?

**3·13**    1. avez-vous/est-ce que vous avez    2. Quelle est    3. habitez-vous/est-ce que vous habitez    4. Quel est    5. ne venez-vous pas/est-ce que vous ne venez pas    6. avez-vous/est-ce que vous avez

**3·14**    1. Où voudriez-vous aller?    2. Combien pouvez-vous dépenser?    3. Qui voyage avec vous?    4. Quelle ligne aérienne préférez-vous?    5. Pourquoi voulez-vous voyager en première classe?

**3·15**    1. qui    2. où    3. Quand/Où/Comment    4. Quel    5. Quand/Où    6. Quand/Comment

**3·16**    1. Quel âge    2. Que    3. Où    4. Qui    5. Que/Pour qui/Où    6. Où    7. Comment    8. Qu'est-ce qu'    9. Qu'est-ce qu'    10. Qu'est-ce qui

**3·17**    1. Laquelle    2. Lequel    3. Lesquels    4. Combien de    5. Combien de    6. Laquelle/Lesquelles

# 4    Exclamatory sentences

**4·1**    1. la lune est belle    2. Nous aimons    3. il fait chaud dehors    4. la limonade est froide    5. Lucie est si fatiguée!    6. Bon! Maintenant nous sommes prêtes!

**4·2**    1. Je suis si mignon(ne)!    2. Je danse si bien!    3. J'ai tant d'amis!    4. Mon patron m'aime beaucoup!    5. Je suis très riche!    6. Tout le monde m'admire!

**4·3**    1. One finds so many pleasures in life!    2. It offers so many surprises!    3. What innocence we see in children!    4. We are so attached to life!    5. How happy we are!    6. How lucky we are!

**4·4**    1. Que ce monsieur conduit vite!    2. Combien d'accidents il y a sur les routes!    3. Comme les chauffards sont dangereux!    4. Que d'obstacles il y a sur la route!    5. Combien de fous brûlent les feux rouges!

**4·5**    1. f    2. e    3. b    4. d    5. a    6. f

**4·6**    Suggested answers: 1. Zut!    2. Au secours!/À l'aide!    3. Super!/Hourra!    4. Attention!    5. Zut!    6. Tant mieux!

**4·7**    1. Chut! Il y a trop de bruit!    2. Ciel! La conférence commence à midi!    3. Hé!/Eh!/Hep! Nous sommes arrivés!    4. Hélas! Je n'ai pas le temps!    5. Tu veux gagner? Espérons!    6. Oh la la! Cette montre est belle!

# 5    Imperative clauses

**5·1**    1. Regarde un bon film!    2. Viens à onze heures!    3. Prends un café!    4. Va chez Paul!    5. Finis cet exercice!    6. Descends au premier étage!

**5·2**    1. pars    2. ne fais pas    3. prends    4. ne téléphone pas    5. rentre

**5·3**    1. 1    2. 1    3. +    4. +    5. +    6. 1

**5·4**    1. Écoute ta maman!    2. Choisis ton film!    3. Descends!    4. Finis tes devoirs!    5. Ne regarde pas ta sœur!    6. Va à ta chambre!

**5·5**    1. Ne criez pas!    2. Fermez la télé!    3. Sortez dans le jardin!    4. Ne salissez pas le divan!    5. Donnez-moi cette serviette!    6. Restez dans votre chambre!

**5·6**    1. Mangeons au restaurant!    2. Invitons Jeanine!    3. Vérifions les horaires des films!    4. Allons-y!    5. Prenons un taxi!

# 6    Independent clauses

**6·1**    1. Jean va arriver ce soir.    2. Nous préparons un bon repas.    3. Tout le monde est content.    4. Il était longtemps absent.    5. Il va dormir dans sa chambre.

**6·2**  1. Brigitte ne dort pas bien.  2. Ginette n'aime plus les gâteaux.  3. Nous ne voulons rien boire.  4. Vous ne pouvez pas lire tout le roman.  5. Elles n'ont rien à dire.  6. Vous n'avez pas encore vingt ans.

**6·3**  1. Est-ce que le ciel est bleu?  2. Est-ce que les oiseaux chantent?  3. Est-ce que le chien court derrière moi?  4. Est-ce que je vais au parc?  5. Est-ce que tu viens avec moi?

**6·4**  1. Décore ta chambre!  2. Peins les murs!  3. Organise le placard!  4. Change les rideaux!  5. Accroche des tableaux!  6. Déplace le lit!

**6·5**  1. A  2. N  3. N  4. A  5. IMP  6. A

**6·6**  1. d  2. e  3. f  4. a  5. b  6. c

**6·7**  1. Toute la journée Mimi était chez ses grands-parents et elle jouait avec leur chien Médor.  2. Je voulais déjeuner avec elle mais elle avait rendez-vous chez le dentiste.  3. Elle a dû aller à son rendez-vous mais elle n'aime pas aller chez le dentiste.  4. Mimi n'a pas mangé toute la journée ni le soir.  5. Aujourd'hui elle doit se sentir mieux sinon elle doit retourner chez le dentiste.  6. Mimi est très gentille mais elle est aussi très indécise.

**6·8**  1. Mes parents restent à la maison le samedi et le dimanche.  2. Papa ne mange pas la viande de bœuf ni le poulet.  3. Maman prépare la salade et la vinaigrette.  4. Nous allons manger vers six heures ou sept heures.  5. Avant le dîner, nous buvons un verre de vin ou un apéritif.  6. Après le dîner, nous faisons du thé ou du café.

**6·9**  1. J'ai envie d'écrire un roman donc je vais au bureau.  2. J'écris mais je n'aime pas le premier chapitre.  3. Je dois récrire le premier chapitre sinon la fin sera impossible.  4. Je peux changer le début ou la fin du chapitre.  5. Je n'ai pas d'idées donc je vais me promener.  6. J'entre dans un café et je commande un express.

**6·10**  1. Tu écris bien et tu parles encore mieux.  2. Le pauvre n'entend ni ne parle.  3. Tu es en retard donc dépêche-toi!  4. Tu arrives et/mais tu repars.  5. Ce manteau est cher mais j'ai assez d'argent pour l'acheter.  6. Le magasin ne ferme ni à six heures ni à sept heures.

**6·11**  1. Zoe se lève, s'habille et se maquille.  2. Elle prend son sac, sort et ferme la porte à clef.  3. Elle prend le vélo, le bus ou le métro.  4. Elle ne boit ni thé ni café, mais elle boit un verre de jus.  5. Il fait de l'orage et il pleut fort, donc elle se dépêche.

**6·12**  1. Quelquefois/Parfois j'aime rester à la maison/chez moi et lire un bon livre.  2. Il y a des jours où je ne veux ni sortir ni parler à personne.  3. Je réponds au téléphone mais seulement si c'est la famille.  4. Je peux voir le nom de mon correspondant, donc je sais qui appelle/téléphone.  5. Je n'ai ni scrupules ni regrets.

# 7 Dependent clauses and the indicative mood

**7·1**  1. affirme = *affirms*  2. rendons compte = *realize*  3. sais = *know*  4. est probable = *is probable*  5. dit = *says*  6. constatent = *notice*

**7·2**  1. qu'il va y avoir une tempête de neige.  2. qu'il a déjà beaucoup neigé pendant la nuit.  3. qu'en hiver cela arrive/se passe.  4. que nous pourrons conduire dans la montagne.  5. que ce sera une bonne journée pour skier.  6. que ce serait une belle journée.

**7·3**  1. qui  2. comment  3. pourquoi  4. que  5. si  6. si

**7·4**  1. d  2. e  3. c  4. b  5. a

**7·5**  1. s'il fera beau  2. comment nous pouvons aller à la plage  3. où nous pouvons prendre un bus  4. où est la plage  5. à quelle heure les bus passent

**7·6**  1. Le monsieur  2. la personne  3. l'ambiance  4. cette ambiance  5. La seule chose  6. Le temps libre  7. la collègue  8. le bureau

**7·7**  1. d  2. b  3. a  4. f  5. c  6. e

**7·8**  1. que *replaces* le stylo  2. qui *replaces* le livre  3. dont *replaces* l'histoire  4. que *replaces* les amis  5. où *replaces* le restaurant

**7·9**  1. Vrai  2. Vrai  3. Vrai  4. Faux  5. Vrai  6. Vrai

**7·10**  1. who lives here  2. I taught him  3. what we would like  4. that is as cute  5. who is calling  6. that resembles Sophia Loren's necklace

**7·11**  1. c  2. a  3. d  4. b  5. e

**7·12**   1. Je cherche un chapeau qui m'aille.   2. Mais je ne vois pas ce qu'il me faut/ce dont j'ai besoin.   3. Je ne vois rien qui me plaise.   4. Peux-tu recommander un magasin que tu aimes bien?   5. Tu sais ce que je veux, n'est-ce pas?   6. Allons au magasin où tu as acheté ton chapeau!

**7·13**   1. Pendant que/Tandis que   2. Depuis qu'/Comme   3. pendant que/tandis que   4. Puisque/Parce que   5. Quand/Dès que   6. Quand/Dès que

**7·14**   1. Quand   2. Puisqu'/Parce qu'   3. Parce qu'/Comme   4. Aussitôt qu'   5. quand/lorsque

**7·15**   1. f   2. b   3. a   4. d   5. c   6. e

**7·16**   1. si je travaille   2. si j'ai le temps   3. si tu viens avec moi   4. si tu restes avec moi   5. si tu décides de ne pas venir   6. si nous trouvons un hôtel bon marché   7. si je n'ai plus d'argent   8. si tout va bien

# 8   Dependent clauses and the subjunctive mood

**8·1**   1. c/d   2. b   3. d/e   4. c/d   5. a   6. c/d

**8·2**   1. puisse   2. es   3. trouviez   4. rends   5. grandisse   6. as

**8·3**   1. Quel âge est-ce que tu crois que grand-maman a?   2. Ah bon! Tu penses qu'elle a soixante ans.   3. En tout cas, je doute qu'elle ait plus de soixante ans.   4. On se demande où elle trouve toute cette énergie.   5. Je souhaite qu'elle vive encore de cette manière pendant longtemps.   6. J'admire qu'elle puisse faire tout ce qu'elle fait.

**8·4**   1. Vive   2. réponde   3. pose   4. entrent   5. finissent   6. s'arrête

**8·5**   1. I am so happy that you are here, Jean.   2. I worried that you might not be able to come.   3. I was afraid that your boss would not want to give you time off.   4. You are impressed that he was so generous, aren't you?   5. Anyway, we better enjoy this weekend.   6. I doubt that this will happen again!

**8·6**   1. de me voir   2. de me trouver   3. de me donner   4. d'entendre   5. de pouvoir

**8·7**   1. C   2. U   3. C   4. U   5. C   6. C

**8·8**   1. suis allé(e)   2. puissiez   3. veux/veuille   4. ai   5. ait

**8·9**   1. It is better to enjoy life.   2. We will have to save the planet.   3. We seem to live with more and more technology.   4. It is natural to want to be happy.   5. It is rare that we do not have a natural disaster somewhere.   6. It is urgent that we slow down pollution.   7. We may invent new technologies.   8. It is not possible to do this in one day.

**8·10**   1. Il vaut mieux jouir de la vie.   2. Il faudra sauver la planète.   3. Nous semblons vivre avec de plus en plus de technologie.   4. Il est naturel de vouloir être heureux.   5. Il est rare de ne pas avoir un désastre naturel quelque part.   6. Il est urgent de ralentir la pollution.   7. Il est possible d'inventer de nouvelles technologies.   8. Il n'est pas possible de faire cela en un jour.

**8·11**   1. pour qu'   2. avant qu'   3. bien qu'   4. pourvu que   5. afin que/pour que   6. afin que/pour que

**8·12**   1. Quoi; *Whatever you do, be honest!*   2. Quelque; *No matter what your mistake is, you can always be forgiven!*   3. Qui; *Whoever is at the door, let the person in!*   4. Où; *Wherever you go, do not forget to call!*   5. Quelque; *However tired you are, eat something before going to bed!*

**8·13**   1. je ne connais personne   2. Je ne peux rien imaginer   3. Je ne connais nul écrivain   4. Je cherche quelqu'un

# 9   Relative clauses

**9·1**   1. qui est garée là; *The motorcycle that is parked there belongs to me.*   2. que je veux acheter; *The car I want to buy is expensive.*   3. qui m'a fait la démonstration; *The salesman who did the demonstration is really great.*   4. qu'il a aidés; *The clients he helped are satisfied.*   5. que je préférerais; *The color I would prefer is red.*   6. que j'aimerais; *The options I would like are the CD player and the retractable roof.*

**9·2**   1. b   2. a   3. d   4. g   5. e   6. h   7. c   8. f

**9·3**   Suggested answers: 1. g   2. f/h   3. f/h   4. c   5. d   6. a/e   7. a/b   8. a/b

**9·4**   1. qui   2. qui   3. qui   4. que   5. que   6. qu'

**9.5** 1. Voici le cadeau que je veux.    2. C'est le vélo qui est dans la vitrine.    3. Regarde! Le vendeur qui était là hier.    4. C'est lui qui m'a montré ce vélo.    5. C'est vraiment le cadeau que je voudrais.    6. C'est même la couleur que j'aime.

**9.6** 1. Voilà les billets que j'ai achetés hier.    2. J'admire les artistes qui vont nous divertir.    3. Ce qui m'étonne, c'est que nos amis ne sont pas encore arrivés.    4. J'ai le temps de boire ce café que j'ai préparé.    5. Ah! J'entends une voiture qui s'arrête devant chez nous.    6. Ce sont nos amis qui arrivent.

**9.7** 1. lequel    2. laquelle    3. qui    4. qui    5. auxquels    6. à laquelle

**9.8** 1. C'est l'ami pour qui je fais cela.    2. C'est le bâtiment dans lequel je travaille.    3. C'est le bureau près duquel il y a un restaurant.    4. C'est la personne grâce à qui j'ai un travail/job.    5. C'est le bureau sur lequel je pose le courrier.    6. C'est le cahier dans lequel j'écris les rendez-vous.

**9.9** 1. dont le chien s'est échappé    2. dont le mari est en voyage    3. dont la fille est si intelligente    4. dont le professeur est fier    5. dont la batterie est vide    6. dont la cuisine est rénovée

**9.10** 1. L'année où Sarkozy est né est 1955.    2. La ville où il est né est Paris.    3. Carla Bruni est la femme avec qui il est marié.    4. La politique est ce qui l'intéresse le plus.    5. Le palais où vivent les présidents français s'appelle l'Elysée.    6. Ce dont il est le plus fier, c'est son titre de président.

# 10 Infinitive and past infinitive clauses

**10.1** 1. sortir en famille    2. nous emmener dans un restaurant chic    3. pouvoir rejoindre mes amis après le dîner    4. passer du temps avec ma famille    5. partir au moment du dessert    6. finir la soirée en disco

**10.2** 1. f    2. c    3. d    4. e    5. b    6. a

**10.3** 1. jouer    2. nager    3. emmener    4. s'amuser    5. tomber    6. faire

**10.4** 1. J'aime me lever tard.    2. Je déteste entendre le réveil sonner le matin.    3. Je préfère prendre le petit déjeuner chez moi.    4. Après le petit déjeuner, je me dépêche de m'habiller.    5. Alors je dois prendre le bus et aller au travail.    6. Je ne laisse pas le boulot devenir ma vie.

**10.5** 1. d'offrir des soins médicaux    2. d'éliminer les taxes    3. d'avoir de bonnes relations    4. gouverner avec sagesse    5. avoir beaucoup d'alliés    6. d'avoir une bonne économie

**10.6** 1. offre des soins médicaux    2. élimine les taxes    3. ait de bonnes relations    4. gouverne avec sagesse    5. ait beaucoup d'alliés    6. ait une bonne économie

**10.7** There is no wrong answer as you choose what describes you.

**10.8** 1. à    2. d'    3. Sans    4. sans    5. à    6. à    7. de    8. Avant de    9. de    10. de

**10.9** 1. d/e    2. h    3. a/f    4. g    5. a/f    6. c/e    7. c/d/e    8. b

**10.10** 1. Ne pas toucher aux allumettes.    2. Ne pas garer les voitures sur le gazon.    3. Respecter la limite de vitesse.    4. Voler est sévèrement puni.    5. Ne pas s'approcher du feu.    6. Conserver les aliments frais au frigo.

**10.11** 1. voyager en train    2. prendre le TGV; aller    3. pouvoir prendre un bain de soleil    4. nager dans la mer    5. prendre des vacances    6. se reposer

**10.12** 1. d    2. c    3. f    4. a    5. b    6. e

**10.13** 1. ne pas avoir étudié    2. avoir reçu une mauvaise note    3. avoir appris quelque chose    4. ne pas avoir triché    5. avoir bien répondu à quelques questions    6. avoir échoué    7. être allé souvent à la bibliothèque    8. y être resté pendant des heures

**10.14** 1. avoir eu    2. avoir fréquenté    3. faire    4. voir    5. comporter

**10.15** 1. à condition d'avoir assez d'argent    2. avant d'avoir fini mes études    3. être allé    4. être retourné    5. pouvoir    6. pouvoir économiser d'argent

**10.16** 1. c    2. h    3. g    4. e    5. a    6. f    7. d    8. b

**10.17** 1. après avoir vu le film    2. après avoir acheté la maison    3. après être monté    4. après avoir fait les achats    5. après être arrivées    6. après avoir fini les devoirs

**10.18** 1. être venue    2. avoir rencontrée    3. avoir eu    4. avoir téléphoné    5. avoir surprise    6. avoir invitée

# 11 Using nouns

**11·1** Un groupe d'étudiants américains suivent un cours de français à la Sorbonne cet été. Leur professeur, M. Maximilien, est un spécialiste de littérature antillaise. Ils vont lire et analyser des écrivains et des poètes tels qu'Aimé Césaire, originaire de la Martinique et Guy Tirolien, originaire de la Guadeloupe. A la fin du cours, tout le monde va se réunir et fêter dans un restaurant antillais très connu par les Parisiens.

**11·2** 1. les Alpes  2. Napoléon Bonaparte  3. l'Atlantique  4. Nicolas Sarkozy  5. le Canada  6. Claude Monet

**11·3** 1. Les Français  2. Alpes; Pyrénées  3. la rocaille; Corse  4. à l'eau  5. Bretons; Manche  6. La beauté; la renommée

**11·4** 1. petite fille  2. pupitre  3. tableau  4. L'institutrice  5. livre  6. l'image

**11·5** 1. à l'école  2. au bureau  3. au parc  4. à la maison  5. Du matin au soir

**11·6** 1. des armées  2. Les équipes  3. le sable  4. farine  5. l'eau  6. l'or

**11·7** 1. L'antagonisme conduit à la violence.  2. Le fanatisme est un obstacle à la paix.  3. Au 17e siècle, la France était une monarchie absolue.  4. La pauvreté est à l'origine de beaucoup de problèmes sociaux.  5. Après avoir menti, nous avons mauvaise conscience.  6. Le bonheur ne s'achète pas.

**11·8** 1. le frère de ma copine  2. Ses parents  3. Mes parents  4. Les beaux rosiers de mon jardin  5. Les grands chats  6. De jolis oiseaux

**11·9** 1. g  2. e  3. a  4. h  5. c  6. d  7. b  8. f

**11·10** 1. des e-mails à Jean  2. les essais à ses étudiants  3. des bises à sa maman  4. des articles à son journal  5. des reproches à son petit garçon  6. des mots d'amour à Gigi

**11·11** 1. Donne-moi un verre d'eau!  2. Je voudrais une robe d'été.  3. Passe-moi cette cuillère à café!  4. Elle a pris congé pour raison de famille.  5. Je vais commander un steak frites.  6. Cherchons le wagon-restaurant!

**11·12** 1. couverte de neige  2. remplie de café chaud  3. comblée de peine  4. écrites en hiéroglyphes  5. réservée aux jeunes mariés  6. conformément à la loi

**11·13** 1. en vacances à la mer  2. à la plage en autobus  3. sur le sable près de la mer  4. chez sa tante qui habite à Nice  5. au téléphone avec sa mère  6. le train pour rentrer chez elle (à la maison) à Paris

**11·14** 1. Achetez des Michelin, pneus durables!  2. «La Vie en rose,» chanson d'Edith Piaf, est connue dans le monde entier.  3. Le Massif Central, région montagneuse, est un endroit rural.  4. Saint-Tropez, berceau des célébrités françaises, est une ville accueillante.  5. Le palais d'Avignon, ancienne résidence des papes, offre des expositions toute l'année.  6. Strasbourg, ville européenne, est le siège du Conseil de l'Europe.  7. MC Solar, né à Dakar, est un chanteur Rap.  8. Sarkozy, président de la république française, a été élu en 2007.

# 12 Using personal pronouns

**12·1** 1. Il  2. Ils  3. nous  4. elle  5. vous  6. ils

**12·2** 1. vous  2. vous  3. tu  4. vous  5. vous  6. vous

**12·3** 1. Elles  2. Vous  3. toi  4. moi  5. Lui  6. Elle  7. eux  8. Nous

**12·4** 1. moi  2. eux  3. nous  4. toi  5. toi/nous  6. vous

**12·5** 1. On est heureux/content  2. On part  3. On apprend  4. On va  5. On ne dit pas  6. On invite/Invite-on

**12·6** 1. me  2. t'  3. te  4. me  5. te

**12·7** 1. vous  2. nous  3. vous  4. nous  5. vous  6. vous

**12·8** 1. les films; les  2. les petits; les  3. le dernier film; le  4. cette actrice; l'  5. Audrey; la

**12·9** 1. le journal; je l'ai acheté  2. la monnaie; il la rend  3. le *Times*; ils le choisissent  4. les magazines; je les préfère  5. ces magazines; je vais les lire dans l'avion  6. les magazines; je vais les jeter à l'arrivée

**12·10** 1. je ne l'ai pas acheté  2. il ne la rend pas  3. ils ne le choisissent pas  4. je ne les préfère pas  5. je ne vais pas les lire dans l'avion  6. je ne vais pas les jeter à l'arrivée

**12·11** 1. aux candidats  2. aux candidats  3. à mon patron  4. aux candidats

**12·12** 1. Je leur ai donné rendez-vous.    2. Je leur ai demandé de fournir un CV à mon patron avant les entretiens.    3. Maintenant je vais lui décrire chaque candidat.    4. Il pourra préparer les questions qu'il leur posera.

**12·13** 1. L'office de tourisme m'a appelé.    2. L'employé m'a dit de venir chercher les billets.    3. Je lui ai demandé si je pouvais venir demain.    4. Il m'a répondu que oui.    5. Les employés de l'office de tourisme nous procurent toujours nos billets.    6. Je vais leur exprimer ma gratitude.

**12·14** 1. à Paris; y; Oui, j'y irai.    2. à Paris; y; Oui, j'y resterai.    3. des souvenirs; en; Oui, j'en achèterai.    4. des bonbons; en; Oui, je t'en apporterai.    5. du vin; en; Oui, j'en boirai tous les jours.    6. des e-mails; en; Oui, je t'en écrirai.

**12·15** 1. le; Suzanne l'a rencontré au cours d'anglais.    2. lui; Elle lui a prêté son livre.    3. leur; Le professeur leur a demandé de faire un projet.    4. les; le; Il les a félicités quand ils l'ont fini.    5. le; Ils l'ont remercié.    6. la; Ils l'ont préparée pendant deux semaines.

**12·16** 1. les; y; les y    2. les; lui; les lui    3. en; leur; leur en    4. en; leur; leur en    5. le; lui; le lui    6. le; y; l'y

**12·17** 1. fais-le    2. prends-le    3. sors-le    4. mets-les    5. montre-les-moi    6. jetez-les

**12·18** 1. montre-le-lui    2. apprends-la-lui    3. donne-la-moi    4. demande m'en    5. chante-la-moi    6. montre-les-moi

**12·19** 1. Ferme-la!    2. Ne le jette pas par terre!    3. Ne l'embête pas!    4. Appelle-les!

**12·20** 1. Où est ton argent? Où l'as-tu mis?/Où est-ce que tu l'as mis?    2. J'ai vu un billet de vingt dollars ici. Où est-il maintenant?    3. Bon! Je te donne un autre billet de vingt dollars. S'il te plaît, ne le perds pas!    4. Trouvons maintenant les fleurs pour ta grand-mère! Où sont-elles?    5. Oui, bien sûr, dans le vase. Donne-les-moi, s'il te plaît!    6. Nous les lui donnerons ensemble.

# 13 Special uses of pronouns

**13·1** 1. c 2. e 3. a 4. h 5. b 6. g 7. f 8. d

**13·2** 1. lui 2. me 3. nous 4. vous 5. vous 6. nous

**13·3** 1. s' 2. se 3. nous 4. nous 5. s' 6. nous

**13·4** 1. te; les 2. se; les 3. se; les 4. nous; les 5. vous; la 6. me; les

**13·5** 1. se 2. X 3. se; se 4. se 5. s' 6. X

**13·6** 1. se 2. se 3. X 4. X 5. X 6. se 7. se 8. X

**13·7** 1. Oui, Suzanne! Préparons-nous!    2. Je sais. Moi aussi, je m'inquiète. Ce temps ne me plaît pas du tout.    3. Oui, mettons-nous au boulot/travail!    4. Bon. Nous allons nous arrêter un moment.

**13·8** Mon cher Michel, tu me manques terriblement. Quand est-ce que tu rentres? Cela me fait de la peine d'être sans toi si longtemps. Il me faut vraiment ta compagnie pour être heureuse. Sans toi, tous les jours sont pareils: je me lève, je m'habille, je me rends au travail, je rentre et je me couche. Les gens qui s'aiment comme nous ne devraient pas être séparés!

# 14 Using adverbs and adverbial phrases

**14·1** 1. f 2. d 3. h 4. g 5. b 6. a 7. e 8. c

**14·2** 1. Nous chantons bien cet hymne.    2. L'artiste sculpte patiemment l'argile./L'artiste sculpte l'argile patiemment.    3. Dînons ensemble ce soir!    4. Les enfants jouent silencieusement.    5. Allons faire des achats ailleurs!    6. Ils désiraient finir leurs études rapidement./Ils désiraient finir rapidement leurs études.

**14·3** 1. trop 2. assez 3. davantage 4. tellement 5. combien 6. moins 7. si

**14·4** 1. La nuit dernière je n'ai pas assez dormi.    2. J'avais trop de choses en tête.    3. Pourtant j'étais si fatigué(e).    4. Aujourd'hui je me sens plus fatigué(e) que jamais.    5. Et j'ai tellement/tant à faire.    6. Je serai si heureux/heureuse quand la journée sera terminée!

**14·5** 1. autant 2. plus 3. aussi sérieusement 4. moins 5. aussi bien 6. le pire 7. mieux 8. le plus 9. le plus souvent 10. mieux

**14·6** 1. si 2. Non 3. Aucunement 4. ni 5. Soit 6. Assurément

**14·7**   1. D'abord; Ensuite; Finalement/Enfin   2. ce matin; Maintenant; Bientôt   3. Hier; Aujourd'hui; Ce soir; tôt   4. en retard; tous les jours; Actuellement; jamais

**14·8**   1. Le petit garçon sait déjà parler.   2. Sa petite sœur parle mal.   3. Le professeur parle intelligemment aux élèves.; Le professeur parle aux élèves intelligemment.   4. Les conférenciers prépareront soigneusement leurs collègues.; Les conférenciers prépareront leurs collègues soigneusement.   5. Les spectateurs assistaient régulièrement aux concerts.; Les spectateurs assistaient aux concerts régulièrement.   6. Les acteurs répètent patiemment la pièce.; Les acteurs répètent la pièce patiemment.

**14·9**   1. J'ai bien aimé ce gâteau.   2. Lise a vite appris son vocabulaire.   3. Gigi a déjà fini son dîner.   4. Nous sommes souvent allés au cinéma.   5. Il a passionnément récité le poème.; Il a récité le poème passionnément.   6. Elle a longuement expliqué la leçon.; Elle a expliqué la leçon longuement.

**14·10**   1. Joëlle ne sait jamais quoi dire.   2. Elle n'ose pas dire la vérité.   3. Elle n'est nullement timide.   4. Mais elle a peur de ne pas plaire aux gens.   5. Elle n'a jamais été sûre d'elle-même.   6. Elle ne s'est pas souvent opposée aux opinions de ses amis.

**14·11**   1. Isi est très fort.   2. Isa est assez jolie.   3. Isi est plus grand qu'Isa.   4. Isa est plus mince qu'Isi.   5. Isi est assez intelligent.   6. Isa est aussi intelligente qu'Isi.

**14·12**   1. PL  2. L  3. PL  4. L  5. PL  6. L

**14·13**   1. avec honnêteté   2. avec politesse   3. avec minutie   4. avec élégance   5. avec diligence   6. avec patience

**14·14**   1. insouciamment   2. familièrement   3. doucement   4. naïvement   5. X   6. X   7. colèreusement

**14·15**   1. d'un air triste   2. d'un air élégant   3. d'un air furieux   4. d'un air joyeux   5. d'un air soigneux   6. d'un air franc

**14·16**   1. ensemble  2. D'abord  3. Ensuite; là-bas  4. longtemps  5. en force  6. à bon marché  7. De plus  8. En général/En particulier; de plus  9. Par contre  10. avec courtoisie

**14·17**   Cher ami/Chère amie, je m'amuse tellement ici en France. Tu n'as pas idée combien de culture et d'histoire j'apprends. J'aurai beaucoup plus de connaissances quand je finirai ce voyage. Je suis si heureux/heureuse d'être ici et je n'ai nul/aucun regret de dépenser tant d'argent. Les Français sont très polis et accueillants. Tu ne peux pas imaginer comme ce voyage est enrichissant! A bientôt!

# 15   Using prepositions and prepositional phrases

**15·1**   1. chez ma tante Irène; en France   2. Á la dernière minute; en Italie   3. pour Rome; au lieu de celui; pour Paris   4. A côté de moi   5. en cours de route   6. Pendant le voyage   7. À la fin du voyage   8. grâce à ma tante Irène

**15·2**   1. Luc est allé au marché pour acheter des légumes.   2. Il a rencontré sa copine Mireille devant le stand des salades.   3. Ils ont fait leurs achats sans beaucoup discuter.   4. Puis ils sont allés au café du coin.   5. Les deux amis ont eu une discussion au sujet d'un projet de vacances.   6. Puis ils sont rentrés chez eux.

**15·3**   1. de Luc   2. à son père   3. à lui   4. Le toit de la maison   5. de la maison   6. de la ville est à son cousin

**15·4**   1. La poupée est à Suzette.   2. Le sac à dos est à l'alpiniste.   3. Le couteau est au boucher.   4. Les valises sont aux passagers.   5. Le sac à main est à la dame.   6. La Peugeot est à M. Lemaire.

**15·5**   1. e  2. d  3. b  4. f  5. a  6. c

**15·6**   1. de/en soie   2. de/en laine   3. de/en caoutchouc   4. de/en cristal   5. d'/en or   6. de/en bois

**15·7**   Suggested answers: 1. à six heures   2. à huit heures   3. à midi   4. à quatorze heures   5. à seize heures   6. à dix-huit heures

**15·8**   1. en Alsace   2. en Champagne   3. à Paris   4. à Strasbourg   5. à Cannes   6. en Provence   7. en Algérie   8. à Montréal

**15·9**   1. de New York   2. d'Allemagne   3. du Mexique   4. d'Australie   5. de Paris   6. de Suisse

**15·10**   1. en France; en avion   2. aux États-Unis; en avion ou en voiture   3. au Mexique; en avion   4. à New York; en métro et en bateau   5. au Texas; en voiture   6. (Insert location of your favorite café); à pied, en autobus, en voiture ou en métro

**15·11**   1. de  2. X  3. à  4. X  5. au  6. du

**15·12**  1. la classe de français   2. la salle de séjour   3. la salade de fruits   4. la table des matières   5. le sujet d'essai   6. le problème de maths

**15·13**  1. à côté de   2. chez toi   3. sans toi   4. pour ces billets   5. De plus/En plus   6. chez ton voisin   7. loin d'ici   8. De quoi   9. avec nous   10. à bientôt

**15·14**  1. Paul habite à Québec.   2. La ville de Québec est au Canada.   3. Il vit encore chez ses parents.   4. Il va au bureau chaque matin.   5. Il commence à travailler à 9 h chaque matin.   6. Le lundi après le travail, il va à l'université.   7. Les autres jours, il rentre chez lui après le travail.   8. Quelquefois il voyage aux États-Unis.

**15·15**  Model response: 1. J'habite à Chicago.   2. La ville de Chicago est aux États-Unis.   3. Je vis encore chez mes parents.   4. Je vais aux cours chaque matin.   5. Je quitte la maison vers 9 h chaque matin.   6. Après mes cours, vers 11 h, je vais au gymnase.

# 16 Using present and past participles

**16·1**  1. allant   2. tombant   3. se dépêchant   4. descendant   5. saisissant   6. réfléchissant

**16·2**  1. sachant   2. préparant   3. passant   4. ayant   5. étant   6. ne pouvant pas

**16·3**  1. Passant   2. Étant   3. Ayant   4. Préparant   5. Ne pouvant pas   6. Sachant

**16·4**  1. terminé   2. passé   3. promis   4. perdu   5. dormi

**16·5**  1. Étant partis trop tôt   2. Ayant annoncé les fiançailles   3. Ayant dansé toute la soirée   4. Ayant entendu la nouvelle   5. Étant déjà rentrés à la maison

**16·6**  1. écrivant   2. regardant   3. marchant   4. promenant   5. regardant   6. faisant

**16·7**  1. conduisant   2. faisant   3. garant   4. essayant   5. écoutant   6. faisant

**16·8**  1. terminé   2. Prévenu   3. lu   4. faite   5. annoncée   6. conclue   7. choisi   8. Arrivés

**16·9**  1. Ayant décidé de correspondre régulièrement avec mon cousin français, j'ai dû réviser mon français.   2. Je peux faire quelques exercices chaque jour en attendant que mon dîner soit prêt.   3. Tout en étudiant, je peux écouter ma musique favorite.   4. Réflexion faite, je suis content(e) d'avoir acheté ce livre.   5. Une fois tous les exercices terminés, j'écrirai bien mieux.

**16·10**  1. est…décrit   2. est reconnu   3. est fasciné   4. est établi   5. Se promenant; sont payées   6. est loué   7. sont estimés

**16·11**  1. La maison est vendue.   2. Les fenêtres sont lavées.   3. Le gazon a été tondu.   4. La cour a été nettoyée.   5. Le panneau a été enlevé.   6. Les buissons ont été taillés.

# 17 Making transitions

**17·1**  1. et   2. ni   3. ou/et   4. mais   5. car   6. donc/et

**17·2**  1. alors que/tandis que   2. pourvu qu'   3. parce que   4. Bien que   5. pendant que/alors que/tandis que   6. parce que

**17·3**  1. mais   2. Puisque   3. tandis que/puisque   4. et/ainsi que   5. donc   6. bien que

**17·4**  1. et/ainsi que   2. et/ainsi qu'   3. Pourtant   4. En effet   5. bien que   6. En fait   7. bientôt   8. Mais actuellement

**17·5**  1. J'ai beaucoup appris mais il me reste encore beaucoup à apprendre.   2. Il faut que j'étudie du vocabulaire ainsi que de la grammaire.   3. Je voudrais aussi comprendre mieux la culture française.   4. Il faut être patient quand on apprend une langue, sinon c'est frustrant.   5. Bien sûr qu'avec un peu de diligence je vais continuer de faire des progrès, en particulier dans l'art d'écrire.   6. Actuellement je sais écrire quelques phrases.   7. Mais bientôt je pourrai écrire un paragraphe entier.

**17·6**  1. Malheureusement   2. c'est pourquoi   3. Cependant   4. même si   5. Puisque   6. Donc

**17·7**  1. Il n'est pas sûr du tout   2. Il est probable   3. Il n'est pas certain   4. Il n'est pas évident   5. Il est contestable

**17·8**  1. À mon avis   2. Je crois   3. Je suis convaincue   4. je crois   5. je pense   6. Selon moi   7. C'est pourquoi   8. Ainsi

**17·9**  1. En premier lieu, je réfléchis et j'organise mes idées.  2. En deuxième lieu, je révise et je finis mon plan.  3. En troisième lieu, je commence à écrire et développer mon essai.  4. En quatrième lieu, je relis et je fais des corrections à mon essai.  5. Finalement, je rends l'essai à mon prof et je quitte la salle de classe.

**17·10**  1. Selon moi, la politique est toujours complexe.  2. Je suis convaincu qu'il est difficile pour un politicien de dire toute la vérité et rien que la vérité.  3. Il est certain que la vérité est quelque fois difficile à admettre.  4. Il va de soi que les gens n'aiment pas entendre la vérité, notamment quand elle est désagréable.  5. Étant donné que peu de politiciens ont le courage de toujours dire la vérité, il faut observer leurs actions de très près.  6. C'est pourquoi je suis les débats et les interviews.

**17·11**  Autrefois/Avant j'étais très timide. Je m'inquiétais beaucoup quand je devais parler, particulièrement devant un groupe de gens. De plus je rougissais toujours devant les gens. Mais bientôt j'ai appris à me calmer. Maintenant je peux même faire des interventions devant une audience. Naturellement cela ne s'est pas passé en un jour.

# 18  Letter writing and messaging

**18·1**  1. Madame Monique Meru
12, avenue Leclerc
59000 Lille
France

2. MM. Royen et Sanson
Société Productrice d'Electricité
10, boulevard Haussman
75009 Paris

3. Hôtel Le Lafayette
5, rue de la Liberté
97200 Fort de France
Martinique

**18·2**  *Suggested answers:*
1. Paris, le 4. 7. 2008
Monsieur le Docteur Mason,
Je vous prie d'agréer, monsieur le Docteur, mes sincères salutations.

2. Metz, le 23. 5. 2009
Chère Jeanine,
Je t'embrasse.

**18·3**  *Sample note:*
Ma chère Marie-Josée,
Depuis que tu es partie à Cannes, je m'ennuie beaucoup. Je n'ai personne pour m'accompagner au cinéma. Tu me manques terriblement. Je ne peux pas attendre que tu reviennes. Enfin, j'espère quand même que tu t'amuses en France. Comment ça te plaît à Cannes? Donne le bonjour à ta tante de ma part.
Bons baisers,
Tina

**18·4**  *Sample letter:*
Chère madame,
J'ai vu votre annonce sur l'Internet pour un appartement à louer. J'aime beaucoup la description et le prix de location mensuel. J'espère que l'appartement est encore à louer. J'aimerais le voir lors de ma visite le 15 juin. Est-ce que cela vous convient? J'attends votre réponse.
Veuillez agréer, madame, mes sentiments distingués,
Georges McKaan

**18·5**  *Sample letter:*
Cher M. Fauchon,
Mon mari et moi sommes restés à votre hôtel à plusieurs occasions. Je voudrais réserver une chambre pour deux semaines au mois de juillet. Nous voudrions notre chambre habituelle avec une vue de la Tour Eiffel. Nous voudrions le petit déjeuner compris dans le prix de la chambre. Pourrions-nous avoir un rabais sur le prix puisque nous sommes des habituels?
Nous vous remercions et vous demandons d'accepter nos cordiales salutations.
Charlotte et James Scott

**18·6**  *Sample e-mail:*
1. Chère Madame Sorot,
Je viens de recevoir le paquet contenant le courrier que vous avez eu la bonté de m'envoyer. Je n'oublierai jamais les jours passés en tant qu'invité dans votre appartement.

Je vous remercie de m'avoir envoyé mon courrier et vous envoie mes salutations cordiales.
Kelly Alexander

2. Cher Jonathan,
Pourrais-tu m'envoyer ton numéro de téléphone en France? Si tu es disponible cet après-midi, je voudrais te parler. Réponds vite!
Arnold

**18·7** *Suggested answer:*
Bjr, toi. J'aime BCP ton KDO. Mr6. Tu veux aller au cine? Rdv 8 h.

# 19 Using colloquial expressions and structures

**19·1** 1. habitudes il a   2. a acheté comme maison   3. as fait comme folies   4. sont gentils/aimables/sympa   5. c'est facile   6. est belle

**19·2** 1. b   2. d   3. c   4. e   5. a

**19·3** 1. Du tout   2. Tu penses bien   3. Mais enfin   4. Je parie que oui   5. Ça se voit   6. Mais évidemment

**19·4** 1. Pas grave   2. Laisse tomber   3. Vrai de vrai   4. Ça marche   5. Ça va   6. Pardi/Évidemment/Bien sûr (que oui)

**19·5** 1. Quoi   2. Comment ça   3. Qu'est-ce que tu racontes   4. Tu dis   5. Et après   6. C'est à dire

**19·6** 1. Les Dupuis se sont acheté une ferme à la campagne.   2. M. Dupuis s'est choisi une vieille ferme pas très chère près de Paris.   3. Mme Dupuis s'est trouvé tout de suite de beaux géraniums.   4. Elle s'est déjà décoré toutes les fenêtres de sa ferme.

**19·7** 1. Nous allons arroser les géraniums aujourd'hui.   2. Nous irons au village acheter des provisions.   3. Après le déjeuner, nous allons tailler les rosiers.   4. En fin d'après-midi, nous ferons une promenade à cheval.   5. Nous brosserons les chevaux demain.

**19·8** 1. Les Dupuis adorent l'équitation.   2. M. Dupuis monte vraiment bien à cheval.   3. Mme Dupuis est encore débutante.   4. Leurs chevaux sont doux.

**19·9** 1. ne   2. Il   3. Il   4. Il   5. n'

# 20 Writing

**20·1** 1. Demain   2. Alors   3. Est-ce que   4. chouette   5. Moi   6. Qui   7. en   8. Vous   9. moi   10. l'

**20·2** *Suggested answers:*
1. Il est plus facile d'apprendre le français en utilisant un livre bien écrit/quand on utilise un livre bien écrit.   2. Pour élargir ma base de français, il faut/il a fallu que je fasse tous les exercices de ce livre.   3. De temps en temps, il faut réviser tout ce qu'on a appris.   4. En même temps, il faut ajouter de nouvelles notions grammaticales et des mots de vocabulaire.   5. Quel plaisir d'utiliser ses connaissances de français en voyageant, en communiquant avec des amis et des collègues et en lisant les journaux!   6. Ne pensez-vous pas que c'est vraiment formidable de comprendre une autre langue et une autre culture?   7. Ce chapitre est plus amusant parce qu'il me permet de m'exprimer d'une façon plus personnelle et plus créative.   8. Après avoir fini ce livre, je voudrais pratiquer avec des amis français.   9. L'année prochaine, si j'ai le temps,/Si j'ai le temps, l'année prochaine, je suivrai/je vais suivre un autre cours de français.   10. Je suis très surpris(e) et content(e) d'avoir compris et appris tant de français!

**20·3** 1. qui voulaient absolument des enfants   2. Alors/Heureusement   3. adorable/très belle   4. l'adoraient.   5. jeunes   6. jolie/belle/adorable   7. Malheureusement   8. la plus vieille   9. vieille   10. a jeté un mauvais sort   11. gentilles/aimables   12. sauvée

**20·4** *Sample answers:*
A. Le jour où j'ai reçu ma première voiture était le plus beau jour de ma vie. Ce matin-là mon père et moi, nous nous sommes levés tôt. Après avoir déjeuné, à huit heures précises, nous étions à la salle de vente des voitures d'occasion. Le représentant qui s'appelait M. Pointu, nous a accueillis chaleureusement et nous a demandé si nous voulions toujours acheter la petite Mazda rouge. Mon père lui a dit que nous étions prêts. À dix heures, nous sommes repartis, moi dans ma petite Mazda rouge, et mon père derrière moi dans sa voiture. J'avais l'impression d'avoir des ailes en conduisant ma petite voiture. Quel cadeau inoubliable!

B. Au mois de mars et puis au mois d'avril, j'attendais toujours de savoir si j'étais accepté à l'université de mon choix. Tous les jours, j'allais ouvrir la boîte à lettres pour voir s'il y avait une lettre pour moi.

Malheureusement les jours passaient sans nouvelles! Et puis, un jour, quelle surprise! Finalement voilà la lettre que j'attendais! Après avoir ouvert la lettre impatiemment et tout en tremblant, j'ai lu l'invitation à me rendre à l'université pour une orientation. Donc j'étais reçu! Incroyable! Mon rêve se réalisait!

**20·5** *Sample answer:*

Moi: Pardonnez-moi, monsieur. Je voudrais me faire rembourser pour ce rasoir électrique.

Vendeur: Oui, monsieur, mais avez-vous votre reçu?

Moi: Bien sûr! Le voilà!

Vendeur: Pourquoi rapportez-vous ce rasoir, monsieur?

Moi: Je me suis coupé ce matin en me rasant.

Vendeur: J'en suis désolé, monsieur.

Moi: Alors, j'ai décidé de continuer de me servir de rasoirs jetables.

Vendeur: Puis-je avoir votre carte de crédit, monsieur?

**20·6** *Sample answer:*

Moi: C'est la première fois que vous venez chez André?

Une connaissance: Oui, tout à fait! Et vous?

Moi: Ah! André et moi, nous sommes de très bons copains. Où est-ce que vous l'avez rencontré?

Une connaissance: Au café de la fac. On faisait la queue. Alors on a bavardé.

Moi: Ah bon! Vous faites du commerce, vous aussi?

Une connaissance: Oui, c'est ça! Et vous, vous faites des études?

Moi: Oui, j'étudie...

**20·7** *Sample answer:*

Moi: Dis donc, Gigi, tu as envie d'aller au ciné ce soir?

Gigi: Je veux bien. Qu'est-ce qui joue de bien en ce moment?

Moi: Y a un nouveau film d'aventure avec Gérard Depardieu au centre-ville.

Gigi: Moi, j'aime pas tellement! Je préfère les comédies. Y a rien d'amusant au ciné?

Moi: Je vais voir sur l'Internet. Je t'envoie un texto dans un moment, d'accord?

Gigi: D'accord. À tout de suite.

**20·8** *Sample answer:*

New York, le 2 septembre 2008

M. Ramoneau,

Je vous écris pour vous remercier de l'accueil merveilleux que vous nous avez fait lors de notre passage à Poitiers le mois dernier.

Mon mari et moi avons passé une semaine de rêve à votre hôtel. C'était la première fois que nous sommes restés au Grand Château qui nous a été recommandé par le syndicat d'initiative de Poitiers.

Je voudrais féliciter en particulier le directeur de votre restaurant, M. Santon. M. Santon nous a accueillis à bras ouverts dans votre magnifique restaurant et a fait en sorte que nous passions des soirées inoubliables. Nous avons dégusté des petits plats absolument divins. De plus, M. Santon nous a fait des réservations dans d'autres restaurants de Poitiers que nous avons énormément appréciés. Lors de notre dernière soirée à votre hôtel, M. Santon nous a offert une bouteille de vin. Quel service et quelle courtoisie!

Je peux vous assurer que mon mari et moi comptons revenir vous voir bientôt et que nous allons recommander votre hôtel à tous nos amis.

Veuillez agréer, monsieur, nos salutations distinguées.

*Lilian Smith*

# 21 Review and extension

**21·1** 1. Nadine regarde souvent des films d'horreur.  2. Elle collectionne des masques d'Halloween.  3. Ses amis donnent toujours des bonbons aux enfants le soir d'Halloween. *or* Le soir d'Halloween, ses amis donnent toujours des bonbons aux enfants.  4. Nadine achète un costume différent chaque année. Or: Cheque année, Nadine achète un costume différent.  5. Elle montre parfois son costume à ses petits frères et à ses petites sœurs.  6. Tout le monde admire les costumes et les masques de Nadine.

**21·2** 1. Nous adorons les stars passionnément.  2. Nous attribuons toutes sortes de qualité à nos stars.  3. De nos jours, les stars représentent des marques publicitaires. *or* Les stars représentent des marques publicitaires de nos jours.  4. Les grandes marques disséminent toujours une image flatteuse de la star.  5. La collaboration de la star avec une marque relance parfois la carrière de la star.  6. On comprend bien la nécessité d'une telle collaboration.

**21·3**
1. Nous ne mangeons jamais d'escargots.   2. Vous n'écoutez personne.   3. Vous ne faites rien le dimanche.   4. Les enfants ne jouent plus.   5. Elle n'a invité personne.   6. Ils n'ont vu qu'un spectacle.   7. Tu ne vas pas au concert?   8. Vous n'allez plus chanter.

**21·4**
1. Aujourd'hui, je ne veux ni fruits ni tarte.   2. Demain, je ne vais inviter personne.   3. Hier, je n'ai rien lu.   4. Maintenant, je ne voudrais plus jouer à ce jeu.   5. L'an dernier, je n'allais jamais au marché.   6. Plus tard ce soir, je ne vais aller nulle part.   7. Généralement, je ne réussis qu'à mes examens de français.   8. Hier, je n'ai ni nagé ni bronzé.

**21·5**
1. je les aime   2. je l'écoute   3. je l'écris   4. je l'ai   5. ils la font   6. on les fait   7. ils la cherchent   8. ils la trouvent

**21·6**
1. ils les ont écrits   2. elle l'a préparé   3. il l'a passé   4. je l'ai lavée   5. ils l'ont sortie   6. je vais bientôt le couper   7. ils vont le nettoyer   8. elle va le finir

**21·7**
1. nous leur obéissons   2. nous allons lui répondre   3. nous lui avons écrit   4. nous leur donnons des cadeaux d'anniversaire   5. nous leur avons envoyé des courriels   6. nous leur promettons des choses   7. nous n'allons pas lui désobéir   8. nous allons lui poser une question

**21·8**
1. elle m'a fait de la peine   2. il va me rester de l'argent   3. une carte de crédit me suffit   4. il nous faut une chambre d'hôtel   5. il me paraît cher   6. elle va nous manquer   7. il m'a plu   8. elle leur plaît

**21·9**
1. je ne les ai pas finis   2. je n'en ai pas eu   3. je les ai aidés   4. je n'y vais pas/plus   5. je ne vais pas t'y accompagner   6. je vais leur expliquer   7. je n'en ai pas besoin   8. je le prends

**21·10**
1. Non, il n'y a pas encore répondu.   2. Non, elle ne l'a peut-être pas envoyé.   3. Non, elle ne m'a montré que le début.   4. Non, je n'en envoie jamais.   5. Non, je ne l'offre jamais à personne.   6. Oui, bien sûr, j'en dis tout le temps.   7. Ah non, je ne les raconte plus.   8. Non, désolé, je ne t'offre rien. Je dois partir.

**21·11**
1. Généralement Monique se promène dans le quartier tôt le matin.   2. Généralement nous nous lavons et nous habillons pendant ce temps.   3. Généralement vous vous arrêtez au café en route.   4. Aujourd'hui vous allez vous préparer dans la chambre.   5. Ce matin, tu t'es bien coiffé(e).   6. Ce matin, je me suis brossé les dents avant toi.   7. Ce matin, papa s'est rasé.   8. Ce matin, nous nous sommes dépêchés.

**21·12**
1. Mireille s'est levée avant le reste de la famille.   2. Moi, son frère, je me suis caché.   3. Mireille s'est dépêchée de sortir.   4. Alec, le copain de Mireille, s'est rendu chez nous.   5. Alec et Mireille se sont rencontrés devant notre maison.   6. Alec et Mireille se sont embrassés.   7. Alec et Mireille se sont promenés un peu ensemble.   8. Alec et Mireille se sont séparés.   9. A neuf heures, Alec et Mireille se sont rendus à l'université séparément.   10. Ils se sont revus au cours de physique.

**21·13**
1. Est-ce qu'Antoine travaille au restaurant?   2. Est-ce qu'il n'a pas de vacances?   3. Est-ce que tu vas en voyage?   4. Est-ce que vous partez aujourd'hui ou demain?   5. Nathalie reste-t-elle à la maison?   6. Les chiens restent-ils chez les voisins?   7. Vas-tu t'amuser tout seul?   8. Peux-tu nous envoyer des texto?

**21·14**
1. Vous dinez avec nous, non?   2. Vous aimez le vin, n'est-ce pas?   3. Vous prenez un apéritif, oui?   4. Vous restez chez nous ce soir, non?   5. On attend les amis, n'est-ce pas?   6. On peut parler de politique, oui?   7. Vous êtes d'accord, non?   8. Vous avez la nationalité française, n'est-ce pas?

**21·15**
1. Quand   2. Où   3. Comment   4. Qui   5. Combien de temps   6. Qu'est-ce que   7. Pourquoi   8. Qu'est-ce qui

**21·16**
1. Qui vas-tu inviter?   2. Pourquoi est-ce que tu ne vas pas inviter Kevin?   3. Comment vas-tu décorer la salle?   4. Où est-ce qu'on va danser?   5. Qu'est-ce que nous allons manger?   6. Qui va être DJ?   7. Qu'est-ce qui va se passer si on boit trop?   8. Combien de temps est-ce que les invités vont rester?

**21·17**
1. J'aime beaucoup ce spectacle.   2. Qu'est-ce que tu penses de la performance?   3. L'actrice principale est géniale.   4. Tu es bien silencieuse.   5. J'aimerais bien.   6. Comment sais-tu?   7. Ne garde pas le silence!   8. Allons-y!

**21·18**
1. Allons nous promener!   2. Il fait beau aujourd'hui.   3. Où veux-tu aller?   4. Il y a un match de football intéressant.   5. Pouvons-nous nous reposer près du zoo plus tard?   6. J'ai envie d'une glace.   7. Donne-moi deux dollars!   8. Que cette glace est bonne!

**21·19**
1. A. Je sais que tu vas arriver à l'heure.   1. B. Je suis content que tu arrives à l'heure.   2. A. Elle pense que c'est élégant.   2. B. Elle veut que ce soit élégant.   3. A. Vous dites qu'il aime ça.   3. B. Vous voudriez qu'il aime ça.   4. A. Le professeur dit que vous allez rendre vos devoirs.   4. B. Le professeur veut que vous rendiez vos devoirs.   5. A. Je suis certain que la voiture va bien marcher.   5. B. Je ne suis pas certain que la voiture marche bien.

**21·20**    1. Je suis content que tu viennes.    2. Il voudrait que tu sois heureux.    3. Elle dit que c'est l'heure de partir.    4. Nous savons que le temps va changer.    5. Vous êtes sûr que le bus est à l'heure.    6. Ils commandent que nous soyons là.    7. Je pense que ces gens sont sympa.    8. Tu réponds que nous pouvons venir.

**21·21**    1. C'est la touriste qui a perdu son sac.    2. Voilà l'avion qu'elle va prendre.    3. C'est le café où on peut prendre le petit déjeuner.    4. Où est le billet que j'ai acheté il y a quelques minutes.    5. Elle cherche la personne qui a trouvé son sac.    6. C'est la porte où il y a beaucoup de gens.    7. Tu vois la personne dont je parlais?    8. C'est un sujet important dont nous avons parlé hier.

**21·22**    1. Je me demande où est notre serveuse.    2. Tu peux commander le plat que j'aime?    3. Je t'invite au café dont je t'ai parlé.    4. Quelqu'un est assis à la table que nous voulions.    5. Voilà la serveuse que nous avons d'habitude.    6. Elle nous apporte les boissons dont nous avons envie.    7. C'est le menu qu'il nous faut.    8. Où est le client qui était assis à notre table?

**21·23**    1. c/e    2. f    3. a/c    4. c/e    5. d    6. b

**21·24**    1. Thomas apprend le français en chantant.    2. Son instructeur l'interroge avant de conclure la leçon.    3. Ses copains veulent jouer avec lui après avoir attendu dans le salon.    4. Les garçons s'amusent en racontant des histoires drôles.    5. Thomas cherche son ballon pour jouer au foot.    6. Sa sœur Béatrice a envie de jouer au foot avec les garçons.    7. Thomas refuse de la laisser jouer.    8. Ses copains lui demandent de la laisser jouer.

**21·25**    1. h    2. f    3. g    4. e    5. d    6. b    7. c    8. a

**21·26**    1. lampe en / de verre    2. service d'assiettes en / de porcelaine    3. feu de bois    4. porte en fer forgé    5. maison de campagne    6. maison de mes grands-parents    7. tapisseries en soie or en soie/ murs de la salle à manger    8. l'horloge de mon grand-père

**21·27**    1. Thomas cherche un pull en laine.    2. Chloé lui en trouve un en coton.    3. Le nouveau pull de Thomas lui va bien.    4. Chloé essaie une robe de soie.    5. La robe de Chloé est jolie.    6. Le rayon de vêtements est super.    7. Ce magasin est dans une zone à circulation restreinte.    8. C'est une chaîne de boutiques haut de gamme.

**21·28**    1. construite en pierre    2. d'une nouvelle toiture en zinc    3. sensible à l'humidité    4. surpris par l'architecture    5. fan de ce style    6. résistant à l'eau    7. effectué par un artisan-couvreur    8. fier de son travail

**21·29**    1. Mon livre de texte est rempli de lectures intéressantes.    2. Il est destiné à des jeunes comme moi.    3. Il est divisé en douze chapitres.    4. Il est riche en analyses culturelles.    5. Les étudiants sont enchantés par la diversité des lectures.    6. Les leçons sont utiles à l'apprentissage.    7. La grammaire est indispensable à l'apprentissage de la langue.    8. Nous sommes très satisfaits de ce livre.

**21·30**    1. Luc va en vacances au Canada.    2. Il va séjourner à Montréal dans une famille d'accueil.    3. Il va rester chez les Richelieu.    4. Les ancêtres des Richelieu viennent de France.    5. Les Richelieu voyagent parfois en France.    6. Luc ne veut pas rester à l'hôtel.    7. Il est plus à l'aise dans sa chambre d'ami.    8. Luc accompagne les Richelieu au marché et à des restaurants en ville.

**21·31**    1. d    2. f    3. g    4. a    5. h    6. b    7. c or e    8. e

**21·32**    1. chez ma cousine    2. du soir    3. vue sur    4. au chien    5. dans ma chambre    6. sur mon lit    7. en ville    8. Pendant la journée    9. au concert    10. avec des amis de Josiane